Decision-Making Techniques and Methods for Sustainable Technological Innovation

Scrivener Publishing
100 Cummings Center, Suite 541J
Beverly, MA 01915-6106

Industry 5.0 Transformation Applications

Series Editors: Dr. S. Balamurugan (sbnbala@gmail) and Dr. Sheng-Lung Peng

The increase in technological advancements in the areas of artificial intelligence (AI), machine learning (ML) and data analytics has led to the next industrial revolution "Industry 5.0". The transformation to Industry 5.0 collaborates human intelligence with machines to customize efficient solutions. This book series covers various subjects under promising application areas of Industry 5.0 such as smart manufacturing, intelligent traffic, cloud manufacturing, real-time productivity optimization, augmented reality and virtual reality, etc., as well as titles supporting technologies for promoting potential applications of Industry 5.0, such as collaborative robots (Cobots), edge computing, Internet of Everything, big data analytics, digital twins, 6G and beyond, blockchain, quantum computing and hyper-intelligent networks.

Publishers at Scrivener
Martin Scrivener (martin@scrivenerpublishing.com)
Phillip Carmical (pcarmical@scrivenerpublishing.com)

Decision-Making Techniques and Methods for Sustainable Technological Innovation

Strategies and Applications in Industry 5.0

Edited by

Kanak Kalita
Dept. of Mechanical Engineering, Rajalakshmi Institute of Technology, Chennai, India

J.V.N. Ramesh
Dept. of Computer Science and Engineering, Koneru Lakshmaiah Education Foundation, Vaddeswaram, India

M. Elangovan
Applied Science Research Centre, Applied Science Private University, Amman, Jordan

and

S. Balamurugan
Research and Development, Intelligent Research Consultancy Service, Coimbatore, India

Scrivener Publishing

WILEY

This edition first published 2025 by John Wiley & Sons, Inc., 111 River Street, Hoboken, NJ 07030, USA and Scrivener Publishing LLC, 100 Cummings Center, Suite 541J, Beverly, MA 01915, USA

For more information about Scrivener publications please visit www.scrivenerpublishing.com.

Wiley Global Headquarters
111 River Street, Hoboken, NJ 07030, USA

For details of our global editorial offices, customer services, and more information about Wiley products visit us at www.wiley.com.

The manufacturer's authorized representative according to the EU General Product Safety Regulation is Wiley-VCH GmbH, Boschstr. 12, 69469 Weinheim, Germany, e-mail: Product_Safety@wiley.com.

Library of Congress Cataloging-in-Publication Data

ISBN 978-1-394-24257-3

Cover image: Generated with AI using Adobe Firefly
Cover design by Russell Richardson

Set in size of 11pt and Minion Pro by Manila Typesetting Company, Makati, Philippines

Printed in the USA

10 9 8 7 6 5 4 3 2 1

Contents

Foreword

In an era marked by rapid technological advancements and an increasing emphasis on sustainability, the role of decision-making in shaping our future has never been more critical. *Decision-Making Techniques and Methods for Sustainable Technological Innovation: Strategies and Applications in Industry 5.0* emerges as a seminal work, offering a nuanced understanding of how cutting-edge decision-making strategies can drive sustainable innovation in this new industrial revolution.

This book is not merely a collection of theoretical concepts; it is a beacon that guides us through the complexities of implementing sustainable technology in various sectors. It beautifully marries the intricacies of advanced technological applications with the principles of sustainability, offering a vision of a future where technology and ecological responsibility coexist harmoniously.

As we delve into the chapters, we are taken on a journey that showcases the dynamic interplay between various facets of Industry 5.0 – from green technology in developing countries to advanced algorithms for enhancing healthcare, security, and legal systems. Each chapter is a testament to the power of innovative decision-making techniques in addressing some of the most pressing challenges of our times, while also paving the way for sustainable solutions.

For researchers, practitioners, and students alike, this book is a valuable compass that navigates the evolving landscape of Industry 5.0. It illuminates the path towards not just technological advancement but also towards creating a sustainable and equitable world.

Let this book serve as your guide and inspiration in exploring the vast potential of sustainable technological innovation. Embrace the journey through these pages and discover the myriad ways in which advanced decision-making strategies can shape a better future for all.

Diego Alberto Oliva
Universidad de Guadalajara, Mexico

Preface

The advent of Industry 5.0 marks a transformative phase in industrial evolution, shifting the focus from automation-driven advancements to sustainability, resilience, and human-centric innovation. In this era, industries are increasingly tasked with balancing technological growth and environmental stewardship, fostering ecosystems where innovation aligns with societal and ecological imperatives. At the core of this transition lies decision-making—an indispensable tool for navigating challenges, prioritizing goals, and crafting impactful strategies.

Decision-Making Techniques and Methods for Sustainable Technological Innovation: Strategies and Applications in Industry 5.0 serves as a comprehensive guide to the multifaceted dimensions of decision-making that empower sustainable technological progress. Drawing on contributions from leading experts in academia and industry, the book synthesizes theoretical frameworks, practical methodologies, and case studies to offer actionable insights. Its chapters collectively demonstrate how decision-making processes can drive innovation, enhance sustainability, and foster inclusive growth across diverse domains.

To ensure coherence and thematic relevance, the book is organized into three parts: *Frameworks for Sustainable Technological Innovation*, *Sustainable Technology and Data Security*, and *AI and Decision-Making in Industry 5.0*. Each part explores critical themes through a series of meticulously curated chapters, bridging foundational concepts with advanced applications.

Part I: Frameworks for Sustainable Technological Innovation

The first part of the book sets the stage for understanding how decision-making frameworks underpin sustainable technological innovation. It introduces models, tools, and methodologies that offer actionable solutions to contemporary challenges.

The opening chapter, *Green Technology Planning in Developing Countries: An Innovative Decision-Making Framework*, addresses the urgent need for systematic approaches to green technology adoption. Using a case study from Pakistan, it presents a strategic framework grounded in SWOT analysis and Grey Analytical Structured Modeling (GASM). By prioritizing 18 sustainable strategies through the G-TOPSIS method, the chapter highlights green technology's potential to boost agricultural output, attract foreign investment, and lower adoption barriers.

The next chapter, *Evaluating Sustainability Indicators for Green Building Manufacture with Fuzzy-MODM Technique*, examines sustainability in the construction sector. Focusing on Malaysia's Green Building Index (GBI), it employs fuzzy DEMATEL to identify energy efficiency and indoor environmental quality as key criteria. This research offers actionable strategies for promoting eco-efficient practices in the building industry, providing valuable insights for manufacturers and policymakers.

Sustainable Energy Options: Qualitative TOPSIS Method for Challenging Scenarios explores energy planning under uncertainty. It proposes a qualitative TOPSIS framework that leverages subjective linguistic evaluations to rank sustainable energy alternatives. Through a case study evaluating energy sources, the chapter illustrates how fuzzy AHP and TOPSIS can facilitate informed decision-making in complex, multi-criteria scenarios.

The final chapter in this part, *Sustainable Education in the Age of 5G and 6G Networks: An Analytical Perspective*, focuses on integrating advanced communication technologies into education. It emphasizes the critical role of teachers in adopting these technologies and presents a hierarchical analysis of barriers and enablers. The chapter offers strategies to inspire educators to embrace environmentally conscious tools, close the digital divide, and enhance learning outcomes.

Part II: Sustainable Technology and Data Security

Part II shifts the focus to the interplay between sustainability and data security, emphasizing the importance of robust technological systems in advancing Industry 5.0 goals.

The chapter *Optimizing Sustainable Image Encryption Strategies in Industry 5.0 Using VIKOR MCDM Methodology* examines image encryption as a critical component of multimedia security. Leveraging the VIKOR methodology, it evaluates substitution boxes for resilience and efficiency, identifying optimal configurations for Industry 5.0 applications. The findings demonstrate how sustainable encryption techniques can enhance data security while adhering to environmental standards.

In *Sustainable Cryptographic Solutions for IoT: Leveraging MOORA in Evaluating Algorithms for Limited-Resource Environments*, cryptographic algorithms for IoT devices are assessed using the MOORA framework. Balancing parameters such as energy efficiency, speed, and security strength, the chapter offers insights into sustainable security solutions for IoT environments, bridging the gap between resource constraints and robust protection.

Optimizing Microwave Device Performance with SPSS Analysis introduces statistical methodologies for enhancing the efficiency of microwave systems. Highlighting components like solid-state amplifiers and wide bandgap devices, the chapter shows how SPSS analysis can optimize performance in high-frequency communication systems, contributing to the advancement of microwave technologies for Industry 5.0.

The study *Enhanced Microgrid Security: Naive Bayes Versus Random Forest in Attack Detection Accuracy* explores algorithms for detecting covert attacks on microgrids. By comparing Naive Bayes and Random Forest models, it establishes the superiority of Naive Bayes in precision and reliability. This chapter underscores the critical role of secure power infrastructures in fostering sustainable technological ecosystems.

Concluding this part is *Enhancing the Accuracy of Detecting Air Pollution Using Random Forest Algorithm Comparison with Support Vector Machine.* This chapter compares Random Forest and SVM models, with Random Forest emerging as the more accurate tool for air pollution detection. It highlights the potential of machine learning in environmental monitoring, offering a blueprint for predictive analytics in sustainability efforts.

Part III: AI and Decision-Making in Industry 5.0

The final part focuses on the transformative role of AI in decision-making, highlighting its applications in security, legal systems, recruitment, and beyond.

Efficient Human Threat Recognition using Novel Logistic Regression Compared over Linear Regression demonstrates the enhanced accuracy of Logistic Regression in threat detection. By integrating neural network techniques, the study achieves significant improvements, offering valuable insights for security applications.

Optimizing Uber Data Analysis: Decision Tree Versus Random Forest evaluates prediction models for ride-sharing data. The study finds Decision Tree algorithms more effective than Random Forest in operational analytics, paving the way for more precise and efficient data-driven decisions in the transportation industry.

Decision-Making in Malware Detection through Advanced Imaging Techniques introduces a deep learning-based approach to identifying malicious software. By training neural networks on extensive datasets, the chapter showcases a high-accuracy model that strengthens cybersecurity within Industry 5.0 environments.

The legal domain also benefits from AI, as explored in *Enhancing Decision-Making in Indian Legal Systems: Automating Document Analysis with Named Entity Recognition*. This chapter proposes a SpaCy-based model for extracting legal entities from court judgments, improving efficiency in legal document processing.

Classification of Indian Legal Judgment Documents through Innovative Technology to Aid in Decision Making extends this exploration by using convolutional neural networks to classify legal documents into predefined categories. The chapter demonstrates how AI can simplify complex legal processes and make justice delivery more efficient.

The closing chapter, *Revolutionizing Recruitment in Industry 5.0: An Efficient AI and Machine Learning-Based Applicant Tracking System*, examines AI-driven recruitment systems. It highlights tools such as applicant tracking systems and video interviews, emphasizing their role in enhancing efficiency and fairness while addressing ethical concerns. The chapter concludes with insights into emerging trends, guiding organizations in adopting technology-driven hiring practices.

This book reflects the collaborative efforts of a diverse group of researchers and practitioners committed to sustainable technological innovation. It stands as a testament to the growing recognition of decision-making as a cornerstone of Industry 5.0—bridging the gap between technological advancement and societal needs.

We extend our gratitude to the authors for their invaluable contributions and to the reviewers for their meticulous feedback. Special thanks to Martin Scrivener and the team at Scrivener Publishing for their support in bringing this project to fruition. We hope this book inspires readers to explore innovative strategies and contribute to a sustainable, inclusive future.

Kanak Kalita
J.V.N. Ramesh
M. Elangovan
S. Balamurugan
July 2025

Part I

FRAMEWORKS FOR SUSTAINABLE TECHNOLOGICAL INNOVATION

1

Green Technology Planning in Developing Countries: An Innovative Decision-Making Framework

Vamsidhar Talasila[1], Chandrashekhar Goswami[2] and Muniyandy Elangovan[3,4*]

[1]*Department of Computer Science and Engineering, Koneru Lakshmaiah Education Foundation, Vaddeswaram, Guntur, India*
[2]*Faculty of Computing and Informatics, Sir Padampat Singhania University, Udaipur, Rajasthan, India*
[3]*Department of Biosciences, Saveetha School of Engineering, Saveetha Institute of Medical and Technical Sciences, Chennai, India*
[4]*Applied Science Research Center, Applied Science Private University, Amman, Jordan*

Abstract

Green technologies are crucial for formulating and creating national environmental and sustainability plans. Development and implementation of approaches for accelerating green technologies in emerging economies are possible as a result of an increasing focus on GT approaches in strategic decision-making. As a result, this research creates comprehensive strategy structure research on SWOT (strengths, weaknesses, opportunities, and threats) analysis for successful planning of the green technology (GT) industry. The SWOT analysis examines both internal and outside factors as well as related aspects that are crucial for Pakistan development of GT. To calculate the weights of the 21 subfactors, the Grey analytical structured model approach is then used. Finally, 18 approaches created for sustainable GT planning are prioritized using the Grey techniques for order performance by similarity to ideal solution. The possibility for high agricultural output, decreased foreign investment because of security and terrorist concerns, declining costs of GTs, and the chance to establish a good reputation are crucial various components for comprehensive GT planning, according to the findings. On the other hand, it has been found that the best approaches involve enhancing

**Corresponding author*: muniyandy.e@gmail.com

Kanak Kalita, J.V.N. Ramesh, M. Elangovan and S. Balamurugan (eds.) Decision-Making Techniques and Methods for Sustainable Technological Innovation: Strategies and Applications in Industry 5.0, (3–24) © 2025 Scrivener Publishing LLC

national security to draw international direct investment, lowering taxes, duties on the import of GT, relaxing regulations for regional businesses going through a transition, and developing plans and initiatives that encourage green innovations in the agricultural sector. The systematic, complete structure for sustainable GT development in Pakistan is being proposed for the first time in this research. Our work closes a gap in the process of preparing and carrying out strategic plans and offers policymakers solutions to deal with roadblocks to adopting GT strategy.

***Keywords*:** Decision-making framework, GT, SWOT, Grey analytical structured model (GASM)

1.1 Introduction

Innovative green technology (GT) is becoming more and more necessary due to the dual restrictions on resources and the environment. Green industrial design may enhance environmental quality, encourage sustainable economic development, and translate technical innovation into GT innovation [1]. GT is a sort of invention that may benefit both the consumers and businesses while also significantly reducing negative environmental impacts. It encompasses technological innovation in areas such as environmental management, waste reduction, waste recycling, and the creation of eco-friendly goods. Due to the rising concern about the status of the environment, innovative GT has consistently attracted attention as a crucial component of green innovation [2]. Environmental regulation has the potential to support the green transformation of the economy *via* two channels: the creation of environmentally friendly technologies and the upgrading of industrial structures. On the other hand, the functions that different degrees of economic growth have in determining the impacts of environmental legislation are often neglected [3]. Sustainable development goals may be attained on a regional and global level due in large part to GT. Additionally, it promotes social advancement and lessens the negative effects of economic growth on the environment. GT has a bright future in fostering economic success in underdeveloped nations. However, the adoption of GT within a particular nation may be impacted by interconnecting environmental as well as social variables [4]. However, it is also accurate that governments, particularly those in developing countries, must continue to work toward promoting economic growth and raising living standards. This is furthermore in addition to the readily apparent fact that diminishing greenhouse gas emissions is important for the long-term sustainability of the global economy [5]. GT planning is a complex process that involves assessing a variety of factors such as technological feasibility, economic viability, environmental impact, and social acceptability. To facilitate this process, an innovative decision-making framework can be used to evaluate the potential benefits and risks associated with different GT options [6]. This framework involves several stages, starting with the identification of key stakeholders and their objectives, followed by the development of a set of criteria to assess the suitability of different GT options. These criteria should be based on a variety of factors, including environmental impact, social and economic benefits, and technological feasibility.

The rest of the essay is structured as follows: related works are discussed in Section 1.2, the suggested approach is explained in Section 1.3, the results and discussion are presented in Section 1.4, and the paper is concluded in Section 1.5.

1.2 Related Works

The four areas in the research [7] of IoT (Internet of Things) applications in agriculture include cattle breeding, environment-controlled planting, open-field planting, aquaculture, and aquaponics. It is advised that the emphasis on deploying agricultural IoT systems be broadened beyond the growing cycle to the life cycle of agricultural products. With the deployment of GTs in mind, operational recognition indications are examined from the standpoint of extended life cycle theory. Fuzzy analytic hierarchy process with triangular fuzzy evaluation is applied to the identifying system following the principles and logic of the suggested recognition system, and a workable computing process is developed [8]. The paper [9] was designed using the DMAIC (define, measure, analyze, improve, and control) technique, and the implementation of the GLS (Green Lean Six Sigma) was suggested based on theoretical components. It was discovered that the integration of GLS is complemented by enablers, a toolkit, and implementation techniques. The suggested architecture offers a route for GLS implementation *via* wise project selection.

The study by Andenæs and colleagues [10] identified and discussed the main building technical issues related to blue–green roofing and to provide a framework for risk management. Research data on blue–green roof faults and their causes have been gathered *via* literature and document analyses, qualitative interviews, and expert meetings. The current study [11] covers a few key sources of bioactive phenol compounds as well as cutting-edge extraction methods. The approaches make use of supercritical, microwave, and ultrasound technologies. The review will also emphasize how to best extract phenolic bioactives from plant-based materials using response surface methodology, a statistical approach. The research [12, 13] provided an integrated GT framework to address a vacuum in the existing body of literature by highlighting the most important characteristics of GTs applicable to Pakistan. The article [13, 14] built a multilayer index system for green building influencing elements and introduced the green financial supporting factor. The WINGS (weighted influence nonlinear gauge system) model is improved with the use of a radial basis function neural network (RBF-WINGS model), which also determines the direct strength–influence matrix. For the assessment of green rating (GR) schemes of current planning bodies (PBs), the research suggests a TOPSIS (technique for order performance by similarity to ideal solution) decision approach based on a cloud model that can get beyond the ambiguity and complexity of scheme selection. The methodology and preparation procedures are explained, and the definitions of the quantitative concepts and parameters are provided [14, 15]. In the study [15–17], the Malmquist index and data envelopment analysis are used to determine how effective GT innovation is in strategically growing sectors.

1.3 Proposed Methodology

In this section, we discuss in detail an innovative decision-making framework for GT planning to facilitate growth in developing countries. GT planning involves the identification of opportunities and approaches to facilitate the development and adoption of GT in developing countries. This includes assessing the current state of technology, identifying areas where GT can be most effective, and developing policies and programs to support its implementation.

By using an innovative decision-making framework, GT planning can be a more effective and efficient process, helping to facilitate the growth of sustainable and environmentally friendly technologies in developing countries.

1.3.1 SWOT, G-TOPSIS and Integrated GASM Methods

In this research, GT approaches are evaluated and prioritized for greater sustainable development in developing countries using SWOT (strengths, weaknesses, opportunities, and threats) analysis, GASM (Grey analytical structured model), and G-TOPSIS (Grey group TOPSIS) technique, which are combined. To identify GTs both inside and outside elements for long-term investment in Pakistan, a SWOT analysis is conducted. As opposed to SWOT analysis, the GASM approach determines the weight of each external as well as internal major element and subfactor. For Pakistan's sustainable development, the G-TOPSIS approach prioritizes and selects the best GT initiatives.

1.3.2 SWOT–GASM Method

In this research, the GASM and SWOT approaches were combined. SWOT is the most extensively used methodical approach and strategic planning method as a building block for long-term planning and factor analysis, both external and internal. Additionally, it cannot give these factors priority throughout the planning and procedure for development. To objectively quantify external and internal elements in the decision-making process, SWOT–GASM integration is used. SWOT analysis development and the process of creating approaches employing the SWOT matrix are the two primary phases of the analysis [18].

The AHP-TOPSIS (analytic hierarchy process-TOPSIS) approach for deciding on design parameters and SWOT-AHP for strategy creation for industries such as certifications for space and forests have been presented in previous research studies as an innovative approach for prioritizing renewable energy resources based on AHP-TOPSIS and AHP-SAW (AHP-simple additive weighting) techniques.

This research did not make use of the Grey combination model approach. This research developed GT solutions for sustainable planning used to fill a gap in the literature; the combined Grey revolutionary model of G-SWOTAHP and G-TOPSIS was developed. The key benefit of utilizing GASM over ordinary AHP is that G-AHP is more adept at handling judgments that are unclear or incomplete. Because G-AHP already takes into account undefined circumstances and can therefore deal with ambiguity when making choices, we chose it over fuzzy analytic hierarchy process.

1.3.3 Process of Grey Analytical Hierarchy

GASM is a powerful tool for making decisions that can be employed in a complicated and unpredictable setting to analyze and rank many criteria and options. This process is especially useful in situations where the decision-making process involves incomplete or uncertain information. The GASM process involves several steps, starting with the identification of the problem to be solved and the decision criteria that will be used to evaluate alternatives. Next, criteria weights are assigned to each decision criterion based on its relative importance. This is followed by the evaluation of each alternative against each decision criterion, using a scoring system or rating scale.

Grey numbers are used to represent uncertain or incomplete information, and these numbers are used to calculate the weighted scores for each alternative. The results of the GASM process can be further analyzed through sensitivity analysis, which tests the robustness of the results by varying the input parameters. The GASM process provides decision-makers with a structured and transparent approach to evaluating and prioritizing alternatives, allowing them to make more informed and objective decisions. By taking into account both quantitative and qualitative factors, the GASM process can help decision-makers to identify the most promising alternatives, even in situations where the decision-making process is complex and uncertain.

GASM provides some benefits over conventional AHP, including excellent accuracy. Additionally, it performs better with a set of expert recommendations and incomplete data. We prefer the GASM technique over fuzzy analytic hierarchy process because it already incorporates fuzzy circumstances and can manage fuzziness in decision-making with ease. Using Grey numerals and unambiguous weight functions that do not rely too much on the expertise of experts, this technique verifies the components of the assessment matrix. The following stages are involved in building GASM.

Step 1: By identifying the research aim, major criteria, and subcriteria, the first stage entails creating a hierarchal structure that offers the best answer for the issue at hand.

Step 2: The second step is creating comparisons between pairwise vectors using the gray scale. M denotes the GASM pairwise contrast matrix, as shown below.

$$N = \begin{bmatrix} \otimes H_{11} \ldots \otimes H_{1m} \\ \vdots \quad \ddots \quad \vdots \\ \otimes H_{n1} \quad \ldots \quad \otimes H_{nm} \end{bmatrix} = \begin{bmatrix} \left(\underline{H_{11}}\overline{H_{11}}\right) & \cdots & \left(\underline{H_{1m}}\overline{H_{1m}}\right) \\ \vdots & \ddots & \vdots \\ \left(\underline{H_{n1}}\overline{H_{n1}}\right) & \cdots & \left(\underline{H_{nm}}\overline{H_{nm}}\right) \end{bmatrix} \tag{1.1}$$

Step 3: The GASM pairing matrix, which is shown in the following table, was normalized.

$$N^* = \begin{bmatrix} \otimes H_{11}^* \ldots \otimes H_{1m}^* \\ \vdots \quad \ddots \quad \vdots \\ \otimes H_{n1}^* \quad \ldots \quad \otimes H_{nm}^* \end{bmatrix} = \begin{bmatrix} \left(\underline{H_{11}}^* \overline{H_{11}^*}\right) & \ldots & \left(\underline{H_{1m}}^* \overline{H_{1m}^*}\right) \\ \vdots & \ddots & \vdots \\ \left(\underline{H_{n1}}^* \overline{H_{n1}^*}\right) & \cdots & \left(\underline{H_{nm}}^* \overline{H_{nm}^*}\right) \end{bmatrix} \tag{1.2}$$

The higher limit is shown by $\overline{\otimes H_{11}^*}$, the lower limit is indicated by $\underline{\otimes H_{11}^*}$, and the normalized limits are produced as follows:

$$\underline{H_{11}^*} = \left[\frac{2\underline{H}_{ji}}{\sum_{j=1}^{n} \underline{H}_{ji} + \sum_{j=1}^{n} \overline{H_{11}}} \right]; \overline{H_{11}^*} = \left[\frac{2\overline{H_{ji}}}{\sum_{j=1}^{n} \underline{H}_{ji} + \sum_{j=1}^{n} \overline{H_{11}}} \right] \tag{1.3}$$

Step 4: The calculation of comparative Grey ratings for the standardized lowest and higher limits is the last step, and the results are shown below.

$$\underline{\otimes T_j} = \frac{\sum \underline{H_{ji}^*}}{m} \tag{1.4}$$

$$T_j = \left[(1-\lambda) * \underline{\otimes T_j} \right] + \left[\lambda * \underline{\otimes T_j} \right] \tag{1.5}$$

The Grey coefficients, whose value is fixed at 0.5, are presented by lower-level approximation approach (LLAA). The Grey coefficient's value might change, depending on the decision-makers' positive and negative inputs.

1.3.4 Grey Numbers

The range between established and unidentified values in an inadequate data system is known as the Grey numbers. The symbol displays the Grey number. In this investigation, we employed three different kinds of Grey numbers: upper bound, internal Grey numbers, and lower bound.

$$\otimes V + \otimes \Upsilon = \left[\underline{V} + \underline{\Upsilon}, \overline{V} + \overline{\Upsilon} \right] \tag{1.6}$$

$$\otimes V - \otimes \Upsilon = \otimes V + (-\otimes V) = [\underline{V} - \bar{\Upsilon}, \bar{V} - \underline{\Upsilon}] \quad (1.7)$$

$$\otimes V \times \otimes \Upsilon = [\text{Min}\{\underline{V}\underline{\Upsilon}, \bar{V}\bar{\Upsilon}, \underline{V}\bar{\Upsilon}, \underline{V}\bar{\Upsilon}\}, \max\{\underline{V}\underline{\Upsilon}, \bar{V}\bar{\Upsilon}, \bar{V}\underline{\Upsilon}, \underline{V}\bar{\Upsilon}\}] \quad (1.8)$$

$$\frac{\otimes V}{\otimes \Upsilon} = \otimes V \times \otimes \Upsilon^{-1} = \left[\text{Min}\left\{\frac{\underline{V}}{\underline{\Upsilon}}, \frac{\underline{V}}{\bar{\Upsilon}}, \frac{\bar{V}}{\underline{\Upsilon}}, \frac{\bar{V}}{\bar{\Upsilon}}\right\}, \max\left\{\frac{\underline{V}}{\underline{\Upsilon}}, \frac{\underline{V}}{\bar{\Upsilon}}, \frac{\bar{V}}{\underline{\Upsilon}}, \frac{\bar{V}}{\bar{\Upsilon}}\right\}\right] \quad (1.9)$$

Equation (1.10) shows how long the Grey number is $\otimes V = [\bar{V}, \underline{V}]$.

$$K(\otimes V) = \bar{V} - \underline{V} \quad (1.10)$$

$\otimes V = [\bar{V},]V, and \otimes \Upsilon[\bar{\Upsilon} - \underline{\Upsilon}]$ are two gray values, then Equation (1.11) may be used to determine the degree of Grey between them. In this research, Grey based on number linguistic factors was employed to assess how GT solutions ranked.

$$O\{\otimes V \leq \otimes \Upsilon\} = \frac{\text{Max}\{0, K^* - \max(0, \bar{V} - \underline{\Upsilon})\}}{K^*} \quad (1.11)$$

where $K^* = K(\otimes V) + K(\otimes \Upsilon)$.

1.3.5 G-TOPSIS Approach

The procedure evaluates *n* options using *m* parameters. This approach has the advantage of measuring both the best positive and negative options for the choice issue. Additionally, in this study, a positive optimum solution demonstrates environmentally friendly growth, whereas the opposite optimum solution demonstrates a reduction in ecological difficulties. The alternative that is closest to the ideal positive answer and farthest from the ideal negative solution is said to be the optimum alternative [19, 20]. To provide correct evaluation and eliminate ambiguity in expert comments, the Grey system theory and TOPSIS are integrated. The following stages make up the Grey TOPSIS method creation.

Step 1: This first phase is calculating each criterion's weight following the opinions of experts as indicated by the use of the Grey linguistic variable. Equation (1.12) may be used to calculate criterion g that weighs alternatives under the assumption that d represents the total amount of decision-makers.

$$\otimes T_h = \frac{1}{c}\left[\otimes g_h^1 + \otimes g_h^2 + \ldots + \otimes g\forall_h^c\right] \tag{1.12}$$

Step 2: Grey linguistic variables are used to ascertain where each choice stands concerning each criterion. The following are the calculations for determining the value of option i if d stands for the number of people who make decisions in criterion j.

$$\otimes H_{ji} = \frac{1}{c}\left[\otimes H_{ji}^1 + \otimes H_{ji}^2 + \ldots + \otimes H_{ji}^c\right] \tag{1.13}$$

Step 3: The following equations serve as a representation of this stage, which utilizes the Grey decision matrix.

$$E = \begin{bmatrix} \otimes H_{11} & \otimes H_{12} & \cdots & \otimes H_{1m} \\ \otimes H_{21} & \otimes H_{11} & \ldots & \otimes H_{2m} \\ \vdots & \vdots & \vdots & \vdots \\ \otimes H_{n1} & \otimes H_{n2} & \ldots & \otimes H_{nm} \end{bmatrix} \tag{1.14}$$

Step 4: The Grey choice matrix is now normalized and represented by the symbol F in Equation (1.15).

$$E = \begin{bmatrix} \otimes H_{11}^* & \otimes H_{12}^* & \cdots & \otimes H_{1m}^* \\ \otimes H_{21}^* & \otimes H_{22}^* & \ldots & \otimes H_{2m}^* \\ \vdots & \vdots & \vdots & \vdots \\ \otimes H_{n1}^* & \otimes H_{n2} & \ldots & \otimes H_{nm}^* \end{bmatrix} \tag{1.15}$$

$$H_{ji}^{*} = \left[\frac{\underline{H}_{ji}}{H_{i}^{\max}}, \frac{\overline{H}_{ji}}{H_{i}^{\max}} \right] \text{ where } H_{i}^{\max} = \max_{1 \le i \le n} \left\{ \overline{H}_{ji} \right\} \tag{1.16}$$

The formula that follows is used for normalizing if the criteria result in reduced characteristics.

$$H_{ji}^{*} = \left[\frac{H_{i}^{\max}}{\overline{H}_{ji}}, \frac{H_{i}^{\min}}{\underline{H}_{ji}} \right] \text{ where } H_{i}^{\min} = \min_{1 \le i \le n} \left\{ \underline{H}_{ji} \right\} \tag{1.17}$$

Step 5: This stage, represented by the letter W in the equation below, entails creating a Grey-weighted normalization decision matrix.

$$U = \begin{bmatrix} \otimes U_{11}^{*} & \otimes U_{12}^{*} & \cdots & \otimes U_{1m}^{*} \\ \otimes U_{21}^{*} & \otimes U_{22}^{*} & \cdots & \otimes U_{2m}^{*} \\ \vdots & \vdots & \vdots & \vdots \\ \otimes U_{n1}^{*} & \otimes U_{n2} & \cdots & \otimes U_{nm}^{*} \end{bmatrix} \text{ where } \otimes U_{ji} = \otimes H_{ji}^{*} \times \otimes t_{i} \tag{1.18}$$

Step 6: Equations (1.19) and (1.20) may be used to determine the best positive and negative answers to the decision-making dilemma.

$$T^{\max} = \left\{ \begin{matrix} \left[\max_{1 \le i \le n} \underline{u}_{j1}, \max_{1 \le i \le n} \overline{u}_{j1} \right], \\ \left[\max_{1 \le i \le n} \underline{u}_{j2}, \max_{1 \le i \le n} \overline{u}_{j2} \right], \ldots, \left[\max_{1 \le i \le n} \underline{u}_{in}, \max_{1 \le i \le n} \overline{u}_{in} \right] \end{matrix} \right\} \tag{1.19}$$

$$T^{\max} = \left\{ \begin{matrix} \left[\max_{1 \le i \le n} \underline{u}_{j1}, \max_{1 \le i \le n} \overline{u}_{j1} \right], \\ \left[\max_{1 \le i \le n} \underline{u}_{j2}, \max_{1 \le i \le n} \overline{u}_{j2} \right], \ldots, \left[\max_{1 \le i \le n} \underline{u}_{in}, \max_{1 \le i \le n} \overline{u}_{in} \right] \end{matrix} \right\} \tag{1.20}$$

Step 7: Equation (1.21) provides the calculation formula for the difference in the level of greyness between the ideal and alternate solutions.

$$O\{T_j \le T^{\max}\} = \frac{1}{m}\sum_{i=1}^{m} O\{\otimes u_{ji} \le \otimes H_i^{\max}\} \quad (1.21)$$

Step 8: The options are then arranged in ascending order following the values obtained in Step 7, meaning that more importance is given to the option with the lowest possible greyness degrees coefficient.

1.4 Results and Discussion

There are two aspects to the study's findings. The analysis and ranking of GT SWOT major components and subfactors according to the relative significance accorded to them by experts are shown in the first part of the findings as SWOT–GASM. G-TOPSIS is used in the second portion of the findings to determine the most important GT initiatives and offers the best option for decision-makers in the direction of development that is long-lasting. Figure 1.1 shows GT in developing nations with the fastest growth.

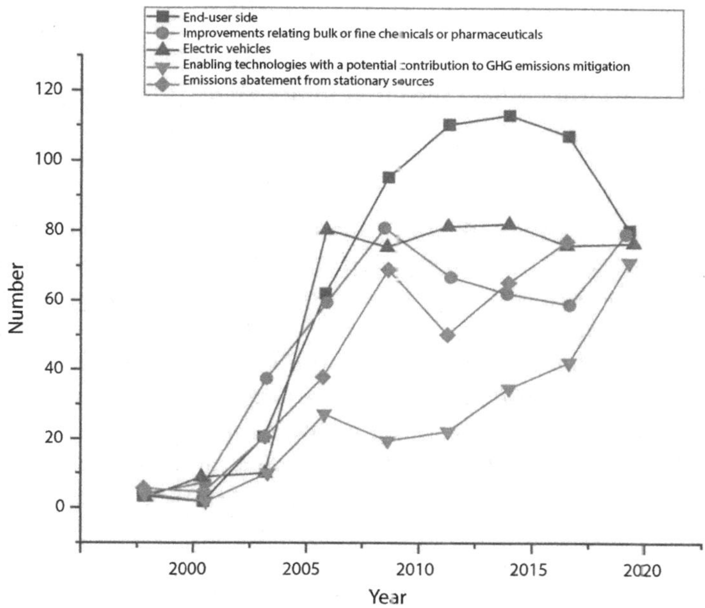

Figure 1.1 GT in developing nations with the fastest growth.

1.4.1 Ranking of SWOT Factors

It is clear that strengths (S) have been given the most weight, receiving a score of 0.35931, followed by opportunities (O), threats (T), a score of 0.21737, and weaknesses, a score of 0.15081. According to GAHP's evaluation of the primary SWOT criteria, the weaknesses, opportunities, and threats strategies were included in the strengths approach. As a result, we may conclude that decision-making requires consideration of all primary SWOT strategies. However, given this country's context, the strength element is crucial for the creation of GT.

1.4.2 Grey Analytical Hierarchical Process Results

Using the matrix of pairwise comparisons of the primary and supporting SWOT factors for the progress of GT in Pakistan, we used a GAHP methodology in the first phase of our study. The study's first section outlines the goal that was attained; the second presents the ranking of GT's SWOT factors and subfactors based on weights calculated using a pairwise comparison matrix; the third reflects an overall ranking of all SWOT subfactors carried out with GAHP, as appropriate.

1.4.2.1 Overall Ranking of SWOT Subfactors

In the area of GT investment, there are a lot of potential chances for Pakistan. Figure 1.2 displays the order of the SWOT opportunities subfactors. GT in society and national policy efforts (O2) were found to be that most significant subfactors, obtaining the maximum weight of 0.3052 in category. The environment has been adversely impacted by the generation of conventional energy, and society increasingly needs alternatives. Green manufacturing methods are a way to reach long-term objectives. Figure 1.3 and Table 1.1 show the international cooperation in the creation of technology connected to the environment.

In addition, people are becoming more knowledgeable about environmental issues and showing awareness regarding ecological stability as a result of people's rising concern on a national and worldwide scale. As a consequence, both domestic and foreign investors have the potential to profit greatly from investments in GTs. Last but not least, with a weight of 0.08115, lowering the cost of GT (O5) was identified as the indication with the least bearing on prospects. In conclusion, experts consider the possibility of knowledge of GT in society and national policy measures (O2) to be the most promising prospect.

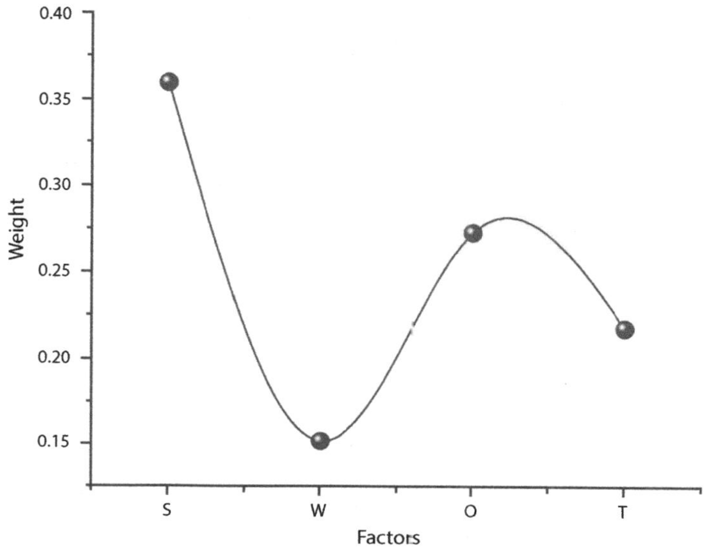

Figure 1.2 SWOT subfactors and main factors.

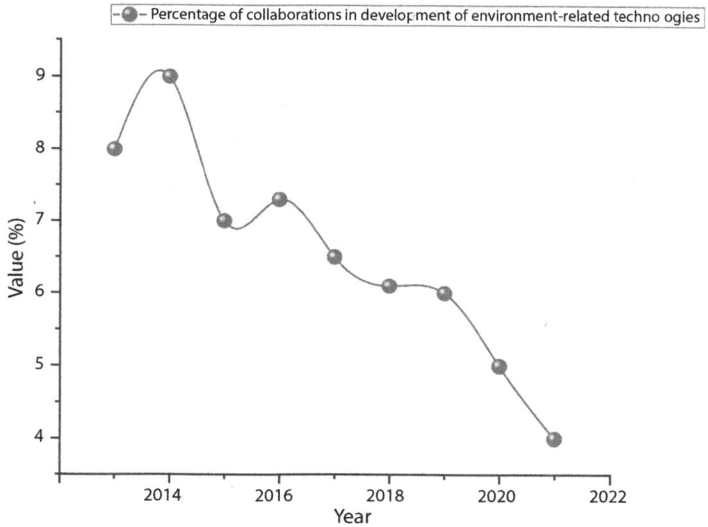

Figure 1.3 International cooperation in the creation of technology connected to the environment.

Table 1.1 Results of technology connected to the environment.

Year	Percentage of collaborations in the development of environment-related technologies
2014	8
2015	9
2016	7
2017	7.3
2018	6.5
2019	6.1
2020	6
2021	5
2022	4

1.4.2.2 Ranking of Threats Subfactors

The order of importance of the subfactors for the SWOT risks category are risks involved with Pakistan's making the switch to a green economy from a regular one. Because it received the highest weight score of 0.3950, foreign investment drops the act of terrorist activity, and safety issues (T4) came in first position. One of the Asian nations impacted by terrorism is Pakistan, which makes luring international investment difficult. It presents a danger to foreign investment as a result. Additionally, after T4, the factors with the highest weights of 0.1362 and 0.1162 were due to population expansion, internal movement from village to urban regions, and unprepared urbanization; there is not enough funding for green energy.

1.4.2.3 Ranking of Opportunities Subfactors

In the realm of GT investment, there are a lot of potential chances for Pakistan. The order of the SWOT opportunities subfactors is as follows: O3 > O1 > O6 > O2 > O4 > O5. GT in society and national policy efforts (O2) were found to have important subfactors, obtaining the maximum weight of 0.3051 within this group. The natural world has been adversely impacted by the generation of traditional power, and society increasingly demands alternatives. Green production methods are a way to reach long-term objectives.

1.4.2.4 Ranking of Weaknesses Subfactors

To maximize the benefits of GT in Pakistan, certain potential vulnerabilities must be addressed. In ranking of the GAHP methods' weakest subfactors, the results show that poor management and high levels of corruption (W2) are the top priorities and have a significant score (0.3919). Pakistan does not score well on the global governance scale, and corruption is one of the main causes.

1.4.2.5 Ranking of Strengths Subfactors

The relative weights of the SWOT subfactors within every category of the primary variable are then multiplied by that weight in order to analyze the overall ranking. The ultimate ranking shown in Table 1.2 is based on the cumulative weight, which is the result of adding each subfactor weight. The following is the final ranking of the subfactors that GT strategy bodies should consider while creating sustainability:

The following order is used: S1 > T4 > O5 > O3 > S4 > T5 > S3 > O1 > T6 > T1 > W2 > W3 > O6 > O2 > S5 > S2 > T7 > O4 > W4 > T3 > W1 > T2.

Our analysis shows that key subfactors for GT strategic planning include the potential for high agricultural productivity (S1), decreased foreign investment due to security and terrorism concerns (T4), declining costs of GTs (O5), and the chance to project a favorable image.

Table 1.2 Final GT subfactor rankings for sustainable planning.

Attributes	Criteria codes	Attribute weights	Consistency ratio
Strengths	S	0.35838	0.0075
Weaknesses	W	0.15083	0.0001
Opportunities	O	0.2725	0.0115
Threats	T	0.21737	0.0035

Main attributes	Subattribute codes	Normalized weights
Strengths	S1	0.08146466
	S2	0.03023022
	S3	0.5508252
	S4	0.06500218
	S5	0.030863624
Weaknesses	W1	0.01391413
	W2	0.04323833
	W3	0.04070664
	W4	0.01762218
Opportunities	O1	0.05339369
	O2	0.034300731
	O3	0.08347129
	O4	0.01930934
	O5	0.08714886
	O6	0.03995127
Threats	T1	0.04904469
	T2	0.01267544
	T3	0.01534383
	T4	0.08821170
	T5	0.06322890
	T6	0.05334007
	T7	0.026710387

1.4.3 Grey TOPSIS Results

Based on SWOT criteria, this study aims to offer SWOT approaches to GT investments in one nation context. First, we used GAHP to prioritize the subfactor after separating out the strengths, weaknesses, opportunities, and threats in GT. In the second step, both internal and external variables are merged, such as strength–opportunity (SO), weakness–opportunity (WO), strength–threat (ST), and weakness–threat (WT). Finally, we used the G-TOPSIS methodology to prioritize 21 GT plans. When used in particular situations, SO techniques can aid in utilizing opportunities with pertinent strengths. WO methods, in contrast, attempt to lessen or eliminate the effects of weakness by properly utilizing opportunity. ST methods offer the chance to defeat potential challenges by appropriately utilizing strength. Opportunities indicate decreasing the ability to fend off possible threats by utilizing the WT model.

1.4.3.1 WO Strategies

In the area of GT investment, there are a lot of potential chances for Pakistan. Figure 1.2 displays the order of the SWOT opportunities subfactors. GT in society and national policy efforts (O2) were found to be important subfactors, obtaining the maximum weight of 0.3051 within the category. The environment has been adversely impacted by the generation of conventional energy, and society increasingly needs alternatives. Green manufacturing methods are a way to reach long-term objectives. Figure 1.4 and Table 1.3 show the international cooperation in the creation of technology connected to the environment.

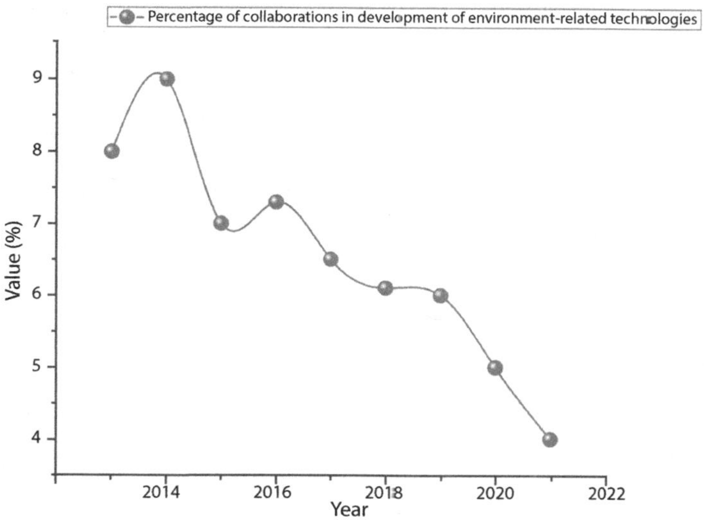

Figure 1.4 International cooperation in the creation of technology connected to the environment.

Table 1.3 Results of technology connected to the environment.

Year	Percentage of collaborations in the development of environment-related technologies
2014	8
2015	9
2016	7
2017	7.3
2018	6.5
2019	6.1
2020	6
2021	5
2022	4

In addition, people are becoming more knowledgeable about environmental issues and showing awareness regarding ecological stability as a result of people's rising concern on a national and worldwide scale. As a consequence, both domestic and foreign investors have the potential to profit greatly from investments in GTs. Last but not least, with a weight of 0.08115, lowering the cost of GT (O5) was identified as the indication with the least bearing on prospects. In conclusion, experts consider the possibility of knowledge of GT in society and national policy measures (O2) to be the most promising prospect.

1.4.3.2 *ST Strategies*

According to the order of importance of the subfactors for the SWOT risks category, there are risks involved with Pakistan's transition from a traditional economy to a green one. Because it received the highest weight score of 0.3950, foreign investment drops the act of terrorism, and safety issues (T4) came in first position. One of the Asian nations impacted by terrorism is Pakistan, which makes luring international investment difficult. It presents a danger to foreign investment as a result. Additionally, after T4, the factors with the highest weights of 0.1362 and 0.1162 were due to population expansion, internal movement from village to urban regions, and unprepared urbanization; there is not enough funding for green energy.

1.4.3.3 SO Strategies

Pakistan is an agricultural nation endowed with a variety of natural resources; thus, it is imperative to make use of this advantage by luring global investment by outside investors in GT. The 15th place with a weight of 0.596673 belonged to launching a platform for detailed suggestions for investing from investors abroad in GT (SO2). Additionally, supporting regional education initiatives to improve local GT industry patents (SO3) looked to be the least significant approach since it obtained a Grey degree of 0.6164829, and assisting nearby industries in switching from conventional to GT (SO4) came in at seventh place. By cutting import tariffs and other levies on subsidies, the government must support local small and medium-sized enterprises (SMEs) in implementing GTs and help the local technology sector in improving their technical work.

1.4.3.4 WT Strategies

Poor governance, ignorance, and corruption aggravated the issue. Foreign investors were repelled by terrorism due to inadequate security arrangements and a lack of cooperation from the government and communities. Every month since 2015 has seen an improvement in the situation, yet the country's economy has been destroyed. Pakistan has boosted security and welcomed foreign direct investment (FDI), but despite substantial efforts, the desired outcome has not yet materialized. Infrastructure at the time, security, poverty, and immorality are all intertwined. To repair the harm inflicted by terrorism in Pakistan, institutions must collaborate. For many years, Pakistan has struggled with severe corruption and poor governance. The government must encourage cooperation and coordination among many entities if GT is to be developed nationally to address environmental issues. To promote foreign direct investment (FDI) in the country, guidelines and approaches must be put into place to improve security conditions. The government must also provide sufficient funding for research and development.

1.5 Conclusion

This is the first research to generate and evaluate the GT approach for long-term development utilizing an integrated SWOT-Grey AHP and G-TOPSIS technique. By integrating SWOT internal and external factors, such as ST, WO, WT, and SO, we rated 21 GT methods. Under each of the four groups of SWOT main factors—strengths, weaknesses, possibilities, and threats—we examined 22 environmentally friendly technology subfactors. We then used a special GASM approach to determine how they were ranked according to their relative importance. The study's findings point the way to acceptable tactics for adopting GT in developing countries, such as ST and SO. ST tactics include budgeting for raising knowledge about how to use renewable energy resources and developing acceptable alternative methods for transitioning from conventional sources of energy to renewable energy supplies. SO comprises designing including public sector support for medium- and small-sized businesses, developing and carrying out development initiatives to encourage GTs, as well as providing instruction on locating and implementing energy generation technology.

References

1. Cuiyun, C. and Chazhong, G., Green development assessment for countries along the belt and road. *J. Environ. Manage.*, 263, 110344, 2020, https://doi.org/10.1016/j.jenvman.2020.110344.
2. Wang, Q., Qu, J., Wang, B., Wang, P., Yang, T., Green technology innovation development in China in 1990–2015. *Sci. Total Environ.*, 696, 134008, 2019, https://doi.org/10.1016/j.scitotenv.2019.134008.
3. Du, K., Cheng, Y., Yao, X., Environmental regulation, green technology innovation, and industrial structure upgrading: The road to the green transformation of Chinese cities. *Energy Econ.*, 98, 105247, 2021, https://doi.org/10.1016/j.eneco.2021.105247.
4. Ikram, M., Sroufe, R., Awan, U., Abid, N., Enabling progress in developing economies: A novel hybrid decision-making model for green technology planning. *Sustainability*, 14, 1, 258, 2021, https://doi.org/10.3390/su14010258.
5. Lv, C., Shao, C., Lee, C.C., Green technology innovation and financial development: Do environmental regulation and innovation output matter? *Energy Econ.*, 98, 105237, 2021, https://doi.org/10.1016/j.eneco.2021.105237.
6. Adnan, N., Nordin, S.M., Rahman, I., Noor, A., The effects of knowledge transfer on farmers decision making toward sustainable agriculture practices:

In view of green fertilizer technology. *World J. Sci. Technol. Sustain. Dev.*, 15, 1, 98–115, 2018, https://doi.org/10.1108/WJSTSD-11-2016-0062.

7. Ruan, J., Wang, Y., Chan, F.T.S., Hu, X., Zhao, M., Zhu, F., Shi, B., Shi, Y., Lin, F., A life cycle framework of green IoT-based agriculture and its finance, operation, and management issues. *IEEE Commun. Mag.*, 57, 3, 90–96, 2019, https://doi.org/10.1109/MCOM.2019.1800332.
8. Lai, C.S., Jia, Y., Dong, Z., Wang, D., Tao, Y., Lai, Q.H., Wong, R.T.K., Zobaa, A.F., Wu, R., Lai, L.L., A review of technical standards for smart cities. *Clean Technol.*, 2, 3, 290–310, 2020, https://doi.org/10.3390/cleantechnol2030019.
9. Kaswan, M.S. and Rathi, R., Green Lean Six Sigma for sustainable development: Integration and framework. *Environ. Impact Assess. Rev.*, 83, 106396, 2020, https://doi.org/10.1016/j.eiar.2020.106396.
10. Andenæs, E., Time, B., Muthanna, T., Asphaug, S., Kvande, T., Risk reduction framework for blue-green roofs. *Buildings*, 11, 5, 185, 2021, https://doi.org/10.3390/buildings11050185.
11. Kumar, M., Dahuja, A., Tiwari, S., Punia, S., Tak, Y., Amarowicz, R., Bhoite, A.G., Singh, S., Joshi, S., Panesar, P.S., Prakash Saini, R.P., Pihlanto, A., Tomar, M., Sharifi-Rad, J., Kaur, C., Recent trends in extraction of plant bioactives using green technologies: A review. *Food Chem.*, 353, 129431, 2021, https://doi.org/10.1016/j.foodchem.2021.129431.
12. Ikram, M., Ferasso, M., Sroufe, R., Zhang, Q., Assessing green technology indicators for cleaner production and sustainable investments in a developing country context. *J. Clean. Prod.*, 322, 129090, 2021, https://doi.org/10.1016/j.jclepro.2021.129090.
13. Wang, W., Tian, Z., Xi, W., Tan, Y.R., Deng, Y., The influencing factors of China's green building development: An analysis using RBF-WINGS method. *Build. Environ.*, 188, 107425, 2021, https://doi.org/10.1016/j.buildenv.2020.107425.
14. Shahsavar, M.M., Akrami, M., Gheibi, M., Kavianpour, B., Fathollahi-Fard, A.M., Behzadian, K., Constructing a smart framework for supplying the biogas energy in green buildings using an integration of response surface methodology, artificial intelligence and Petri net modelling. *Energy Convers. Manage.*, 248, 114794, 2021, https://doi.org/10.1016/j.enconman.2021.114794.
15. Luo, Q., Miao, C., Sun, L., Meng, X., Duan, M., Efficiency evaluation of green technology innovation of China's strategic emerging industries: An empirical analysis based on Malmquist-data envelopment analysis index. *J. Clean. Prod.*, 238, 117782, 2019, https://doi.org/10.1016/j.jclepro.2019.117782.
16. Manikandan, S., Vickram, S., Subbaiya, R., Karmegam, N., Woong Chang, S., Ravindran, B., Kumar Awasthi, M., Comprehensive review on recent production trends and applications of biochar for greener environment. *Bioresour. Technol.*, 388, 129725, 2023, https://doi.org/10.1016/j.biortech.2023.129725.

17. Manikandan, S., Krishnan, R.Y., Vickram, S., Subbaiya, R., Kim, W., Govarthanan, M., Karmegam, N., Emerging nanotechnology in renewable biogas production from biowastes: Impact and optimization strategies–A review. *Renew. Sustain. Energy Rev.*, 181, 113345, 2023, https://doi.org/10.1016/j.rser.2023.113345.
18. Kalita, K., Pal, S., Haldar, S., Chakraborty, S., A Hybrid TOPSIS-PR-GWO Approach for Multi-objective Process Parameter Optimization. *Process Integr. Optim. Sustain.*, 6, 4, 1011–1026, 2022, Springer. DOI: 10.1007/s41660-022-00256-0.
19. Diyaley, S., Shilal, P., Shivakoti, I., Ghadai, R.K., Kalita, K., PSI and TOPSIS Based Selection of Process Parameters in WEDM. *Period. Polytech., Mech. Eng.*, 61, 4, 255–260, 2017, Budapest University of Technology and Economics. DOI: 10.3311/PPme.10431.
20. Shivakoti, I., Pradhan, B.B., Diyaley, S., Ghadai, R.K., Kalita, K., Fuzzy-TOPSIS Based Selection of Laser Beam Micro Marking Process Parameters. *Arabian J. Sci. Eng.*, 42, 11, 4825–4831, 2017, Springer. DOI: 10.1007/s13369-017-2673-1.

2

Evaluating Sustainability Indicators for Green Building Manufacture with Fuzzy-Based MODM Technique

Chandrshekhar Goswami[1], Muniyandy Elangovan[2,3*] and Puppala Ramya[4]

[1]Faculty of Computing and Informatics, Sir Padampat Singhania University, Udaipur, Rajasthan, India
[2]Department of Biosciences, Saveetha School of Engineering, Saveetha Institute of Medical and Technical Sciences, Chennai, India
[3]Applied Science Research Center, Applied Science Private University, Amman, Jordan
[4]Department of Computer Science and Engineering, Koneru Lakshmaiah Education Foundation, Vaddeswaram, Guntur, India

Abstract

Despite its contribution to the expansion of the national economy over the past few decades, building manufacturing has had negative effects on the environment. As a result, many governments take into account the use of green manufacturing buildings and technology when establishing strategic plans for economic development as important contributors to a greener economy and reduced carbon emissions. The implementation of eco-efficiency concepts in the building products industry, however, has received very little attention so far. In actuality, environmental sustainability is still in its infancy as it relates to construction projects and delivery. As a result, this research considers the Green Building Index, which is the greatest widely used ranking for sustainability instruments in the nation, to define and evaluate the markers of sustainability for evaluating the green construction industry in Malaysia. The relevance level and correlations in terms of sustainability in the production of green buildings are revealed using data gathered from an expert group and enhanced fuzzy Decision-Making Trial and Evaluation Laboratory. In evaluating the manufacture of green buildings in Malaysia, the results indicate that the most important criteria are energy savings and indoor environmental quality,

**Corresponding author*: muniyandy.e@gmail.com

Kanak Kalita, J.V.N. Ramesh, M. Elangovan and S. Balamurugan (eds.) Decision-Making Techniques and Methods for Sustainable Technological Innovation: Strategies and Applications in Industry 5.0, (25–44) © 2025 Scrivener Publishing LLC

whereas innovation and water efficiency are less crucial. This research may operate as a guide to help manufacturers choose and promote the best strategies for producing green buildings.

***Keywords*:** Fuzzy logic, DEMATEL, green building, building manufacturing

2.1 Introduction

Countries have continuously prioritized combating global warming in their efforts to develop. According to reports, the building industry accounts for almost 30% of all greenhouse gas outputs, with 40% of all power consumption being from developed countries Therefore, reducing greenhouse gas emissions while designing the sector is essential for combating climate change. In reality, promoting green construction by reducing waste, regulating energy use, and enhancing the eco-friendliness of buildings has drawn the attention of all parties, including governments, research organizations, universities, and emerging and developed countries [1]. According to the World Green Building Council, a "green" building has the potential to have positive impacts on our climate and natural environment during design, construction, or operation. Aiming to increase buildings' energy efficiency (EE), recent developments in green building (GB) design integrate both passive and active technology [2]. The relevance of sustainability in the construction industry is increasing, and it must be taken into account not only during the design phase but also during the whole lifespan of a building. Building information modeling enables administration of the whole lifetime (from design to demolition), but up to now, the majority of investigation has been concentrated on the design stage. Service and demolition phases often get less attention, despite the fact that all lifespan stages should be taken into account to optimize the process [3].

In this context, "green building" may be used to refer to the process of creating and utilizing healthier and more resource-efficient techniques of construction, renovation, operations, regular consumption, and demolition. It could be a gerund to refer to the GB technique or a noun to refer to the actual building [4]. GB manufacturing incorporates a variety of practices and technologies, such as the use of sustainable building practices, energy-efficient building systems, and renewable energy sources. By incorporating these elements into the building design and construction, it is possible to reduce the amount of energy and resources required during the building's lifetime [5]. Quality assurance and assurance of achievement are the strategies for quality performance. While the latter category entails activities to assess and modify manufacturing and constructing processes to meet a level of quality for the end product, the former includes systematic actions necessary to provide a level of confidence that the building components will perform admirably in service. To verify that the components installed in GBs comply with the design team's objective, more frequent inspections are conducted throughout the construction process [6].

The goal of GB is to provide people access to ecologically friendly buildings that effectively use resources such as water and energy. Reduced operating costs are another benefit of a GB. As a result, both emerging and industrialized nations are emphasizing the idea of green construction. Building sustainability depends on choosing the right materials while taking certain environmental, social, and economic factors into account [7]. In a fuzzy-based MODM approach, multiple objectives are considered simultaneously, and their relative importance and interdependence are analyzed to find a trade-off solution that optimizes the overall performance of the building. This approach can help to balance conflicting objectives and evaluate different alternatives based on the available data and expert opinion [8]. The approach could take into account factors such as energy consumption, material waste, carbon footprint, and social impact, among others. By using fuzzy logic, it is possible to account for uncertainty and imprecision in the data and prioritize different objectives based on their relative importance.

The rest of this paper is follows: Section 2.2 is literature review, Section 2.3 contains the proposed method explained, Section 2.4 includes the results and analysis, and Section 2.5 discusses the conclusion.

2.2 Related Works

The study [9] revealed the synthesis between artificial intelligence and GB and was done on trends and knowledge gaps that may be addressed in future studies. Utilizing 383 research papers from Scopus, a quantitative bibliometric assessment was done to impartially identify the primary research hotspots, trends, knowledge gaps, and upcoming research requirements. According to the study [10], a machining process plan may be decided upon using a multiobjective strategy. First, using an input process output model, the resource use and emissions that affect the environment of the machining process are examined. A weight is calculated using both subjective and objective weights, taking into account the criteria significance by intercriteria correlation (CRITIC) approach and the analytical hierarchy process (AHP) as part of the calculation. The goal of the research [11] was to identify and rank the criteria, subcriteria, and related indicators that should be used to analyze GB universities in Malaysia. The criteria and the accompanying indicators were determined using the Green Building Index (GBI), the greatest sustainability grading methodology for buildings in Malaysia. A significant portion of the expanding global energy consumption is made up of the construction industry. A key objective is to increase EE in the stock of existing buildings. So, the current study presents a parallel processing structure and results-saving archive for a multiobjective optimization framework based on simulation [12].

Building material equipment group enterprises often have issues with variable production quality and limited delivery capacity, and manufacturing quality has a significant impact on these businesses' ability to deliver goods on schedule. Therefore, the main strategy to increase their core competitiveness is to improve manufacturing quality control capabilities [13]. For the purpose [14] of evaluating GBs in China, the research creates a set of social sustainability indicators that are accurate and valid. Some research needs to be supported by GB indicators, and these indicators may also help practitioners comprehend social sustainability indicators. The fuzzy Delphi approach is thus used to assess these indicators. In addition, important factors include accessibility, comfort, and health. The research [15] proposed a new framework for adapting GB evaluation methodologies for geographical areas or nations with different climatic conditions [16–18]. The system combines the silhouette value for clustering verification, the K-means approach to group the region's diverse climates into groups, and the expert judgment of locals for local customization of GB evaluation tools [19]. The rules are modified for each climatic zone using the fuzzy AHP [20, 21].

2.3 Proposed Method

In this section, we discuss in detail the enhanced fuzzy Decision-Making Trial and Evaluation Laboratory (DEMATEL) technique to evaluate sustainability indicators for GB manufacture, and the group decision approach from multi criteria decision making (MCDM) was used in this research to establish the relative relevance of the rules for Malaysian GB production. This method has proved successful in solving problems with decision-making. It is often used in GB industry evaluation systems since it is a strong systematic tool for looking into complicated choices despite having a simple assessment process. It seems it has an easy assessment process, but it is a strong systematic approach for looking into complex choices; it is frequently utilized in relation to GB rating systems.

2.3.1 Enhanced Fuzzy DEMATEL

In terms, a fuzzy decision matrix is a decision-making tool that uses linguistics and logically fuzzy variables to examine and evaluate options. While linguistic variables use linguistic phrases or descriptions to convey individual views and preferences, fuzzy logic allows for the representation and manipulation of inaccurate or ambiguous data. A sophisticated method of decision-making called enhanced fuzzy decision-making combines fuzzy logic with a number of improvement methods in order to increase the precision and efficiency of decision-making processes. In complicated decision-making systems, enhanced DEMATEL has shown to be one of the efficient MCDM strategies for tackling practical issues. This method is reliable for identifying the connections between system criteria and their interdependencies, assisting decision-makers in understanding how these criteria affect output. Fuzzy logic may more effectively address the difficulties of uncertainty, ambiguity, and information leakage when determining the subjective weight of criteria, even though sharp-type enhanced DEMATEL has been employed by MCDM decision-maker situations on a large scale. Assume that the experts will be asked to examine a number of criteria, such as $D = D_1, D_1, \ldots, D_i, \ldots D_n$. $F = F_1, F_1, \ldots, F_i \ldots, F$. According to the influence level shown in Table 2.1, each expert E may provide his or her opinion about the impact of criteria D_j on criterion D_i.

Table 2.1 The DEMATEL impact level for fuzzy triangles of numbers.

Linguistic variable	Triangular fuzzy number	Abbreviations
Very high influence	VL	VH: (0.75,1,1)
High influence	HL	HL: (0.5,0.75,1)
Very low influence	VL	VL: (0,0.25,0.5)
Low influence	L	L: (0.25,0.5,0.75)
No influence	NI	NI: (0,0,0.25)

Note: Very high influence (VL), high influence (HL), very low influence (VL), low influence (L), no influence (NI), triangular fuzzy number (TFN).

Step 1: The initially fuzzy direct-influence matrix S is built in the first stage. For the impact of D_j on D_i supplied by the expert l, $s_{ji}^l = \left(s_{ji}^l, s_{ji}^l, s_{ji}^l, s_{ji}^l\right)$ is the outcome of the comparison of a direct effect and is derived based on the matching fuzzy triangles of numbers. Observe that such a diagonal component of the T will have zero. The initial average fuzzy matrix of direct impact, denoted by S in Equation (2.2), may be computed by applying aggregated operations on Equation (2.1)'s equations.

$$s_{ji} = s_{ji}^1 \oplus s_{ji}^2 \ldots \oplus s_{ji}^l / l$$

$$D_1 D_2 \ldots D_m \tag{2.1}$$

$$\tilde{S} = \begin{matrix} D_1 \\ D_2 \\ \ldots \\ D_j \end{matrix} \begin{bmatrix} 0 & s_{ji} & \ldots & s_{ji} \\ s_{ji} & 0 & \ldots & s_{ji} \\ \ldots & \ldots & \ldots & \ldots \\ s_{ji} & s_{ji} & \ldots & 0 \end{bmatrix} \tag{2.2}$$

Step 2: In this step, Equation (2.3) is used to calculate the matrix M (matrix of fuzzy normalized direct influence).

$$\widetilde{n_{ji}} = {}^{s_{ji}}\!/_{T} = \left(s_{ji}^K / t, s_{ji}^N / t, s_{ji}^V / t\right)$$

$$T = \underbrace{\max}_{1 \le j \le m} \left(\sum\nolimits_{i=1}^{m} s_{ji}^v\right) \tag{2.3}$$

Step 3: The following equations are used in this stage to compute the approximate total-influence matrix $\tilde{O}$. $(n \times n)$ is a square matrix in these equations, and its diagonal members are 1.

$$\tilde{O} = lim_{l\to\infty}\tilde{N} \oplus \tilde{N}^2 \oplus \ldots \oplus \tilde{N}^l = \tilde{N}(J-\tilde{N})^{-1}$$

$$\begin{aligned}\left[o_{ji}^K\right] &= N_k \times (J-N_k)^{-1},\\ \left[o_{ji}^N\right] &= N_N \times (J-N_N)^{-1},\\ \left[o_{ji}^V\right] &= N_V \times (J-N_V)^{-1}\end{aligned} \tag{2.4}$$

Step 4: By calculating $\tilde{C}_j$ and $\tilde{Q}_j$, the subjective weights are determined at this stage. The matrix of fuzziness for total-influence $\tilde{O}$ is then used to get $\tilde{C}_j$ and $\tilde{Q}_j$, which are the sums of rows and columns, respectively, using Equations (2.5) and (2.6). The ordered pairs $(\tilde{C}_j+\tilde{Q}_j, \tilde{C}_j-\tilde{Q}_j)$, $\tilde{C}_j+\tilde{Q}_j$ and $\tilde{C}_j-\tilde{Q}_j$, are then formed by deriving $\tilde{C}_j+\tilde{Q}_j$ and $\tilde{C}_j-\tilde{Q}_j$ from $\tilde{C}_j$ and $\tilde{Q}_j$.

$$\tilde{C} = \left(\widetilde{C_j}\right)_{m\times 1} = \left[\sum_{i=1}^{m}\widetilde{o_{ji}}\right]_{m\times 1} \tag{2.5}$$

$$\tilde{Q} = \left(\widetilde{Q_j}\right)_{m\times 1} = \left[\sum_{i=1}^{m}\widetilde{o_{ji}}\right]_{m\times 1} \tag{2.6}$$

In this stage, the crisp ordered pairs $\tilde{C}_j+\tilde{Q}_j{}^{def}, \tilde{C}_j-\tilde{Q}_j{}^{def}$ are generated from the ordered pairs of fuzzy $\tilde{C}_j+\tilde{Q}_j; \tilde{C}_j-\tilde{Q}_j$ using a defuzzification technique. As a result, Equation (2.7) is used to determine the relative subjective relevance of each criterion.

$$x_{j0} = \left[\tilde{C}_j+\tilde{Q}_j)(\tilde{C}_j+\tilde{Q}_j)^2+\tilde{C}_j+\tilde{Q}_j)^2\right]^{1/2} \tag{2.7}$$

Finally, by using Equation 2.8 to the direct influence relationship, we can get the subjective weight.

$$x_j^t = {x_{j0}}\Big/{\sum_{j=1}^{m}x_{j0}} \tag{2.8}$$

2.4 Results and Discussion

An enhanced fuzzy DEMATEL-based questionnaire was developed and provided to specialists at some Malaysian institutions and construction enterprises scholars and experts in the fields of building management, green construction, and computerization in construction. This was done to verify the sustainability elements and determine their relative importance. The paired question format was used in the construction of the enhanced fuzzy DEMATEL questionnaire. The process of making decisions on sustainability-related issues is multifaceted and challenging. Therefore, selecting experts with the necessary expertise, training, and experience is more crucial than selecting a large-enough sample size because it is not the latter significant in MCDM techniques.

The evaluation MCDM model's hierarchical structure is shown in Table 2.2 and consists of 6 major criteria, 54 items, and 17 subcriteria. The questions in pairs were created to allow comparisons by the experts by expressing the relative relevance of one aspect when compared to each measurement, its supporting criteria, and its corresponding indicators. Each measurement, criterion, and subcriterion affect how many contrasting ideas are used. Experts give these comparisons for the dimensions using 0- to 4-point scale measurements.

Table 2.2 GBI Integrated Environmental Building's criteria, subcriteria and indicators.

Part	Criteria	Item (indicator)	Subcriterion
1	Innovation	Innovation and environmental design initiatives Facilitator of the Green Building Index Water efficient—irrigation/ landscaping	
2	Water efficiency	Water recycling System for metering and leak detection Water reduction	Water harvesting and recycling Increased efficiency

(*Continued*)

Table 2.2 GBI Integrated Environmental Building's criteria, subcriteria and indicators. (*Continued*)

Part	Criteria	Item (indicator)	Subcriterion
3	Materials reuse	Materials with recycled content Materials selection and reuse Sustainable timber Regional resources Building waste management Keeping and collecting recyclables Clean agents and refrigerants	Recycled and reused materials Sources of sustainability Waste control Organic products
4	Energy efficiency (EE)	Submetering for electricity Lowest EE performance Postoccupancy commissioning is ongoing Enhanced commissioning Sustainable maintenance EE verification	Design Commissioning Verification and maintenance
5	Environmental quality indoors	Control of tobacco smoke in the environment Control and monitoring of carbon dioxide Breakout areas Design and controllability of thermal comfort systems Level of electric lighting	Air quality Thermal comfort Comfortable lighting, visibility, and acoustics
6	Planning and management of sustainable sites	Community connectivity and development density Noise pollution Construction activity pollution control: earthworks Worker's site amenities Vehicle priority: green Route and proximity of the cargo delivery Plant life and roof Building user's guide	Site planning Construction management Transportation Design

The findings elucidate that, from the standpoint of experts, EE (weight 6.651) and environmental quality (EQ) (weight 6.154) are the paramount criteria within the GBI for Integrated Environmental Building (IEB) (refer Table 2.3). Within the EE dimension, the subcriterion "design and performance" emerges as the most significant, possessing a weight of 7.21 (refer Table 2.4). Furthermore, "advanced or improved EE performance—building energy intensity (BEI) and/or energy use intensity (EUI)" is identified as the most critical indicator within "design and performance," with a weight of 0.43.

In the EQ dimension (refer Table 2.5), "lighting, visual, and acoustic comfort" is deemed to hold greater significance than other criteria, with a weight of 8.65. The indicators "daylighting" and "external views" achieve the highest weights within "lighting, visual, and acoustic comfort," with weights of 8.65 and 0.34, respectively. In the site management category (refer Table 2.6), "site planning," with a weight of 7.21, is regarded as more crucial compared to the other criteria. The indicators "environmental management" and "noise pollution" are recognized as two vital elements within this category.

In the materials reuse (MR) dimension (refer Table 2.7), "reused and recycled materials" is recognized as a significant criterion, with a weight of 8.13. Within this dimension, the criterion "materials reuse and selection" is deemed more critical than others, holding a weight of 0.75. In the WE category (refer Table 2.8), "water harvesting and recycling" stands out as the most essential criterion. Within this framework, "rainwater harvesting" is prioritized over "water recycling," with a weight of 7.31.

Table 2.3 DEMATEL results for criteria importance level.

Criteria	$(D_i + R_i)^{def}$	$(D_i - R_i)^{def}$
SSPM	5.954	0.021
IEQ	6.154	0.542
EE	6.651	0.456
WE	5.056	0.845
MR	5.860	0.794
Innovation	4.346	0.123

Note: Energy efficiency (EE), indoor environmental quality (IEQ), sustainable site planning and management (SSPM), materials reuse (MR), water efficiency (WE).

Lastly, in the innovation (IN) dimension, "innovation in design and environmental design initiatives" achieves the highest significance concerning the "GBI-accredited facilitator" indicator.

Table 2.4 DEMATEL results for subcriteria importance level (energy efficiency).

Subcriteria	$(D_i + R_i)^{def}$	$(D_i - R_i)^{def}$
DP	7.21	0.43
Commissioning	5.63	0.86
VM	5.13	0.26

Note: Design and performance (DP), verification and maintenance (VM).

Table 2.5 DEMATEL results for subcriteria importance level (indoor environmental quality).

Subcriteria	$(D_i + R_i)^{def}$	$(D_i - R_i)^{def}$
AQ	6.54	0.77
OC	4.32	0.52
Verification	6.15	1.24
LVAC	8.65	0.34

Note: Air quality (AQ), occupant comfort (OC), lighting, visual, and acoustic comfort (LVAC).

Table 2.6 DEMATEL results for subcriteria importance level (sustainable site planning and management).

Subcriteria	$(D_i + R_i)^{def}$	$(D_i - R_i)^{def}$
Transportation	3.16	0.51
SP	7.21	0.37
Design	5.04	0.21
CM	5.13	0.34

Note: Site planning (SP), construction management (CM).

Table 2.7 DEMATEL results for subcriteria importance level (materials reuse).

Subcriteria	$(D_i + R_i)^{def}$	$(D_i - R_i)^{def}$
GP	7.33	0.16
SR	7.41	0.23
RRM	8.13	0.75
WM	7.39	0.94

Note: Reused and recycled materials (RRM), sustainable resources (SR), waste management (WM), green products (GP).

Table 2.8 DEMATEL results for subcriteria importance level (water efficiency).

Subcriteria	$(D_i + R_i)^{def}$	$(D_i - R_i)^{def}$
WHR	7.31	0.52
IE	5.22	0.24

Note: Water harvesting and recycling (WHR), increased efficiency (IE).

Energy efficiency

The production of GBs and their EE refers to the ability of building materials and products to use less energy while maintaining or improving their performance compared to traditional materials. Figure 2.1 and Table 2.9 depict the EE of the proposed method.

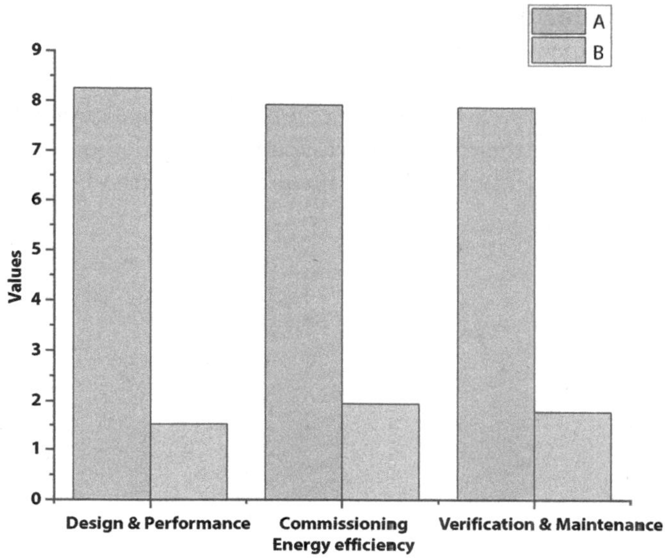

Figure 2.1 Results from DEMATEL for the EE.

Table 2.9 Result of energy efficiency.

Energy efficiency	Values	
	A	**B**
Design and performance	8.25	1.52
Commissioning	7.92	1.95
Verification and maintenance	7.87	1.78

Indoor environmental quality

Indoor environmental quality (IEQ) in the context of GB manufacturing refers to interior building conditions that have an impact on residents' comfort, health, and well-being. It encompasses a range of factors such as air quality, lighting, thermal comfort, acoustics, and ergonomics. Figure 2.2 and Table 2.10 denote the IEQ of the proposed method.

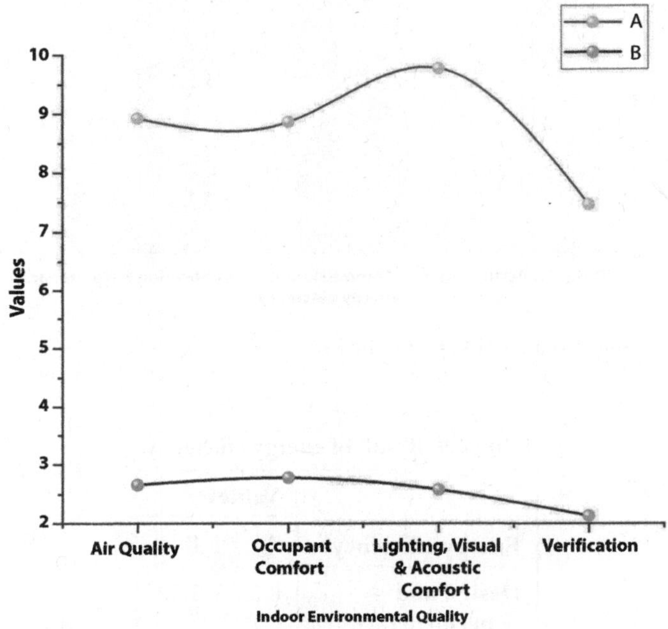

Figure 2.2 Results from DEMATEL for the indoor environmental quality.

Table 2.10 Results of indoor environmental quality.

Indoor environmental quality	Values	
	A	B
Occupant comfort	8.86	2.78
Lighting, visual, and acoustic comfort	9.77	2.58
Air quality	8.92	2.66
Verification	7.46	2.13

Water efficiency

WE in the context of GB manufacturing refers to the efficient use of water in and around buildings, as well as the reduction of water waste and the impact of the building on the surrounding water resources. Figure 2.3 and Table 2.11 show the water efficiency of the proposed method. By using water-efficient fixtures and appliances, collecting and using nonpotable water, implementing efficient landscaping, and monitoring water usage, the building can operate more sustainably and reduce its overall environmental footprint.

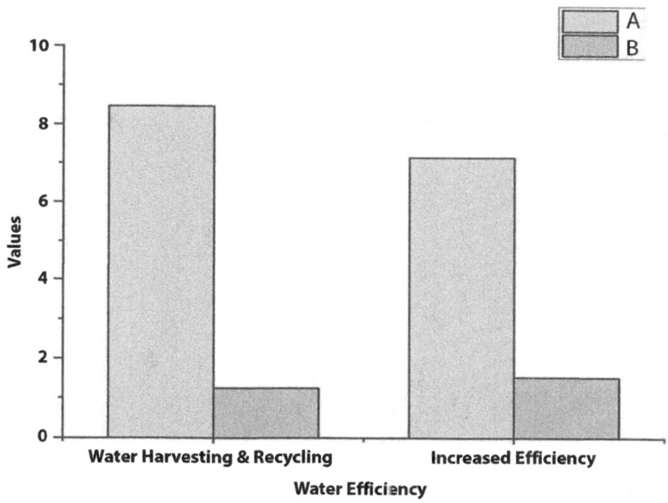

Figure 2.3 Results from DEMATEL for the water efficiency.

Table 2.11 Results of water efficiency.

	Values	
Water efficiency	**A**	**B**
Water harvesting and recycling	8.46	1.24
Increased efficiency	7.15	1.52

Innovation

The use of sustainable materials, such as recycled or low-impact materials, and sustainable construction practices, such as prefabrication and modular construction leads to reduced waste and improved efficiency. Figure 2.4 and Table 2.12 demonstrate the innovation of the proposed method. The application of a coordinated design strategy that engages all parties involved in the planning and building phases, such as architects, engineers, builders, and building owners should be implemented in order to maximize the efficiency and sustainability of the structure.

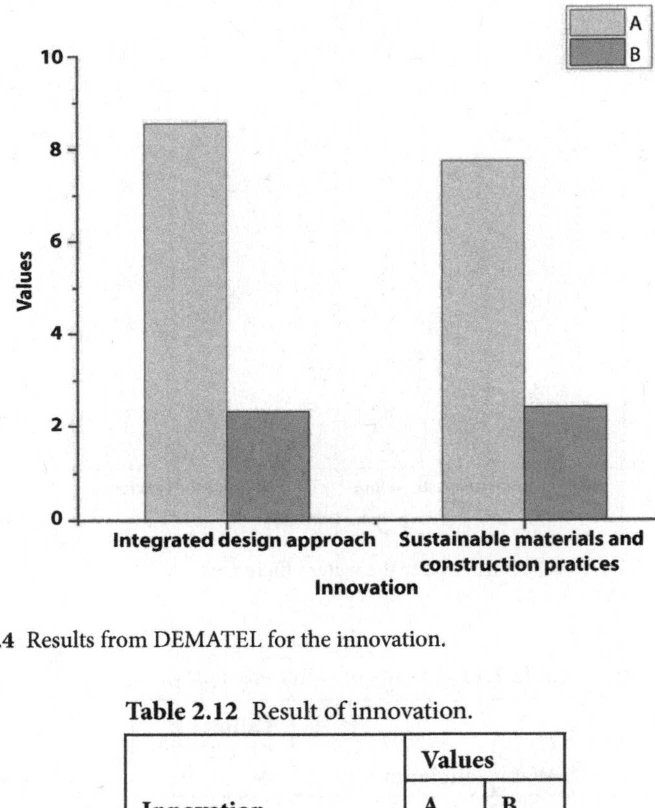

Figure 2.4 Results from DEMATEL for the innovation.

Table 2.12 Result of innovation.

Innovation	Values	
	A	B
Integrated design approach	8.55	2.32
Sustainable materials and construction practices	7.73	2.41

2.5 Conclusion

The preservation of the environment has elevated to the top of global cultures' agendas over the past few decades. Manufacturing companies are under more pressure to engage in environmentally conscious practices because they are the primary sources of worldwide degradation of the environment. Eco-efficiency techniques to provide excellent products and services while minimizing their adverse effects on the natural world is need of the hour. Despite its importance to nation growth, it has reportedly had negative environmental effects. The production of buildings has begun to adopt eco-friendly evaluation processes and procedures. However, there has not been a lot of research done on the production of GBs. Less has been written about using green building rating systems (GBRSs) to decide on and prioritize sustainability metrics that are acceptable for evaluating industrial GB performance. Because GBI is the most widely used sustainable rating instrument in the nation, this study's objective was to define and rate the criteria for evaluating GB manufacture in Malaysia. As a result, using GBI, 5 primary criteria, 15 subcriteria, and 53 associated sustainability indicators were chosen, and information was gathered from a group of experts. Fuzzy DEMATEL was used, and the findings suggested that EE and EQ are the most crucial factors in GBI-IEB. The study determined "designing and efficiency" in the EE dimensions as the most crucial subcriterion, while "lighting, visual, and acoustic comfort" in the EQ dimensions is more crucial than other considerations. WE and IN were found to be the least crucial criteria.

References

1. Yadegaridehkordi, E., Hourmand, M., Nilashi, M., Alsolami, E., Samad, S., Mahmoud, M., Alarood, A.A., Zainol, A., Majeed, H.D., Shuib, L., Assessment of sustainability indicators for green building manufacturing using fuzzy multi-criteria decision-making approach. *J. Clean. Prod.*, 277, 122905, 2020, https://doi.org/10.1016/j.jclepro.2020.122905.
2. Jami, T., Karade, S.R., Singh, L.P., A review of the properties of hemp concrete for green building applications. *J. Clean. Prod.*, 239, 117852, 2019, https://doi.org/10.1016/j.jclepro.2019.117852.
3. Muller, M.F., Esmanioto, F., Huber, N., Loures, E.R., Canciglieri, O.C., A systematic literature review of interoperability in the green Building Information Modeling lifecycle. *J. Clean. Prod.*, 223, 397–412, 2019, https://doi.org/10.1016/j.jclepro.2019.03.114.

4. Lu, W., Chi, B., Bao, Z., Zetkulic, A., Evaluating the effects of green building on construction waste management: A comparative study of three green building rating systems. *Build. Environ.*, 155, 247–256, 2019, https://doi.org/10.1016/j.buildenv.2019.03.050.
5. Meena, C.S., Kumar, A., Jain, S., Rehman, A.U., Mishra, S., Sharma, N.K., Bajaj, M., Shafiq, M., Eldin, E.T., Innovation in green building sector for sustainable future. *Energies*, 15, 18, 6631, 2022, https://doi.org/10.3390/en15186631.
6. Raouf, A.M. and Al-Ghamdi, S.G., Framework to evaluate the quality performance of green building delivery: Construction and operational stage. *Int. J. Construct. Manage.*, 23, 2, 253–267, 2023, https://doi.org/10.1080/15623599.2020.1858539.
7. Al-Atesh, E.A., Rahmawati, Y., Zawawi, N.A.W.A., Utomo, C., A decision-making model for supporting a selection of green building materials. *Int. J. Construct. Manage.*, 23, 5, 922–933, 2023, https://doi.org/10.1080/15623599.2021.1944548.
8. Huang, C.F., Chen, W.T., Kao, C.K., Chang, H.J., Kao, P.M., Wan, T.J., Application of fuzzy multi-objective programming to regional sewer system planning. *Processes*, 11, 1, 183, 2023, https://doi.org/10.3390/pr11010183.
9. Debrah, C., Chan, A.P.C., Darko, A., Artificial intelligence in green building. *Autom. Constr.*, 137, 104192, 2022, https://doi.org/10.1016/j.autcon.2022.104192.
10. Lv, L., Deng, Z., Meng, H., Liu, T., Wan, L., A multi-objective decision-making method for machining process plan and an application. *J. Clean. Prod.*, 260, 121072, 2020, https://doi.org/10.1016/j.jclepro.2020.121072.
11. Yadegaridehkordi, E. and Nilashi, M., Moving towards green university: A method of analysis based on multi-criteria decision-making approach to assess sustainability indicators. *Int. J. Environ. Sci. Technol.*, 19, 9, 8207–8230, 2022, https://doi.org/10.1007/s13762-022-04086-y.
12. Tavakolan, M., Mostafazadeh, F., Jalilzadeh Eirdmousa, S.J., Safari, A., Mirzaei, K., A Parallel computing simulation-based multi-objective optimization framework for economic analysis of building energy retrofit: A case study in Iran. *J. Build. Eng.*, 45, 103485, 2022, https://doi.org/10.1016/j.jobe.2021.103485.
13. Xu, W., Wu, R., Wang, L., Zhao, X., Li, X., Solving a multi-objective distributed scheduling problem for building material equipment group enterprises by measuring quality indicators with a product gene evaluation approach. *Comput. Ind. Eng.*, 168, 108142, 2022, https://doi.org/10.1016/j.cie.2022.108142.
14. Tseng, M.L., Li, S.X., Lin, C.R., Chiu, A.S., Validating green building social sustainability indicators in China using the fuzzy Delphi method. *J. Ind. Prod. Eng.*, 40, 1, 35–53, 2023, https://doi.org/10.1080/21681015.2022.2070934.

15. Sadeghi, M., Naghedi, R., Behzadian, K., Shamshirgaran, A., Tabrizi, M.R., Maknoon, R., Customization of green buildings assessment tools based on climatic zoning and experts' judgment using K-means clustering and fuzzy AHP. *Build. Environ.*, 223, 109473, 2022, https://doi.org/10.1016/j.buildenv.2022.109473.
16. Kalita, K., Ganesh, N., Shankar, R., Chakraborty, S., A fuzzy Marcos-based analysis of dragonfly algorithm variants in industrial optimization problems. *Informatica*, 35, 1, 155–178, 2024, https://doi.org/10.15388/23-INFOR538. DOI: 10.15388/23-INFOR538.
17. Shanmugasundar, G., Mahanta, T.K., Čep, R., Kalita, K., Novel fuzzy measurement alternatives and ranking according to the compromise solution based green machining optimization. *Processes*, MDPI, 10, 12, 2022, https://doi.org/10.3390/pr10122645.
18. Bansod, A.V., Patil, A.P., Kalita, K., Deshmukh, B.D., Khobragade, N., Fuzzy multicriteria decision-making-based optimal Zn-Al alloy selection in corrosive environment. *Int. J. Mater. Res.*, 111, 11, 953–963, 2020, https://doi.org/10.3139/146.111957.
19. Shivakoti, I., Pradhan, B.B., Diyaley, S., Ghadai, R.K., Kalita, K., Fuzzy TOPSIS-based selection of laser beam micro-marking process parameters. *Arabian J. Sci. Eng.*, 42, 11, 4825–4831, 2017, https://doi.org/10.1007/s13369-017-2673-1.
20. Manikandan, S., Vickram, S., Subbaiya, R., Karmegam, N., Woong Chang, S., Ravindran, B., Kumar Awasthi, M., Comprehensive review on recent production trends and applications of biochar for greener environment. *Bioresour. Technol.*, 388, 129725, 2023, https://doi.org/10.1016/j.biortech.2023.129725.
21. Manikandan, S., Krishnan, R.Y., Vickram, S., Subbaiya, R., Kim, W., Govarthanan, M., Karmegam, N., Emerging nanotechnology in renewable biogas production from biowastes: Impact and optimization strategies–A review. *Renew. Sustain. Energy Rev.*, 181, 113345, 2023, https://doi.org/10.1016/j.rser.2023.113345.

3

Sustainable Energy Options: Qualitative TOPSIS Method for Challenging Scenarios

Muniyandy Elangovan[1,2*], Puppala Ramya[3] and Chandrashekhar Goswami[4]

[1]*Department of Biosciences, Saveetha School of Engineering, Saveetha Institute of Medical and Technical Sciences, Chennai, India*
[2]*Applied Science Research Center, Applied Science Private University, Amman, Jordan*
[3]*Department of Computer Science and Engineering, Koneru Lakshmaiah Education Foundation, Vaddeswaram, Guntur, India*
[4]*Faculty of Computing and Informatics, Sir Padampat Singhania University, Udaipur, Rajasthan, India*

Abstract

Multicriteria decision-making techniques give managers important information at every stage of the choice-making procedure. However, because unpredictability exists in reality, criteria are not always absolute. Fuzzy structures and multiple-criteria decisions involving uncertainties are recognized as appropriate approaches to solving conflicting issues that defy numerical representation, particularly in planning and analysis for power. In this research, a modified TOPSIS (technique for order performance by similarity to ideal solution) method with qualitative linguistic labels for group decision-making with several criteria is proposed. This approach takes into account various degrees of precision when addressing uncertainty. Subjective linguistics identifiers represent every choice maker's assessment of the efficiency of options in relation to each criterion. Without any prior collection, the new method uses linguistic data supplied by the decision-makers. To produce a complete ranking of alternatives, the suggested method incorporates decision-maker judgments. As an illustrated investigation where power strategy possibilities are ranked, an application in energy planning is provided. Three environmental and energy specialists examined seven alternative energy sources based on nine criteria. Fuzzy analytical hierarchy process is used to calculate the weights of the criterion, while qualitative TOPSIS is used to establish the order

**Corresponding author*: muniyandy.e@gmail.com

Kanak Kalita, J.V.N. Ramesh, M. Elangovan and S. Balamurugan (eds.) Decision-Making Techniques and Methods for Sustainable Technological Innovation: Strategies and Applications in Industry 5.0, (45–68) © 2025 Scrivener Publishing LLC

of the possibilities. The advantages of the proposed methodology for managing linguistic evaluations to create a framework uncertainties and imprecision are demonstrated by comparison with a customized fuzzy TOPSIS technique. While the latest strategy involves less mental work from individuals, it nonetheless produces comparable outcomes.

***Keywords*:** TOPSIS, qualitative reasoning, multicriteria choices, linguistic labeling, energy management

3.1 Introduction

Due to its ability to promote advantages on the social, environmental, and economic fronts, sustainable development (SD) has gained enormous relevance in the modern world. The idea supports fulfilling immediate demands while maintaining a generation's potential to provide for itself in the future. However, since it involves taking a number of elements considered and stakeholder perspectives, decision-making in SD is inherently complex. In this regard, multicriteria decision-making (MCDM) techniques offer a useful strategy for tackling the complexities of decision-making in SD. As a result of these methodologies' facilitation of the examination of many criteria, decision-makers are better equipped to make educated and thorough judgments that take into account the various aspects that go into sustainably [1].

In numerous political papers [2], one of the most significant issues is the creation of sustainable energy sources. The building industry, which accounts for 10% of CO_2 emissions and 40% of all primary energy consumption, is crucial in resolving these problems. Building renovation is a top objective of the EU Renovation Wave Strategies. The Renovation Wave Strategy seeks to drastically cut down on greenhouse gas emissions and boost energy effectiveness in buildings by doubling or more current renovation rates over the next 10 years. As a result, reducing energy use in buildings is crucial in the fight against global warming. Heating, ventilation, and air conditioning use up the majority of the energy in a structure. By selecting the right building design options, significant energy savings in buildings can be obtained. Structures' improved insulating capabilities significantly cut thermal expenditure; as a result, many societies' national energy programs now place a high priority on improving energy savings in buildings.

Discussions about the production of power have arisen as a result of the recent increase in energy consumption caused by demographic change and increased economic activity. There is more focus based on the assumption that energy usage and manufacturing ought to reflect the principle of SD as a consequence of the rising consumption of power, the finite energy supplies, and the severe usage of fossil fuels that have been having detrimental environmental effects. Based on the assumption that energy usage and manufacturing ought to reflect the principle of SD, many nations are working to develop them, accelerating the global renewable energy sector's growth with success [3].

A comprehensive and integrated approach to the functions of the economy, society, and environment is known as "sustainable development." An SD strategy aims to deliver services that satisfy current, fundamental human needs in a cleaner, more effective manner while maintaining the requirements of coming generations. Energy today has a significant environmental impact and is unquestionably crucial for achieving the SD and the success of a society. The achievement of SD can be greatly aided by improvements in the energy efficiency of processes using sustainable resources. The adoption of energy sources that produce the fewest environmental pollution is highly advised by SD. To substitute for or limit the usage of fossil fuels for electricity, alternative sources of energy must be developed [4].

The ability of MCDM to incorporate scientific data and multistakeholder value into decision-making procedures based on building information modeling is beginning to be demonstrated. It integrates component indications from all available data sources into one comprehensive picture indication to compare and rank decision-making processes. These component indicators are frequently at odds with one another. The MCDM is composed of three key steps: (1) identify pertinent substitutions and features; (2) connect numerical measurements to the relative weights of various attributes and how alternatives affect them; and (3) use numerical measures to rank and order various alternatives. The AEC business is plagued by a number of MCDM issues. Through its synergy with building information modeling, MCDM's potential in the AEC industry can be more effectively encouraged [5].

Using a variety of parameters to make decisions, MCDM was among the most widely used decision approaches in those fields, which included the business, sciences, engineering, and government. The effectiveness of choices can be improved by using MCDM techniques, which make forming the decision-making process more clear, logical, and efficient. The need for manufacturers to react swiftly was implied by the rapid technological advancements in the creation of goods. The selection decisions are complex since decision-making is becoming increasingly challenging. A variety of methodologies have been widely used in recent years in many different fields in various circumstances for MCDM [6, 7].

3.2 Related Works

The article [8] examined a research that used MCDM techniques as a significant tool to assess household renewable energy technology. The results of the research are grouped in accordance with the goals that were pursued, and the evaluation criteria are described. The article also breaks down the key benefits and drawbacks of utilizing MCDM techniques to assess household technology. It also includes an overview and in-depth examination of these techniques.

In the article [9], the use of MCDM in several SD engineering fields has gained a lot of attention. There are numerous studies of MCDM techniques; however, there are not many comprehensive reviews of MCDM in the fields of low-carbon transportation and sustainable logistics. This work conducts a systematic evaluation of more than 190 publications published between 2010 and 2022 in order to address these gaps in the state of the art. It also builds a broader framework of MCDM methodologies for this academic issue, gives a thorough analysis, reviews present procedures, and simplifies them.

The research [10] discussed the life cycle assessment (LCA) and MCDM methods for evaluating the sustainability of waste management systems. They provide a framework for combining LCA–MCDM methods. In order to emphasize the technical and sustainability criteria applied in the research, they first identified the most popular MCDM approaches for disposal techniques described in academic publications. Then, important LCA study findings regarding waste management systems were examined and discussed. According to the review's findings, there are not many studies that combine LCA and MCDM to evaluate the sustainability of waste management systems. Additionally, less than half of the studies that used the combined technique were unsuccessful to take into account all three sustainability pillars.

The article [11] analyzes the methodologies that the scientific community has employed over the last 10 years to assess the sustainability of renewable energy sources. This work's main goals are to confirm that a methodological framework that comprised a combination of LCA and MCDM is the best one for evaluating a collection of sustainable indicators, assessment methods, and the settings in which they are used, which are needed to evaluate the long-term viability of sustainable power sources.

One hundred fifty-five examples of sustainable energy infrastructure evaluations were used to develop a knowledge repository with an emphasis on solar panels.

The study [12] suggests an approach that highlights the effects of each cleaning method and links it to the sustainable development goals and the targets that go along with it. The solar photovoltaic (PV) plant depends on the PV panels' output and efficiency. In addition to excessive heat and natural shadowing, certain geographical areas are more prone to unfavorable dust accumulating on the surfaces of PV panels.

The study [13] offers an automated MCDM method coupled with a geographic information system to address the complex nature of recognizing locations and priority challenges brought on by the existence of several indications, including economics, surroundings, technology, problems with society, and risk factors. The field of bioenergy falls under the purview of multiple ministries, particularly those of energy, agriculture, the environment, industry, and commerce, making decisions in this area challenging. Surrounding and physically, the biomass feedstocks are dispersed.

In some studies [14, 15], the best cleaning procedure for Dubai is determined using the MCDM technique known as the Comparison of Preferences to the Perfect Solutions. This strategy prioritizes the choices by taking into account the deciding elements and their relative significance to the cleaning techniques. The work's objective is to take social, economic, and environmental factors into account while deciding on the best cleaning technique for solar PV panels.

In the articles [16–18], uses of MCDM in sustainable production were presented in an organized manner. In the current study, papers from the Scopus database that discussed the use of various MCDM approaches in the field of sustainable manufacturing were reviewed. The study emphasizes the advantages of using MCDM methodologies for decision-making in the industrial industry.

3.3 Methods and Materials

A mathematical formulation is created to aid in evaluating choices when dealing with multifaceted and collective choices for ordering issues. The technique provided in this article has been modified from the technique used in the investigation to summarize the TOPSIS (technique for order performance by similarity to ideal solution) approach's best and worst reference points for assessing alternatives based on comparing distances to a single ideal indicator [19, 20]. To achieve this, following the introduction of some preliminary materials, the suggested TOPSIS approach, known as qualitative TOPSIS (Q-TOPSIS), is described [21].

3.3.1 Preliminaries

3.3.1.1 *Models of Absolute Qualitative Order of Magnitude*

In order to create the models of absolute order of magnitude, an interval that determines the set of fundamental labels is partitioned. A collection of actual monuments serves to define the separation. The term qualitative algebra refers to a broad mathematical framework that integrates the concepts of sign algebra and interval arithmetic.

Definition 1. Let $\left[e_1, e_{m+1}\right]$ a genuine time period and $\{e_1, \ldots, e_{m+1}\}$ some actual places, with $e_1 < .. < e_{m+1}$. Simple labels are defined by $A_j = \left[e_j, e_{m+1}\right], j = 1,..,m$.

Definition 2. The nonbasic labels designating various degrees of precision are as follows: $\left[A_j, A_i\right] = \left[e_j, e_{m+1}\right]$, where $j,i = 1,\ldots,m$, and $j < i$. The label $\left[E_j, E_i\right]$ complies with the idea "between A_j and A_i."

A point-of-reference method affected the qualitative approach that was used to evaluate alternatives. This method rates many possibilities $\{E_1,.., E_1\}$ utilizing a distance-based formula. It relies on subjective linguistic evaluations and aims to minimize the distance between each alternative and a predefined reference point that best represents the ideal performance for each criterion. According to the methodology, every option is determined by a set of *k* criteria, and each of those criteria is assessed by the opinions of a group of *n* specialists. These assessments are made with the aid of a collection of numerical labels with varied degrees of accuracy that correspond to a particular order-of-magnitude space $\mathbb{G}_m = \{\left[E_j, E_i\right] \mid j,i = 1, m+1, j \leq i\}$ considering $\left[E_j, E_i\right] = A_j$.

In this approach, every potential $E_j, j = 1,\ldots f$, is depicted by an *r*-dimensional description vector in $\left(\mathbb{G}_m\right)^r, E_j \leftrightarrow \left(E_{j_{1n}}, \ldots, E_{j_{k1}}, \ldots, E_{j_{kn}}\right)$, *r* considering the result of quantity of requirements, and the quantity of professionals: $r = k,n$. The position of the value $\mathbb{G}_m$, which facilitates shifting from a normal scale to a numerical size, is described as follows. This technique yields the distances between linguistics *r*-dimensional vector of basic and nonbasic labels.

Definition 3. The expression $l: \mathbb{G}_m \rightarrow \mathbb{H}^2$ that is the location function definition in $\mathbb{G}_m$.

$$f\left(\left[E_j, E_i\right]\right) = \left(-\sum\nolimits_{g=1}^{j-1} \mu\left(P_g\right), \sum\nolimits_{g=i+1}^{m} \mu\left(P_g\right)\right) \tag{3.1}$$

where μ is any specified measure over the collection of fundamental labels, such as $\mu\left(P_j\right) = \mu\left(\left[e_j, e_{j+1}\right]\right) = e_{j+1} - e_j$.

In this case, both sets of real values are employed to represent the opposite of a combination of the fundamental labeling measures to the left and to the right, respectively. As a result, the position of the in variables of a subjectively label is defined by the mixture of both of these sets of actual numbers $\left[E_j, E_i\right]$.

Every possible solution E_j is encoded using a $2r$-dimensional matrix of integers by assigning an equation f to every element of the r-dimensional vector of labels: $F\left(E_j\right) = \left(f\left(E_{j11.}\right), \ldots, f\left(E_{j1n.}\right), \ldots, f\left(E_{jk1.}\right), \ldots f\left(E_{jkn.}\right)\right)$.

3.4 Analytical Hierarchy Process Method to Compute Weights

In the MCDM writing, particular focus has been placed on the formulation of the weighted criterion for aggregating procedures. To determine the general deciding value of the possibilities, evaluations assigned to various criteria are particularly crucial. The criteria weights can be applied in many ways, depending on how MCDM models are aggregated. Weights can be interpreted as indicators of the significance or trade-offs among variables. In multi-criteria decision-making (MCDM) techniques that utilize distance metrics, weights are often determined through pairwise comparisons to achieve a balanced evaluation of criteria. In this investigation, the analytic hierarchy process (AHP) is specifically employed to determine the weights of criteria used to assess various energy sources.

It employs an organizational structure system to determine the relative relevance of every condition to the other. The framework's organization, contrasting assessment of the standards, and synthesis of the priorities form the foundation of the AHP technique. A complex problem is divided into an organization in the first stage, with a goal serving as the main aim and criteria, and their subsections arranged like an ancestral tree's stages and lower levels. To identify the comparative relevance of the criteria within each level, the second stage starts with a prioritization technique. It goes from the second level to the lowest one and is evaluated using pairings to determine the decision maker (DM) inclinations. Every matrix's respective weights are as follows: identified and adjusted in the final stage. The AHP is regarded as a single strategy for synthesizing criteria.

Both qualitative and quantitative factors might be used in this procedure. Additionally, a fuzzy conduct of the AHP technique was created for dealing with unknowns visible in some complex problems. When the judgments of the specialists are represented by linguistic variables, the fuzziness and ambiguity of the decision-makers are taken into account by the fuzzy AHP. Generally speaking, experts employ linguistic phrases, which are converted to fuzzy; triangle fuzzier integers are used to lastly present evaluation rankings and weights.

3.5 The Proposed Q-TOPSIS Technique

Order-of-magnitude systems with perfect quality are the framework that originated in subdivision and can be processed using the TOPSIS method named Q-TOPSIS, which is proposed in this work. Imagine a collection of $\{E_1,\ldots,E_1\}$ options, each of which is determined by a set of r requirements that are evaluated by a group of m specialists. These assessments are made using a collection using descriptive adjectives of varying degrees of precision that fall under a specific magnitude-order region $\mathbb{G}_m$. A labeled k-dimensional vector, where k is the sum of the quantity of requirements, and the quantity of specialists is used for representing each choice, $E_j, j=1,..,f$ and $r=k{\cdot}n$:

$$E_j \leftrightarrow \left(E_{j11},\ldots,E_{j1n},\ldots,E_{jk1},\ldots E_{jkn}\right), E_{jiz} \in \mathbb{G}_m, i=1,\ldots,f, i=1,..,k,$$
$$z=1,\ldots,n$$

We define the qualitative positive reference label (QPRL) as an r-dimensional vector, denoted as (QPRL) $E^*=\left(P_m,\ldots,P_m\right)$. Similarly, the qualitative negative reference label (QNRL) is represented as a k-dimensional matrix (QNRL) $E^-=(P_1,\ldots,P_1)$. These reference points serve as standard benchmarks and are used to compute the range of values for evaluating alternatives. They function as reference positions for assessing the performance of service numbers across different criteria.

$$F\left(E^*\right)=\left(-\sum_{g=1}^{m-1}\mu\left(P_g\right),0,\ldots,-\sum_{g=1}^{m-1}\mu\left(P_g\right),0\right) \tag{3.2}$$

$$F\left(E^{-}\right)=\left(0,\sum_{g=2}^{m}\mu\left(P_g\right),\ldots,0\sum_{g=2}^{m}\mu\left(P_g\right)\right) \tag{3.3}$$

The weighted Euclidean radius of every potential site $F(E_j), j=1,\ldots,f$ to E^* and E^- places is determined after that; therefore, $t\left(F(E_j),F(E^*)\right)$ *and* $t\left(F(E_j),F(E^-)\right)$ by applying Equation (3.4) to the vectors and $\left(y,x\right)=t\left(F(E_j),F(E^*)\right)$ and $\left(Y,X\right)=t\left(F(E_j),F\left(E^-\right)\right)$, respectively:

$$t\left(Y,X\right)=\sqrt{\sum_{j=1}^{k}U_j\sum_{j=1}^{2n}\left(Y_{ij}-X_{ij}\right)^2} \tag{3.4}$$

where $Y_{ij}, X_{ij}, i=1,\ldots,2n, j=1,\ldots,k$, and U_j, the weight corresponding to the $j-th$ indicator, are the corresponding elements of Y and X. Finally, using Equation (3.5), the possibilities are ordered in decreasing order of the QCC_j values to calculate each possibility's quantitative proximity score.

$$QCC_j=\frac{t_j^-}{t_j^*+t_j^-}, j=1,2,\ldots,1. \tag{3.5}$$

where the distances compared to the alternate location $F(E_j)$, the QPRL location $F\left(E^*\right)$, and the QNRL location $F\left(E^-\right)$ are denoted by t_j^* and t_j^-, accordingly. The preorder defined by the values of QCC_j can be used to rank options; the value of QCC_j increases with the alternative's proximity to and distance from E^* and E^-, respectively. In this situation, which occurs frequently when using the TOPSIS methodology, the alternative E_j with the highest QCC_j is selected as the optimal option.

3.6 Results and Discussion

3.6.1 A Q-TOPSIS Investigation that Demonstrates How to Choose Sustainable Energy Sources

An application for choosing alternate sources of sustainable energy is provided to show the possibilities of this approach. The presented approach is demonstrated using an instance example based on the supplied data. With the use of this case study, they are able to demonstrate the key benefits of the Q-TOPSIS approach over the already used techniques, such as conventional TOPSIS and fuzzy TOPSIS. In particular, representing ambiguity in human thoughts and allowing professionals to use "different levels of precision" in assessments are two key features of the suggested method. The applicability of this for choosing sustainable energy alternatives is evident despite the fact that it is not specifically relevant to energy concerns and may be applicable generally for selecting the best among possibilities. When some experts do not have sufficient understanding of a certain topic, it is essential to use psychological declarations with varying degrees of precision for expert evaluation.

3.6.1.1 Alternatives, Criteria, and Indicators for Sustainability Assessment

The present article looked at seven alternatives: nuclear, wind, biomass, conventional, solar, hydraulic, and combined heat and power (CHP). To evaluate the offered possibilities, nine indicators were chosen, taking into consideration the most popular technological, economic, environmental, and social aspects. Note that the same metrics were used in this study, so that results could be compared; other significant biological indicators such as carbon monoxide (CO), sulfur dioxide (SO_2), and suspended particulate matter (SPM) pollutants as well as health and dangers to the environment are taken into account. Because of this, the Q-TOPSIS approach is used based on the weighted average of these 9 factors, as determined by a panel of three experts.

Efficiency, investment cost, energy, CO_2 emission, operation and NOX emission, maintenance cost, and environmental indicators and land use; job creation and social characteristics; the production of jobs; and acceptance in society are the ones that are applied into account for every factor. Figure 3.1 shows the modification of the CO_2 emission standard.

3.6.2 Results

The Q-TOPSIS algorithm stages are carried out when the indicators, weights, and alternatives have been defined and described, along with the criterion evaluations. The Q-TOPSIS methodology used in this case employs seven fundamental subjective labels. Table 3.1 displays these descriptive labels and their placements while taking into account the assessment over the set of fundamental labeled 1 for 2.

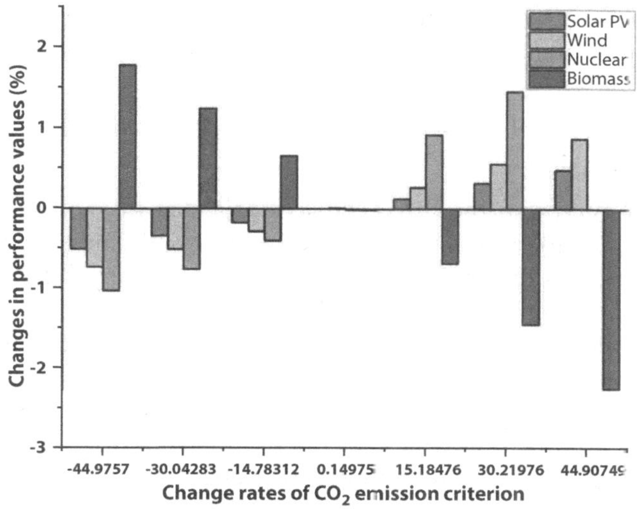

Figure 3.1 Performance modifications of the CO_2 emission standard.

Table 3.1 Evaluation scores.

Qualitative labels	Linguistic terms	Locations
VP	B_1	(0,6)
P	B_2	(−1,5)
MP	B_3	(−2,4)
F	B_4	(−3,3)
MG	B_5	(−4,2)
G	B_6	(−5,1)
VG	B_7	(−6,0)

Note: Very poor (VP), poor (P), medium poor (MP), fair (F), medium good (MG), good (G), very good (VG).

Every specialist uses nine qualitative labels (one for each indication) to evaluate every option. As a result, a vector of qualitative labels in 27 dimensions is used for representing each option A.

$$E \leftrightarrow \left(A_{1,1},\ldots,A_{1,9},A_{2,1},\ldots A_{2,9},A_{3,1},\ldots,A_{3,9}\right) \tag{3.6}$$

After that, every possibility is codified by the position algorithm applying a 54-dimensional integer vectors, as was previously indicated.

$$E \leftrightarrow \left(X,\ldots,X_{1,18},X_{2,1},\ldots X_{2,18},X,\ldots,X_{3,18}\right) \tag{3.7}$$

Keep in mind that the three matrices provided in Table 3.2's *i*th row were combined to create the vector in Equation (3.7) for each possibility. Table 3.2 displays the analysis matrix for the options by highlighting the positions of the nine indicators while taking into account independently the judgments given by the E1, E2, and E3 constituting three energy management specialists.

When calculating distances, the two vectors,..., 0,6,...,0,6 and,..., 6,0,..., 6,0, are taken into consideration as the regards designations. Then, using Equation (3.8), one can determine the statistical Euclidean separation between each option and the QPRL and QNRL.

$$t\left(E,\tilde{E}\right)=\sqrt{\sum\nolimits_{j=1}^{9} U_j \sum\nolimits_{j=1}^{6}\left(Y_{ij}-\tilde{X}_{ij}\right)^2} \tag{3.8}$$

The process described in subsection Q-TOPSIS methodology was used, and the following weights are taken into consideration: 0.09; 0.1, 0.1, 0.11, 0.13, 0.15, 0.11, 0.09, and 0.12. Table 3.2 displays the values of the QPRL and QNRL distances to each possibility as well as the values of the 111.

The modified fuzzy TOPSIS methodology is contrasted with Q-TOPSIS in two various manners. The outcomes of the Q-TOPSIS utilization (Table 3.3) for choosing sustainable energy substitutes in Subsection A are compared with those of the outcomes gathered using the modified fuzzy TOPSIS developed in the second subsection. In the section, they theoretically compared both techniques. Since both the suggested approach and the modified fuzzy TOPSIS are TOPSIS methods that express ambiguity with language identifiers, these two methods can be compared. They chose the modified fuzzy TOPSIS technique for the comparison since it is, in certain technical aspects, similar to Q-TOPSIS in order to show the novel contributions of our methodology.

3.6.3 Method Comparison

A well-liked tool for analyzing the best option is an altered version of fuzzy TOPSIS that takes as input a fuzzy judgment matrix that has been assessed.

Table 3.2 Decision matrices that are qualitative.

E_1	Q_1	Q_2	Q_3	Q_4	Q_5	Q_6	Q_7	Q_8	Q_9
A_1	(−7,1)	(−5,3)	(−6,2)	(−4,4)	(1,7)	(−3,5)	(1,7)	(−3,6)	(−6,2)
A_2	(−6,1)	(−7,1)	(1,7)	(−7,1)	(−3,5)	(−3,5)	(1,7)	(−3,5)	(−6,2)
A_3	(−3,5)	(−4,4)	(−5,3)	(−4,4)	(−7,1)	(−6,2)	(−6,2)	(−6,2)	(−5,2)
A_4	(−4,4)	(−6,2)	(−6,2)	(−6,2)	(−6,2)	(−7,1)	(−6,2)	(−7,1)	(−4,4)
A_5	(−4,4)	(−6,2)	(−5,3)	(−4,4)	(−3,5)	(−2,6)	(−3,5)	(−4,4)	(−6,2)
A_6	(−4,4)	(−4,4)	(−5,3)	(−4,4)	(−6,2)	(−6,2)	(−5,3)	(−6,2)	(−6,2)
A_7	(−5,3)	(−4,4)	(−5,4)	(−3,5)	(−4,4)	(−4,4)	(−6,2)	(−5,3)	(−5,3)
E_2	P_1	P_2	P_3	P_4	P_5	P_6	P_7	P_8	P_9
A_1	(−6,2)	(−6,2)	(−5,3)	(−5,3)	(1,7)	(1,7)	(−2,6)	(−3,5)	(−5,3)
A_2	(−7,1)	(−4,3)	(1,7)	(−7,1)	(−4,4)	(−4,4)	(−4,4)	(−2,6)	(−6,1)
A_3	(−4,4)	(−4,4)	(−4,4)	(−5,4)	(−5,1)	(−6,2)	(−7,1)	(−6,2	(−4,4)
A_4	(−3,5)	(−6,3)	(−4,2)	(−6,2)	(−6,2)	(−7,1)	(−7,1)	(−6,2)	(−4,4)
A_5	(−6,3)	(−6,2)	(−5,3)	(−4,4)	(−3,5)	(−2,6)	(−3,5)	(−4,4)	(−6,2)
A_6	(−4,4)	(−5,3)	(−5,3)	(−4,4)	(−6,2)	(−6,2)	(−5,3)	(−6,2)	(−6,2)
A_7	(−4,3)	(−5,3)	(−4,4)	(−3,5)	(−4,4)	(−4,4)	(−5,3)	(−6,2)	(−6,2)
E_3	P_1	P_2	P_3	P_4	C_5	P_6	P_7	P_8	P_9
A_1	(−6,2)	(−6,2)	(−5,3)	(−5,3)	(0,7)	(0,7)	(−3,6)	(−3,5)	(−5,3)
A_2	(−7,1)	(−4,3)	(1,7)	(−7,1)	(−4,4)	(−4,4)	(−5,4)	(−2,6)	(−6,1)
A_3	(−2,4)	(−4,4)	(−4,4)	(−4,4)	(−7,1)	(−6,2)	(−8,1)	(−6,2	(−4,4)
A_4	(−3,5)	(−5,3)	(−6,2)	(−6,2)	(−6,2)	(−7,1)	(−8,1)	(−6,2)	(−2,4)
A_5	(−6,3)	(−6,2)	(−5,3)	(−4,4)	(−3,5)	(−2,6)	(−4,5)	(−4,4)	(−6,2)
A_6	(−4,4)	(−5,3)	(−5,3)	(−4,4)	(−6,2)	(−6,2)	(−6,3)	(−6,2)	(−6,2)
A_7	(−4,3)	(−5,3)	(−4,4)	(−3,5)	(−2,4)	(−4,4)	(−6,3)	(−6,2)	(−5,2)

Table 3.3 Qualitative TOPSIS results.

	t_j^-	t_j^*	QCC_j
A_1	8.615	9.034	0.488
A_2	10.288	9.658	0.515
A_3	11.538	6.421	0.642
A_4	13.120	5.437	0.707
A_5	9.205	8.974	0.506
A_6	11.492	5.878	0.661
A_7	10.138	7.496	0.574

Distances between the fuzzy-positive and fuzzy-negative ideal solutions are calculated; this MCDM technique calculates the optimal alternative based on a compilation of the experts' ratings on fuzzy assessments. Linguistic preferences are transformed into fuzzy triangle numbers in modified fuzzy TOPSIS. The key distinctions between the modified fuzzy TOPSIS and Q-TOPSIS methodology are shown in Table 3.4. The variations listed in Table 3.4 represent four noteworthy upgrades from enhanced fuzzy TOPSIS.

Both methods utilize linguistic variables, but in distinct ways. Q-TOPSIS employs triangular fuzzy numbers to represent qualitative indicators with varying degrees of precision, whereas fuzzy TOPSIS applies a more generalized fuzzy logic framework for evaluation. In both approaches, the distance of each alternative from the ideal (best) and anti-ideal (worst) solutions is calculated using aggregated results. Although both methods aim to rank alternatives based on closeness to these reference points, they differ in their computational mechanisms and representation of uncertainty.

Table 3.4 Nuances between the two techniques.

Differences	Fuzzy TOPSIS	Q-TOPSIS
Aggregation step	Weighted mean	Without prior aggregation
Granularity	Fixed granularity	Multigranularity
Normalization	Normalization	Without prior normalization
Scale	Fuzzy triangle numbers	Qualitative labels

First off, because the computations are done directly with the labels using position operations, the Q-TOPSIS strategy for creating the first qualitative concepts does not call for any prior separation or naming of features. The modified fuzzy TOPSIS, in contrast, uses cutoff points to define fuzzy labels that must be specified before any aggregate triangle fuzzy numbers. Second, several levels of accuracy can be addressed using the Q-TOPSIS approach, from the most basic, exact, and most specific label, which is used to indicate elements that are uncertain. As previously indicated, decision-makers occasionally create errors if they are pushed to make more exact judgments considering the alternatives that knowledge permits. In this manner, experts are not pressured to make judgments that are more accurate than they are capable of. Finally, an aggregate of opinions from experts or a previous normalization is not required for the Q-TOPSIS technique calculations. The latter reduces discrepancies by condensing expert opinions into a specific range, whereas the former includes a loss of knowledge. But as can be seen in the following subsection, the outcomes of using both approaches are comparable.

3.6.4 Results Comparison and Sensitivity Analysis

Adapted fuzzy A case-example application of Q-TOPSIS has been used to apply TOPSIS to the data obtained in order to choose sustainable energy choices. Three specialists assessed 9 linguistically specified triangular numeric indications of the technological, economic, environmental, and social kinds shown in Table 3.5 with respect to all of the seven energy options: conventional, biomass, biomass, solar, nuclear, hydraulic, and CHP.

The adjusted fuzzy TOPSIS generated the appropriate alternative ranking for the specific scenario (1.09, 1.1, 1.1, 0.1, 1.11, 1.13, 1.15, 1.11, 1.09, and 1.12): "wind > biomass > solar > CHP > hydraulic > nuclear > conventional energy." The same data were used for both methods, and for this specific scenario, according to both surveys, wind power was deemed to be the best kind of sustainable production. Despite the fact that the two MCDM linguistic techniques handle uncertainty in different ways, their outcomes generate evaluations that are identical.

Additionally, a sensitivity analysis was performed to examine the outcomes when using both approaches, taking into account the four additional scenarios while altering the weights taken into account for each criterion, shown in Table 3.6. An important step in any multiple-criteria

Table 3.5 The alternatives' fuzzy ratings.

Linguistic terms	Fuzzy numbers
Fair (F)	(4,6,8)
Poor (P)	(10,11,12)
Very good (VG)	(1,1,2)
Good (G)	(8,10,11)
Medium poor (MP)	(3,5,6)
Very poor (VP)	(1,1,2)
Medium good (MG)	(6,8,10)

Table 3.6 Indications with varying weights for five layouts.

	Lay 1	Lay 2	Lay 3	Lay 4	Lay 5
Q_1	1.10	1.3	1.3	1.06	1.4
Q_2	1.2	1.1	1.16	1.06	1.06
Q_3	1.2	1.06	1.06	1.2	1.06
Q_4	1.12	1.06	1.06	1.2	1.06
Q_5	1.14	1.2	1.3	1.16	1.3
Q_6	1.16	1.2	1.06	1.16	1.06
Q_7	1.12	1.2	1.06	1.16	1.06
Q_8	1.10	1.2	1.06	1.16	1.06
Q_9	1.13	1.3	1.3	1.2	1.3

problem approach is determining whether the outcome rating is based on and sensitive to the estimations of the criteria scores.

Table 3.7 provides an overview of the outcomes of utilizing both strategies. Only the cells in the darker areas showed variations. Every time the initial thing is displayed, the subsequent element and the Q-TOPSIS outcome display an altered fuzzy TOPSIS result, in each shaded cell.

Table 3.7 Sensitivity analysis.

Lay 1	Lay 2	Lay 3	Lay 4	Lay 5
B	W	W	BS/S	S
C	C	C	C	C/Water
W	B	B	W	B
N/water	N	N/CHP	Water	N/CHP
Water/N	Water	Water	N	Water/C
CHP	CHP	CHP/N	CHP	CHP/N
Solar	S	S	S/B	W

Note: Biomass (B), convent (C), wind (W), nuclear (N), solar (S).

Table 3.7 demonstrates that, in the first choice, the findings from the two techniques always agree, and that, generally speaking, they produce comparable rankings of the alternatives. Particularly, both methodologies yield the exact same ranking in Scenario 2. In the final scenario, there were further differences discovered. This observation may be explained on the grounds since the proportions used in the last scenario's variance deviations are noticeably higher than those of the other situations. Furthermore, shifting the weight of C1's criteria shifts the place of winds as a substitute in the earlier scenarios, demonstrating how heavily the weights of metric for effectiveness affect this choice. The options that were moved into different locations were more responsive to changes in the weights of the criterion. Figure 3.2 shows the performance modification of water consumption criterion.

Last but not least, a simulation was run with 30 additional situations in which the weights taken into account varied at random for each criterion in order to compare the similarities between the two ranking algorithms. The correlation coefficient values from the 30 situations are displayed in Figure 3.3. For each of the 30 cases, the association values for Spearman ρ and Kendall τ were determined to be extremely relevant qualities, with 0.05 p values reported in each situation. For these coefficients, the average and variation from the mean were $\rho = 0.97$ and $r = 0.93$, and $S = 0.037$ and $S_c = 0.082$, respectively. The findings show that the outcomes from the two strategies have a strong association.

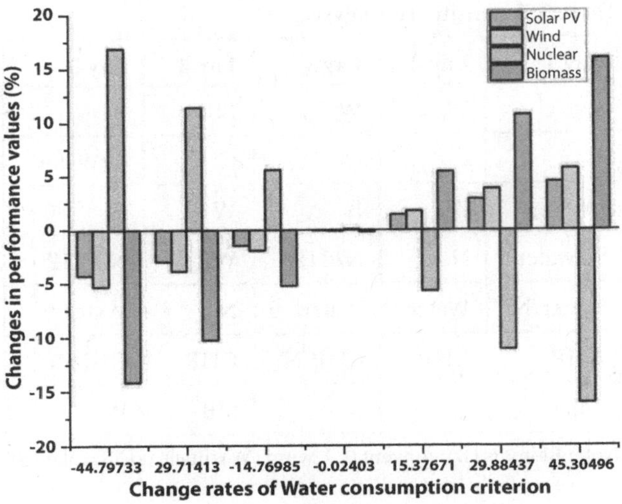

Figure 3.2 Performance modifications of water consumption criterion.

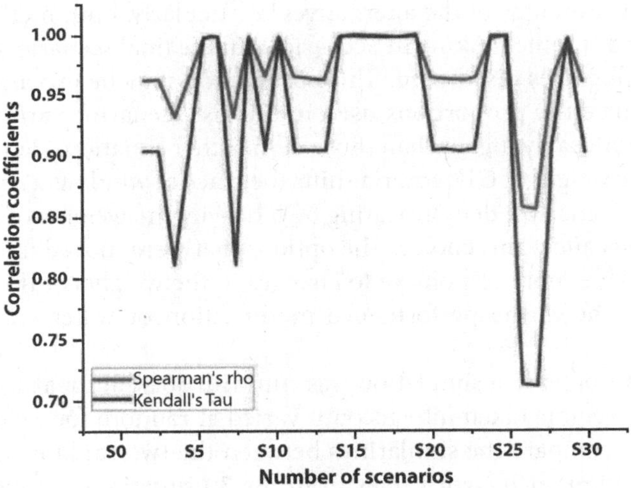

Figure 3.3 Kendall τ and Spearman ρ correlation coefficients.

3.6.5 Enabling Specialists to Employ Various Degrees of Precision

We demonstrate the method's capability to effectively depict the inherent ambiguity of human thinking by illustrating a modeled extension of

Scenario 1, in which analysts are allowed to use different levels of accuracy in their evaluations. Costs, societal acceptance, and job creation are frequently the variables with the greatest degree of unpredictability, which implies that results and forecasts may differ greatly. As a result, we believe that Expert 1 makes ambiguous judgments while evaluating criteria (C9, C3, C8, and C4) in Scenario 1. Table 3.8 shows the prior values evaluated for Expert 1 evaluations in relation to these four criteria, the locations of which are shown in Table 3.4, as well as the new assessments with varying levels of precision.

The final rating remains unchanged from the previous one, with wind energy coming in first, followed by CHP, biomass, hydraulic, solar, nuclear, and then conventional energy (Table 3.7). Q-TOPSIS can be utilized for calculating these consequences. This method is recommended in the present investigation, as the adapted fuzzy TOPSIS approach is not capable of handling such types of assessments.

This example demonstrates the uniqueness and value of the suggested method because, although allowing experts to communicate their doubt through approximate rankings, it still produces the same end rating, allowing for the same findings to be attained with less data. Additionally, this supports the claim that the suggested method can be applied to actual circumstances more readily and with fewer attempts at thinking in the opinion of the professionals. But obviously, if the evaluations are less accurate,

Table 3.8 Expert 1 evaluation using terms that are not basic.

	A_3		A_4		A_8		A_9	
E_1	BL	N-BL	BL	N-BL	BL	N-BL	BL	N-BL
Q_1	P_5	$[P_2–P_6]$	P_3	P_3	P_5	P_5	P_5	$[P_3–P_6]$
Q_2	P_1	P_1	P_2	$[P_1–P_3]$	P_7	P_7	P_6	P_6
Q_3	P_4	$[P_3–P_5]$	P_6	P_6	P_4	$[P_3–P_5]$	P_4	$[P_3–P_5]$
Q_4	P_6	P_6	P_7	P_7	P_6	P_6	P_4	P_4
Q_5	P_5	$[P_4–P_6]$	P_4	$[P_3–P_5]$	P_4	$[P_1–P_7]$	P_6	P_6
Q_6	P_4	$[P_3–P_5]$	P_6	$[P_5–P_6]$	P_4	$[P_3–P_5]$	P_6	P_6
Q_7	P_4	$[P_1–P_7]$	P_6	P_6	P_3	$[P_1–P_4]$	P_5	$[P_4–P_5]$

Note: Basic labels (BL), nonbasic labels (N-BL).

Table 3.9 Expert 1's evaluation of more unconventional labels.

	A_9		A_4		A_8		A_3	
E_1	BL	N-BL	BL	N-BL	BL	N-BL	BL	N-BL
Q_1	P_5	$[P_3–P_5]$	P_5	P_5	P_3	P_3	P_5	$[P_4–P_6]$
Q_2	P_6	$[P_4–P_6]$	P_7	$[P_1–P_3]$	P_2	$[P_1–P_3]$	P_1	$[P_1$-$p_2]$
Q_3	P_4	$[P_4–P_6]$	P_4	$[P_4–P_6]$	P_6	$[P_6–P_7]$	P_4	$[P_4–P_7]$
Q_4	P_4	$[P_4–P_6]$	P_6	$[P_6–P_7]$	P_7	P_7	P_6	$[P_6–P_7]$
Q_5	P_6	$[P_4–P_7]$	P_4	$[P_4–P_6]$	P_4	$[P_4–P_6]$	P_5	$[P_5–P_6]$
Q_6	P_6	$[P_4–P_6]$	P_4	$[P_3–P_5]$	P_6	$[P_4–P_6]$	P_4	P_4
Q_7	P_5	$[p_4–P_6]$	P_3	$[P_4–P_5]$	P_6	P_6	P_4	$[P_2–P_6]$

the resultant ranking can differ, as is the case in the scenario shown in Table 3.9.

According to these updated rankings, hydroelectricity is superior to solar energy, biomass energy, CHP energy, nuclear energy, and traditional electricity. The relative positions of solar/biomass and hydro/nuclear are flipped in a fresh sequence.

3.7 Conclusion

It is necessary to study and measure various sorts of factors containing inaccuracy while taking into account natural, economic, technological, and social elements. These aspects, particularly the social nations, are not always accurate because the real world is full of ambiguities and imprecisions. Consequently, in order to give relevant information from professionals, to assist decision-makers in all phases of their decision-making process with unclear values, a new MCDM technique is provided. The use of linguistic factors involving quantitative labeling with varying degrees of precision allows for the capturing of this imprecision. This strategy, which is based on order-of-magnitude qualitative ranking, offers an approach that can get outcomes based on nonnumeric data.

The quantitative TOPSIS technique, which is introduced and used in a case study on energy, is the primary contribution of this research. Management for sustainable energy involves making significant choices in an array of dynamic complications that take competing the environment, financial, social, and technical variables into consideration. This approach takes preference strength into consideration and equips professionals to evaluate options in the face of ambiguity by articulating their opinions through linguistic factors incorporating quantitative labeling. In order to create methods that energy managers can easily utilize for evaluation procedures, it is advantageous to use quantitative labels with varying degrees of accuracy. This approach may capture the uncertainty already present in human reasoning and solves the issue while maintaining the importance of the principle: Each variable is appraised with the appropriate level of accuracy.

The modified fuzzy TOPSIS approach, which makes use of a different set of linguistic factors, is contrasted with the suggested Q-TOPSIS method in this study. The enhanced fuzzy TOPSIS method makes use of fuzzy linguistic factors to assess the options. The most suitable sustainable energy option for a certain geographic location will be identified for further study using the suggested Q-TOPSIS approach and real data. Furthermore, with regard to the program for choosing sustainable energy alternatives, the theoretical framework can be greatly expanded to include other factors, such as handling waste, additional environmental pollutions (SO_2, GHG, CO, and SPM), public health and risk to the environment, and the effects of potential mishaps. These indicators are essential in energy studies. For investments in any sources of energy that be taken into consideration in potential applications, other factors such as the internal rate of returns and payoff duration are crucial economic criteria.

References

1. Rane, N.L., Achari, A., Choudhary, S.P., Multi-criteria decision-making (MCDM) as a powerful tool for sustainable development: Effective applications of ahp, fahp, topsis, electre, and vikor in sustainability.
2. Siksnelyte-Butkiene, I., Streimikiene, D., Balezentis, T., Skulskis, V., A systematic literature review of multi-criteria decision-making methods for sustainable selection of insulation materials in buildings. *Sustainability*, 13, 2, 737, 2021, https://doi.org/10.3390/su13020737.
3. Rediske, G., Siluk, J.C.M., Michels, L., Rigo, P.D., Rosa, C.B., Cugler, G., Multi-criteria decision-making model for assessment of large photovoltaic farms in Brazil. *Energy*, 197, 117167, 2020, https://doi.org/10.1016/j.energy.2020.117167.
4. Rezaei, M., A multi-criteria decision-making approach for sustainable energy prioritization. *Environ. Energy Econ. Res.*, 6, 1, 1–19, 2021.

5. Tan, T., Mills, G., Papadonikolaki, E., Liu, Z., Combining multi-criteria decision making (MCDM) methods with building information modelling (BIM): A review. *Autom. Constr.*, 121, 103451, 2021, https://doi.org/10.1016/j.autcon.2020.103451.
6. Hindi, R., El-Assal, A., Sabry, I., Multi-criteria decision-making methods comparative analysis in fuzzy environment: Article review. *Benha J. Appl. Sci.*, 7, 5, 227–235, 2022, https://doi.org/10.21608/bjas.2022.260612.
7. Wu, Z. and Abdul-Nour, G., Comparison of multi-criteria group decision-making methods for urban sewer network plan selection. *CivilEng*, 1, 1, 26–48, 2020, https://doi.org/10.3390/civileng1010003.
8. Siksnelyte-Butkiene, I., Zavadskas, E.K., Streimikiene, D., Multi-criteria decision-making (MCDM) for the assessment of renewable energy technologies in a household: A review. *Energies*, 13, 5, 1164, 2020, https://doi.org/10.3390/en13051164.
9. Tian, G., Lu, W., Zhang, X., Zhan, M., Dulebenets, M.A., Aleksandrov, A., Fathollahi-Fard, A.M., Ivanov, M., A survey of multi-criteria decision-making techniques for green logistics and low-carbon transportation systems. *Environ. Sci. Pollut. Res. Int.*, 30, 20, 57279–57301, 2023, https://doi.org/10.1007/s11356-023-26577-2.
10. Torkayesh, A.E., Rajaeifar, M.A., Rostom, M., Malmir, B., Yazdani, M., Suh, S., Heidrich, O., Integrating life cycle assessment and multi criteria decision making for sustainable waste management: Key issues and recommendations for future studies. *Renew. Sustain. Energy Rev.*, 168, 112819, 2022, https://doi.org/10.1016/j.rser.2022.112819.
11. Campos-Guzmán, V., García-Cáscales, M.S., Espinosa, N., Urbina, A., Life Cycle Analysis with Multi-Criteria Decision Making: A review of approaches for the sustainability evaluation of renewable energy technologies. *Renew. Sustain. Energy Rev.*, 104, 343–366, 2019, https://doi.org/10.1016/j.rser.2019.01.031.
12. Aljaghoub, H., Abumadi, F., AlMallahi, M.N., Obaideen, K., Alami, A.H., Solar PV cleaning techniques contribute to Sustainable Development Goals (SDGs) using multi-criteria decision-making (MCDM): Assessment and review. *Int. J. Thermofluids*, 16, 100233, 2022, https://doi.org/10.1016/j.ijft.2022.100233.
13. Zhao, B., Wang, H., Huang, Z., Sun, Q., Location mapping for constructing biomass power plant using multi-criteria decision-making method. *Sustain. Energy Technol. Assess.*, 49, 101707, 2022, https://doi.org/10.1016/j.seta.2021.101707.
14. Rediske, G., Siluk, J.C.M., Michels, L., Rigo, P.D., Rosa, C.B., Cugler, G., Multi-criteria decision-making model for assessment of large photovoltaic farms in Brazil. *Energy*, 197, 117167, 2020, https://doi.org/10.1016/j.energy.2020.117167.
15. Jamwal, A., Agrawal, R., Sharma, M., Kumar, V., Review on multi-criteria decision analysis in sustainable manufacturing decision making. *Int. J.*

Sustain. Eng., 14, 3, 202–225, 2021, https://doi.org/10.1080/19397038.2020.1866708.

16. Kalita, K., Pal, S., Haldar, S., Chakraborty, S., A hybrid TOPSIS-PR-GWO approach for multi-objective process parameter optimization. *Process Integr. Optim. Sustain.*, 6, 4, 1011–1026, 2022, https://doi.org/10.1007/s41660-022-00256-0.
17. Diyaley, S., Shilal, P., Shivakoti, I., Ghadai, R.K., Kalita, K., PSI and TOPSIS based selection of process parameters in WEDM. *Period. Polytech., Mech. Eng.*, 61, 4, 255–260, 2017, https://doi.org/10.3311/PPme.10431.
18. Manikandan, S., Vickram, S., Sirohi, R., Subbaiya, R., Krishnan, R.Y., Karmegam, N., Sumathijones, C., Rajagopal, R., Chang, S.W., Ravindran, B., Awasthi, M.K., Critical review of biochemical pathways to transformation of waste and biomass into bioenergy. *Bioresour. Technol.*, 372, 128679, 2023, https://doi.org/10.1016/j.biortech.2023.128679.
19. Thanigaivel, S., Vickram, S., Manikandan, S., Deena, S.R., Subbaiya, R., Karmegam, N., Govarthanan, M., Kim, W., Sustainability and carbon neutralization trends in microalgae bioenergy production from wastewater treatment: A review. *Bioresour. Technol.*, 364, 128057, 2022, https://doi.org/10.1016/j.biortech.2022.128057.
20. Dey, N., Kumar, G., Vickram, A.S., Mohan, M., Singhania, R.R., Patel, A.K., Dong, C.D., Anbarasu, K., Thanigaivel, S., Ponnusamy, V.K., Nanotechnology-assisted production of value-added biopotent energy-yielding products from lignocellulosic biomass refinery–a review. *Bioresour. Technol.*, 344, A, 126171, 2022, https://doi.org/10.1016/j.biortech.2021.126171.
21. Jamuna, G., Yasodha, S., Thamarai, P., Vickram, A.S., Swaminaathan, P., Saravanan, A., Yaashikaa, P.R., Design strategies, utilization and applications of nano-engineered biomaterials for the enhancement of bioenergy: A sustainable approach. *Biochem. Eng. J.*, 200, 109104, 2023, https://doi.org/10.1016/j.bej.2023.109104.

4

Sustainable Education in the Age of 5G and 6G Networks: An Analytical Perspective

Kambala Vijaya Kumar[1]*, Yalanati Ayyappa[2], T. Preethi Rangamani[3], Eswar Patnala[1], Vinay Kumar Dasari[1] and Gudipalli Tejo Lakshmi[1]

[1]*Department of Computer Science and Engineering, Koneru Lakshmaiah Education Foundation, Vaddeswaram, Guntur, India*
[2]*Department of Computer Science and Engineering, Vel Tech Rangarajan Dr. Sagunthala R&D Institute of Science and Technology, Avadi, India*
[3]*Freshman Engineering Department, P.V.P Siddhartha Institute of Technology, Vijayawada, India*

Abstract

Based on biological growth and social frameworks, students develop physiologically and socially. Students enhance their knowledge *via* thought and action as they grow, receiving ongoing feedback. Teachers need to be comfortable using new technologies, especially in today's classroom. Learning is now time- and space-unlimited to technology. As a result, incorporating modern technology and teaching techniques gives teachers access to workable and extremely beneficial educational tools. In this research, we analyze the sustainable education in the age of fifth-generation (5G) and sixth-generation (6G) networks. This study primarily focuses on the teacher's role as it investigates the implementation of new communication technology in education. The analysis hierarchical technique was employed through interviews and questionnaire surveys to examine the variables influencing the use of contemporary communication technologies. In education, 5G technology is one of the newer innovations that helps make learning accessible and efficient. The significance of the criterion layer demonstrates that, with the right support, it is possible to integrate new technology into education. Teachers are wary of utilizing new technology because of the effort, time, and resources required to develop suitable content. Despite the numerous benefits of modern technology, including 5G, its issues prevent teachers from actively utilizing it. The

**Corresponding author*: kvijayakumar@kluniversity.in

Kanak Kalita, J.V.N. Ramesh, M. Elangovan and S. Balamurugan (eds.) Decision-Making Techniques and Methods for Sustainable Technological Innovation: Strategies and Applications in Industry 5.0, (69–84) © 2025 Scrivener Publishing LLC

conclusions of this study provide a fundamental understanding of the need to inspire instructors to effectively integrate technological advances into education, particularly teaching, and to support the promotion employing environmentally conscious educational technologies to close the success divide.

Keywords: Sustainable education, age of 5G and 6G networks, analytical hierarchy process (AHP), teachers, students

4.1 Introduction

The requirement for sustainable practices in fifth-generation (5G) networks and smart cities has increased due to technical developments in network services, telephony, intelligent cities, and the Internet of Things (IoT). According to the Brundtland Report, developing resources effectively enables contemporary requirements to be met without endangering the capacity of future generations [1]. Additionally, sixth-generation (6G) wireless networks are being suggested to more efficiently address and facilitate the societal sustainable development goals required. The recommended 6G network specifications might include 1 Tbps of ultrafast data rates, less than 1 ms of low latency, enhanced coverage and mobility, flexibility and practical connections between items at the trillion-level 60 b/s per Hz peak spectral efficiency high-system dependability, and enhanced network safety [2]. Studies for 6G have generated a lot of interest from academia and business focused on discovering key drivers, performance requirements, and technology breakthroughs for 6G of mobile cellular networks during the global commercialization of 5G [3]. 5G technological devices, although just developed, have the qualities to address these issues; it is defined by improved interaction, individualization, and diversification. For industry, academia, and education, it is mostly employed in multimedia communication. The huge data volume, quick data transmission, and capacity to support significantly reduced latency between interconnected devices are the main features of 5G technology that are used in applications [4]. The latest innovations and techniques will make fully remote education of full distance learning competitive with the established modes of instruction and learning. Digital duplicates, a technology with the potential to revolutionize teaching and learning, are additionally briefly introduced [5]. This study primarily focuses on the teacher's role as it investigates the implementation of new communication technology in education. The analysis hierarchical technique was employed through interviews and questionnaire surveys to examine the variables influencing the use of contemporary communication technologies. In education,

5G technology is one of the newer innovations that helps make learning accessible and efficient.

4.2 Related Work

The goal of the study by Vanelli-Coralli *et al.* [6] is to provide for our society's growing demand for ubiquitous and constant connectivity services in all facets of our lives, from education to banking, politics to health, and entertainment to environmental protection; the evolution of 5G technology toward above 5G and 6G networks is intended. According to a research [7] considering the requirement for specialized data as well as the enormous number of connected devices, developing businesses working on technologies that will replace 5G have extra options to take into account. Specialists are working on the architecture of next 6G networks to continue advancement in next-generation communication. The goal of the study by Tariq *et al.* [8] is to provide predictions on cutting-edge technologies that could bring about the tectonic disturbances required for 6G to advance the idea of 5G to more ambitious future scenarios. In a research [9], there is no dispute that the quantity of network infrastructure and the number of connected terminals will increase during the course of the current 5G and upcoming 6G decades, which will have an impact on the rise in energy prices. In the objective of the study by Gohar and Nencioni [10], the growth of new industries and subindustries, the implementation of cost-saving measures, and enhancements to the quality of goods and services will all be made possible by the high bandwidth and secondary latency characteristics of 5G. They covered the current advancements toward enabling 6G wireless systems, proposed an extensive classification based on many criteria, and highlighted several unresolved issues and crucial advice. They concluded that 6G systems enable the Internet of Everything–based innovative services. Consequently, intelligent cities' full potential will be realized [11]. Machine learning (ML), in particular, and artificial intelligence (AI), in general, can significantly aid in developing 6G network applications. They provided an overview of ML methods used in 6G wireless communication systems in this study and a recent analysis of ML methods [12]. The vehicular network is attracting significant interest from businesses and academia to facilitate the development of intelligent transportation systems, autonomous driving, and smart cities [13]. The advancement of information and communication technology and its applications, such as blockchain technology, AI, virtual reality, and the IoT, have impacted the creation of the 6G communication infrastructure [14].

Only after a country can be considered adaptive for sustainable development is technological advancement vital. To satisfy future demand, these papers describe an IoT-based smart grid that aids energy conservation [15].

4.3 Methodology

4.3.1 Elements for Hierarchical Structure

Education happens as professors and students converse and interact in a classroom context. The growth and individuality of each student are the main concerns of emotional learning. Emotional learning requires an uncentralized, informal root structure for student-centered education.

4.3.2 Students

Considering that every student incorporates a distinct personality, they frequently internalize the characteristics of their classifications. Students in schools rely on the manifestation of this commonality for learning. However, because they relate the course material to their thinking methods, students prefer emotional learning. The framework of environmental concept emphasizes the value of the outdoors in teaching and learning. Individual connection and growth take place inside intricate, interrelated ecological systems. Instructors may now focus a greater extent on their learners in the educational setting, thanks to the IoT and 5G technologies. They support teachers in developing students' abilities and responsibilities while seeing each student as an individual and the primary educational element.

4.3.3 Teachers

By fostering two-way relationships with their students, teachers have a significant impact on them. Thus, teachers' and students' behavior are influenced by their personalities and abilities. The teacher's goal when instructing in a classroom setting is to support each student's personal growth. Teachers must possess specialized knowledge to guide pupils in learning for this. Teachers today must mediate between students and technology, as well as gain the tools needed providing innovative application approaches and tools that boost the growth of students, contented with learning and performance.

4.3.4 Relationship Between Learning and Teaching

In consideration of the effortlessness, expediency, and sharing of instructional materials in the age of 5G, schools must develop an innovative concept of learning. To do this, schools must be rebuilt, as well as a high-quality learning databank and a national center for educational resources. For learning to occur with the new paradigm, barriers between schools, schools, social education institutions, and families must be removed. To create a new notion of learning, it is necessary to reform the educational system and create an education model focused on the future inside a new educational ecosystem integrating cutting-edge technologies like 5G, big data, and AI. Professors have the greatest ability to lead. There are attempts to create an environment of educators and learners where communication and harmony depend on mutual understanding. The foundation of this cooperation is interpersonal communication and the use of learning tools for instruction.

4.3.5 Teacher: Intermediary Between Students and Technology

Considering the many ways that technology has improved learning, instructors' primary concerns still remain ensuring that students are receiving the proper information. The use of the internet and e-learning technologies by 5G technology has accelerated the advancements in educational technology. It offers limitless information saved on numerous media and lowers the cost of knowledge. Consequently, teachers must act as a bridge between students, knowledge, and technology. To sustain students' emotional learning, teachers must refrain from influencing them with their personalities. To educate effectively with the right technology, teachers must put in extra effort.

4.3.6 Analytical Hierarchy Process

Saaty created the analytical hierarchy process (AHP). Although AHP has been found to have several flaws, it has been frequently used in education to define weights and criteria to determine the best options from a set of probable ones. As a result, the problem analysis in this study was conducted using the chosen AHP research approach. It was created to address decision-making issues and develop standards for rating the making of decisions, performance, and planning. Salty suggested using AHP for politics, decision-making, organizing, alternative decision-making, setting priorities, allocating resources, determining risks, creating systems, monitoring performance, maintaining system stability, and optimizing systems. The primary application of AHP is the analysis of systems or issues that involve interactions at several levels. AHP establishes an organizational framework by classifying the variables that affect a system into different groups. An AHP was developed as the consequence of the results of a poll that inquired about the aforementioned variables.

4.4 Result and Discussion

4.4.1 Target Layer

Expectations to "select and integrate innovative technology" and "maintain conventional instructional methods" are part of the AHP's target layer, which contrasts the preferences of teachers and students. We compared the target layers and came up with the consistency index in the manner described below to establish their relative importance. Employ and integrate modern technology and "maintain traditional teaching method" as the two subfactors weights, respectively,

$$DJ = \frac{\lambda \max - m}{m-1} \tag{4.1}$$

where $\lambda \max$ is the highest grade determined using Equation (4.2).

$$\lambda_n = \left(\frac{u_1}{u_1'} + \frac{u_2}{u_2'} + \frac{u_3}{u_3'}, \ldots + \frac{u_m}{u_m'} \right) \tag{4.2}$$

$$DQ = \frac{DJ}{QJ} \tag{4.3}$$

Indicate both related to the components' weights ("choose and combine new technology" and "maintain traditional teaching method"). The "maintain traditional teaching method" element has a weight of 0.668, which is higher than the weight of the other factor. Table 4.1 represents the desired area's evaluations for two components. Figure 4.1 illustrates the combined weights of two subfactors for the target area. This indicates that instructors desire to continue using conventional techniques of instruction. However, when the analysis considers the component 'teachers as

Table 4.1 The desired region's weights for two components.

Factor	Selecting and combining fresh innovations from the aspects	Maintain traditional teaching methods	Weight (W)	Geometric mean
Selecting and combining fresh innovations from the aspects	3	1/2	0.332	0.708
Maintaining traditional teaching methods	2	3	0.668	1.415
Total			1.000	2.123

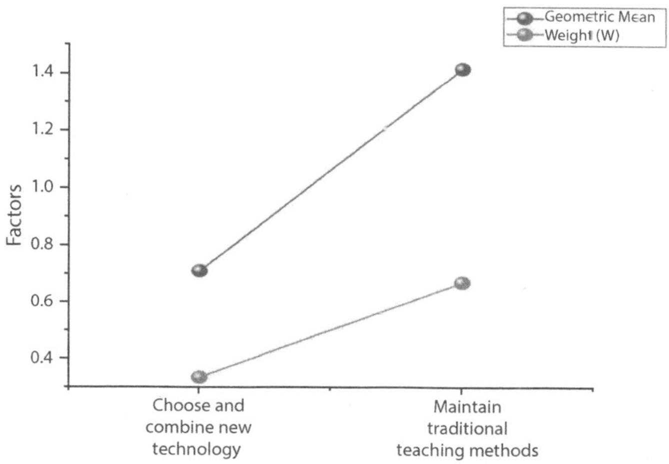

Figure 4.1 The combined weights of two subfactors for the target area.

the intermediary between students and technology,' it reveals that this factor holds the highest weight among the three, highlighting the essential role of teachers in technological integration. Table 4.2 represents that instructors are incorporated in the target layer's weights as intermediate learners and technology are in between. Figure 4.2 illustrates instructors

Table 4.2 Instructors are incorporated in the target layer's weights as intermediate learners and technology are in between.

Factor	Maintain traditional teaching method	Teachers as the intermediary	Selecting and combining fresh innovations from the aspects	Geometric mean	Weight (W)
Maintain traditional teaching method	1	1	1	1.000	0.329
Selecting and combining fresh innovations from the aspects	1	1/2	2	0.798	0.265
Teachers as the intermediary	2	2	3	1.265	0.415
Total				3.063	1.019

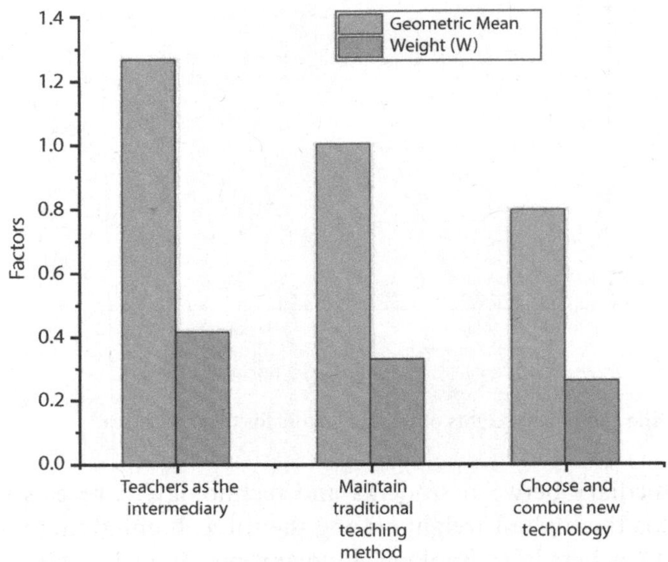

Figure 4.2 Instructors as the intermediaries for learners and technologies constitutes one of the target layer's weights.

as the intermediaries for learners, and technology constitutes one of the target layer's weights.

4.4.2 Layer of Criteria

The criteria layer outlines the relevant conditions influencing the integration of new technologies. Key factors include instructor experience, sense of achievement, incentives, school service support, and technological familiarity. The development of educational content is related to the statements "maintain traditional teaching method part as well as other factors like investing in innovative teaching understanding the technology and measurements." This outcome demonstrates the significance of supporting teachers and their interactions with students to integrate new technologies into the classroom successfully. Therefore, it is necessary to reward and inspire teachers through their pupils' attitudes toward learning. When it relates to picking and integrating new technology, the factors motivated included employees' decades of experience and satisfaction with achievement, educational services and support, and technological integration, which all carry significant weight. Investment in creative pedagogy is another factor to consider. One of the key components supporting the conventional teaching approach is the preparation of instructional materials during vacation time. This outcome demonstrates the significance of supporting teachers and their interactions with students to integrate new technologies into the classroom successfully. Therefore, it is necessary to reward and inspire teachers through their pupils' attitudes toward learning. Table 4.3 shows the explanation of the criteria layer's weights and factors. Figure 4.3 illustrates a description of the requirement layer's weights and factors.

4.4.3 Discussion

As mentioned previously, traditional teaching approaches are still regarded by educators as effective teaching instruments. Three elements are used in the target layer to define how teachers function as a bridge between students and new technology and traditional teaching methods [16]. The measurements show that traditional teaching methods are still preferred by both teachers and students over modern technologies. These results corroborated instructor case studies about the use of technology. Researchers confirmed that teachers could operate educational institutions employing conventional methods while still implementing an educational program centered on technology. The requirement layer's weighted elements

Table 4.3 The explanation of the criteria layer's weights and factors.

Factors	Weight	
	Maintain traditional teaching method	**Choose and combine new technology**
Preparation of teaching material during vacations	1.505	1.515
School's service	1.255	1.755
Understanding technology	1.505	1.515
Investing in innovative teaching	1.501	1.501
School's support	1.337	1.668
Interaction with students	1.334	1.669
Incentive	1.335	1.668
Teacher experience and sense of accomplishment	1.335	1.665

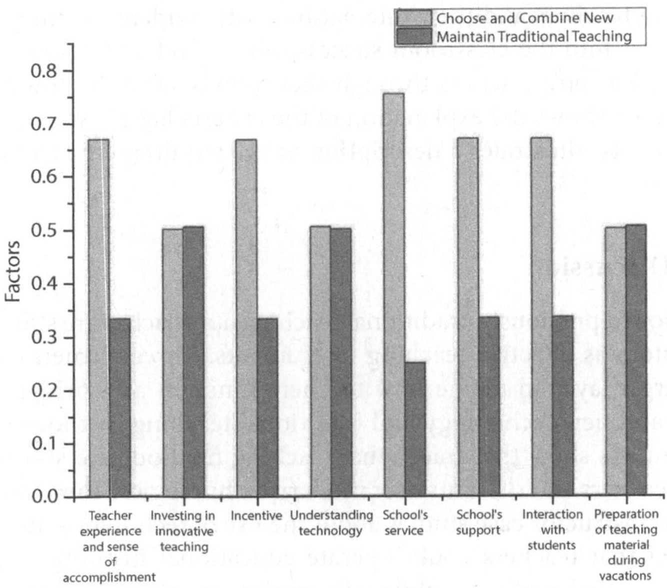

Figure 4.3 A description of the requirement layer's weights and factors.

represent the probability of incorporating technological improvements into education with suitable support and incentives, thereby encouraging educators to make use of cutting-edge tools [17]. Regarding the work, time, and resources they devote to creating suitable materials and resources, teachers appear impartial. Although five of the eight criteria-layer components include strengths that are high, the solution still employs traditional teaching methods [18]. Consequently, the IoT has significantly advanced the fields of sensors, networks, and communication technologies, including WSN (wireless sensor networks), 5G, and LTE (long-term evolution) [19]. Although 5G utilizes high-frequency millimeter waves that enable faster communication, they suffer from a limitation of short transmission range. Rapid and low-quality connections with a large number of connections can only be offered with the correct number of base stations. The 5G network's faster and larger data transmission rates help to improve the functionality of educational apps, particularly those used for remote mobile instruction. Big data, virtual reality, and AI are already widely used, thanks to advanced 5G technology. However, 5G technology continues to be hampered by a lack of infrastructure, expensive costs, and a small number of mobile devices that support it [20]. Although 5G technology is believed to be a platform for citizen empowerment, the technology is an element of a complex social-technical environment that also includes educational institutions, learners, educators, resources, and information ecologies. Despite modern communications technology, teachers are still the only sources of students' learning at the moment, such as 5G technology, which affects how knowledge is acquired. Learning becomes centered on the professionalism and growth of the teachers. Teachers must serve as search engines in the classroom by linking students with learning materials. Teachers must improve their information literacy to help students adjust their learning preferences and become accustomed to using digital resources, as well as to serve as evaluators and facilitators of learning [21]. Instructors must adapt their teaching strategies to foster active and in-depth learning in a new learning environment enabled by 5G technology, necessitating that they take on the role of mediators. Modern communication has primarily been used outside school, while traditional communication has dominated classrooms. In addition to this, instructors need to serve as intermediaries to resolve problems when there are needs for modern and conventional methods of communication [22]. Instructors must take the initiative to embrace proper technology to use the 5G platform for education. Then, to provide knowledge direction, value development, activity organization, and learning feedback, instructors must engage with students and technology. Social contact is necessary to develop knowledge and values, and teachers must play a significant role in that relationship. Teachers direct other teachers and connect students to learning resources [23]. As an effort to overcome these constraints, 5G technology merges all four types of intelligent technology, virtual reality, augmented reality, and the IoT. The challenges that traditional teaching is confronted with are simulation and instructional practice in addition to the time difference. It emphasizes that, especially for sustainable education, learning has no bounds and is not limited by time or the study of geography [24]. Despite the infrastructure of 5G technology continuing to expand, instructors must learn how to use it autonomously. Therefore, innovative approaches to motivating and assisting educators in acquiring and using new communication tools are required [25]. The conclusions of this investigation's AHP analysis reflect this. New communication technologies, including 5G, have issues that limit how widely they may be used as alternatives to conventional teaching strategies.

4.5 Conclusions

This study investigated how emerging communication technologies, such 5G technology, might affect teachers and their instructions. The AHP analysis, along with questionnaires and surveys regarding interviews, was completed for this. The three elements are listed under "The instructor provides a connection between students and technology" AHP structure, along with "Pick and integrate new technology" while "preserving traditional teaching method." Eight criteria are included in the criterion layer: "teacher experience and accomplishments," "investing in innovative teaching," "understanding the technology," "incentives," "promotions," "school's service," "school's support," and "interaction time with technology." "A fresh technology and platform" and "traditional instructional tools" are described as two aspects in the solution area. The relative weighting of each layer demonstrates the preference for conventional over innovative educational methods and resources. The requirements for the layer's weight factors explain this. The elements that relate to the encouragement and rewards for instructors who attempt to use technology in the classroom are given more weight than those that relate to the efforts and services of teachers. This finding suggests that sufficient guidance is necessary for successfully integrating technological advances in communication into education, particularly in the learning environment. Despite the many benefits of technologies like 5G, there are still issues that need to be resolved before teachers can actively use the technology. Adequate assistance is required for teachers to accept the present 5G technology on a broad scale. This study offers a fundamental understanding of what is needed to motivate educators to integrate this new technology into learning, mainly teaching correctly. The position of the educator needs to be given top priority, especially when introducing new technology because the purpose of education is to develop students' capacity for accepting varied knowledge and technologies. If revolutionary technologies such as 5G or 6G are developed, the conclusions of this study then allow for the quick deployment of sustainable education to reduce educational inequality.

References

1. Shehab, M.J., Kassem, I., Kutty, A.A., Kucukvar, M., Onat, N., Khattab, T., 5G networks towards intelligent and sustainable cities: A review of recent developments, applications, and future perspectives. *IEEE Access*, 10, 2987–3006, 2021.
2. Imoize, A.L., Adedeji, O., Tandiya, N., Shetty, S., 6G enabled smart infrastructure for a sustainable society: Opportunities, challenges, and research road map. *Sensors*, 21, 5, 1709, 2021, https://doi.org/10.3390/s21051709.
3. Zhou, Y., Liu, L., Wang, L., Hui, N., Cui, X., Wu, J., Peng, Y., Qi, Y., Xing, C., Service-aware 6G: An intelligent and open network based on the convergence of communication, computing, and caching. *Digit. Commun. Netw.*, 6, 3, 253–260, 2020, https://doi.org/10.1016/j.dcan.2020.05.003.
4. Wang, X.Y., Li, G., Tu, J.F., Khuyen, N T.T., Chang, C.Y., Sustainable education using new communication technology: Assessment with analytical hierarchy process (AHP). *Sustainability*, 13, 17, 9640, 2021, https://doi.org/10.3390/su13179640.
5. Strinati, E.C., Alexandropoulos, G.C., Wymeersch, H., Denis, B., Sciancalepore, V., D'Errico, R., Clemente, A., Phan-Huy, D.T., De Carvalho, E., Popovski, P., Reconfigurable, intelligent, and sustainable wireless environments for 6G smart connectivity. *IEEE Commun. Mag.*, 59, 10, 99–105, 2021, https://doi.org/10.1109/MCOM.001.2100070.
6. Vanelli-Coralli, A., Guidotti, A., Foggi, T., Colavolpe, G., Montorsi, G., 5G and Beyond 5G Non-Terrestrial Networks: Trends and research challenges, in: *3rd 5G World Forum (5GWF)*, 2020, September, IEEE Publications, pp. 163–169, 2020, https://doi.org/10.1109/5GWF49715.2020.9221119.
7. Bajpai, A. and Balodi, A., Role of 6-g networks: Use cases and research directions, in: *IEEE Bangalore Humanitarian Technology Conference (B-HTC)*, 2020, October, IEEE Publications, pp. 1–5, 2020, https://doi.org/10.1109/B-HTC50970.2020.9298017.

8. Tariq, F., Khandaker, M.R.A., Wong, K.K., Imran, M.A., Bennis, M., Debbah, M., A theoretical study on 6G. *IEEE Wirel. Commun.*, 27, 4, 118–125, 2020, https://doi.org/10.1109/MWC.001.1900488.
9. Mao, B., Tang, F., Yuichi, K., Kato, N., AI-based service management for 6G green communications, *arXiv preprint arXiv:2101.01588*, 2021.
10. Gohar, A. and Nencioni, G., The role of 5G technologies in a smart city: The case for the intelligent transportation system. *Sustainability*, 13, 9, 5188, 2021, https://doi.org/10.3390/su13095188.
11. Khan, L.U., Yaqoob, I., Imran, M., Han, Z., Hong, C.S., 6G wireless systems: A vision, architectural elements, and future directions. *IEEE Access*, 8, 147029–147044, 2020, https://doi.org/10.1109/ACCESS.2020.3015289.
12. Rekkas, V.P., Sotiroudis, S., Sarigiannidis, P., Wan, S., Karagiannidis, G.K., Goudos, S.K., Machine learning in beyond 5-G/6G networks—State-of-the-art and future trends. *Electronics*, 10, 22, 2786, 2021, https://doi.org/10.3390/electronics10222786.
13. Nguyen, H.T., Nguyen, M.T., Do, H.T., Hua, H.T., Nguyen, C.V., DRL-based intelligent resource allocation for diverse quality of service in 5G and toward 6G vehicular networks: A comprehensive survey. *Wirel. Commun. Mobile Comput.*, 2021, 1–21, 2021.
14. Meena, P., Pal, M.B., Jain, P.K., Pamula, R., 6G communication networks: Introduction, vision, challenges, and future directions. *Wireless Pers. Commun.*, 125, 2, 1097–1123, 2022, https://doi.org/10.1007/s11277-022-09590-5.
15. Renegade, N., Saravanan, S., Sudha, C., IoT-based intelligent energy grid for sustainable cities. *Mater. Today Proc.*, 2021.
16. Szymkowiak, A., Melović, B., Dabić, M., Jeganathan, K., Kundi, G.S., Information Technology and Gen Z: The Role of Teachers, the Internet, and technology in the Education of young people. *Technol. Soc.*, 65, 101565, 2021, https://doi.org/10.1016/j.techsoc.2021.101565.
17. Hero, J.L., The Impact of Technology Integration in Teaching Performance. *Int. J. Sci.: Basic Appl. Res. (IJSBAR)*, 48, 1, 101–114, 2019.
18. Selvaraj, A., Radhin, V., Ka, N., Benson, N., Mathew, A.J., Effect of pandemic-based online education on teaching and learning system. *Int. J. Educ. Dev.*, 85, 102444, 2021, https://doi.org/10.1016/j.ijedudev.2021.102444.
19. Singh, P., Elmi, Z., Krishna Meriga, V.K., Pasha, J., Dulebenets, M.A., Internet of Things for sustainable railway transportation: Past, present, and future. *Clean. Logist. Supply Chain*, 4, 100065, 2022, https://doi.org/10.1016/j.clscn.2022.100065.
20. Semiari, O., Saad, W., Bennis, M., Debbah, M., Integrated millimeter wave and sub-6 GHz wireless networks: A roadmap for joint mobile broadband and ultra-reliable low-latency communications. *IEEE Wirel. Commun.*, 26, 2, 109–115, 2019, https://doi.org/10.1109/MWC.2019.1800039.

21. Oughton, E.J., Lehr, W., Katsaros, K., Selinis, I., Bubley, D., Kusuma, J., Revisiting wireless internet connectivity: 5G vs wi-fi 6. *Telecommun. Policy*, 45, 5, 102127, 2021, https://doi.org/10.1016/j.telpol.2021.102127.
22. Sharma, P., Jain, S., Gupta, S., Chamola V., Role of machine learning and deep learning in securing 5G-driven industrial IoT applications. *Ad Hoc Networks*, 123, 102685, 2021, https://doi.org/10.1016/j.adhoc.2021.102685.
23. Xu, X., Li, D., Sun, M., Yang, S., Yu, S., Manogaran, G., Mastorakis, G., Mavromoustakis, C.X., Research on key technologies of intelligent campus teaching platform based on 5G network. *IEEE Access*, 7, 20664–20675, 2019, https://doi.org/10.1109/ACCESS.2019.2894129.
24. Kioupi, V. and Voulvoulis, N., Education for sustainable development: A systemic framework for connecting the SDGs to educational outcomes. *Sustainability*, 11, 21, 6104, 2019, https://doi.org/10.3390/su11216104.
25. Guo, J., Wang, L., Zhou, W., Wei, C., Powering green digitalization: Evidence from 5G network infrastructure in China. *Resour. Conserv. Recycl.*, 182, 106286, 2022, https://doi.org/10.1016/j.resconrec.2022.106286.

Part II

SUSTAINABLE TECHNOLOGY AND DATA SECURITY

5

Optimizing Sustainable Image Encryption Strategies in Industry 5.0 Using VIKOR MCDM Methodology

I. Shiek Arafat[1], R. Premkumar[2], M. Vidhyalakshmi[3], C. Priya[4] and Muniyandy Elangovan[5,6*]

[1]Department of Electronics and Communications Engineering, Vel Tech Rangarajan Dr. Sagunthala R&D Institute of Science and Technology, Chennai, India
[2]Department of Electronics and Communications Engineering, Faculty of Engineering and Technology, Jain University, Bengaluru, India
[3]Department of Electronics and Communications Engineering, SRM Institute of Science and Technology, Bharathi Salai, Ramapuram, Chennai, India
[4]Department of Electronics and Communications Engineering, Siddharth Institute of Engineering & Technology, Puttur, India
[5]Department of Biosciences, Saveetha School of Engineering, Saveetha Institute of Medical and Technical Sciences, Chennai, India
[6]Applied Science Research Center, Applied Science Private University, Amman, Jordan

Abstract

In the realm of Industry 5.0, where sustainability intertwines with technological innovation, the security of digital images is paramount. This chapter explores the optimization of image encryption techniques, a cornerstone in safeguarding multimedia applications. We delve into a spectrum of optical image encryption methods, adopting the VIKOR (VIseKriterijumska Optimizacija I Kompromisno Resenje) approach for a comprehensive analysis. Our focus is to evaluate and refine substitution boxes (S-boxes), which are fundamental in enhancing image encryption's resilience. By examining the properties of various S-boxes through a VIKOR-based framework, we aim to identify the most effective configurations for sustainable image security. The chapter presents an innovative method of transforming color image matrices, incorporating nonlinear elements and the novel

**Corresponding author*: muniyandy.e@gmail.com

Kanak Kalita, J.V.N. Ramesh, M. Elangovan and S. Balamurugan (eds.) Decision-Making Techniques and Methods for Sustainable Technological Innovation: Strategies and Applications in Industry 5.0, (87–100) © 2025 Scrivener Publishing LLC

concept of credibility complex fuzzy sets. This leads to the identification of the optimal GRAY S-box for image encryption, not only ensuring enhanced security but also aligning with sustainable practices in Industry 5.0. The results showcase the selected S-box's effectiveness in improving the readability and integrity of image data, furthering the sustainable technological advancement in image encryption techniques.

Keywords: Sustainable image encryption, Industry 5.0, VIKOR, multiple-criteria decision-making

Introduction

Image encryption techniques are vital for ensuring the security and confidentiality of digital images, especially in scenarios where sensitive or classified information is involved. These techniques employ various cryptographic methods to protect image data from unauthorized access [1]. A commonly used method involves symmetric key encryption, wherein a confidential key is employed for both the encryption and decryption of the image. Block ciphers, like advanced encryption standard (AES), are often employed for their efficiency and security. Asymmetric key encryption, using techniques such as RSA (Rivest–Shamir–Adleman), can also be utilized for secure key exchange between parties. In addition to these fundamental encryption methods, steganography can be incorporated to hide image data within another image, providing an extra layer of protection. In the contemporary digital era, image encryption methods are of paramount importance in preserving the confidentiality and authenticity of digital images. Furthermore, DRPE (double random phase encodings) has been explored for its applicability in encrypting multiple images and color images. Image scrambling techniques, akin to numerical preprocessing procedures, have also been integrated with the DRPE system, employing methods like JT (Jigsaw transform) and ART (Arnold transform). Image encryption algorithms represent the primary means of safeguarding images [2]. Steganography, on the other hand, involves the embedding of specific information into a cover medium, such as digital images, audio signals, or videos, with the objective of concealing its presence. Consequently, steganography accomplishes the concealment of information to the extent that only the intended recipient can discern the existence of the data [3]. This article offers an overview of contemporary image encryption methods, highlighting their advantages and disadvantages. The paper has three primary objectives: One of the main motivations for this study is the scarcity of literature regarding image encryption techniques based on metaheuristics. This lack of understanding prompted us to conduct a thorough evaluation of current image encryption approaches [4]. Image encryption techniques based on metaheuristics demonstrate notably better performance in comparison to established methods, especially when it comes to their resistance against diverse forms of cryptanalysis. Consequently, it is imperative to investigate the existing cryptanalysis techniques to understand their strengths and limitations. Every image encryption method comes with its unique set of strengths and weaknesses [5]. While certain techniques exhibit robustness against a range of attacks, they may experience a decrease in computational efficiency [6–9]. Therefore, it becomes essential to evaluate the trade-off between computational speed and the ability to withstand different security threats. This paper offers several notable contributions: It conducts an extensive exploration of diverse image encryption methods, with a specific emphasis on metaheuristic encryption approaches. The paper undertakes a comprehensive examination of various attack types and performance metrics related to image encryption methods. Current techniques are scrutinized regarding their susceptibility to differential, statistical, and key analyses. Additionally, the paper investigates potential directions for future research that could contribute to the advancement of efficient image encryption methods. The establishment of effective evaluation measures is crucial for assessing the effectiveness of image encryption techniques, enabling the examination of different aspects of an image encryption algorithm. In this communication, a novel method is suggested for secure image encryption, encompassing the concurrent rearrangement of pixel positions and modification of the grayscale values of image pixels.

Image Encryption

Image encryption methods aim to transform an original image into an obscured version that is difficult to interpret, ensuring the confidentiality of the image between authorized users. In essence, it is crucial to prevent anyone from understanding the image's content without the appropriate decryption key [10–12]. Furthermore, the secure management and transmission of digital images play a pivotal role in a wide range of applications, encompassing cable TV, online personal photo collections, medical imaging systems, military image exchanges, and confidential video conferencing. In response to these demands, a multitude of image encryption techniques have been introduced. These image encryption algorithms can be broadly classified into three primary categories: (1) position permutation-based algorithms, (2) value transformation-based algorithms, and (3) visual transformation–based algorithms. The preceding subsections provide detailed descriptions of the image encryption techniques falling into these categories [13]. Additionally, a comparative analysis of these techniques is conducted using specific performance metrics, including image energy, image contrast, average image correlation, and image homogeneity. The paper also focuses on the study of particular block ciphers, namely, AES, advanced permutation algorithm (APA), Gray, Lui, Residue Prime, and S8. In their research, authors [14] introduced an inventive method for implementing the substitution box (S-box) using a chaotic approach, incorporating affine and Lorenz transforms. This pioneering technique aimed to improve the algebraic and statistical properties of the S-box. The S-box is primarily utilized in block encryption to introduce pixel-level confusion, providing an efficient means to reinforce both confusion and diffusion, thereby strengthening the input image against security vulnerabilities. In another investigation conducted by Chen and their team, they harnessed the concept of multibeam interference in conjunction with vector composition to achieve optical image encryption. This innovative approach entails the creation of a series of n phase masks, which are subsequently used as encryption keys. The encrypted image is generated through multibeam interference and vector composition. During the decryption process, the original image is reconstructed by illuminating n beams at specific modulation points (POMs) on the output plane following a Fourier transform. This method presents a distinctive and secure strategy for encrypting and decrypting optical images.

Chen and their team proposed a technique to transform a grayscale image into a color ciphertext using the common vector composition (CVC) method and a three-beam interference approach. The CVC method divides the initial grayscale image into three segments, each carrying amplitude and phase data, which are then employed to produce a colored ciphertext. Subsequently, the three-beam interference method is utilized to restore the grayscale image from the colored ciphertext, presenting a novel approach for manipulating and safeguarding image data. In a distinct research effort, Tran and colleagues delved into the precision and real-world utility of S-boxes in image encryption. They scrutinized the encryption procedure by assigning various input values to different types of S-boxes, aiming to pinpoint the most appropriate GRAY S-boxes. To tackle this challenge, they devised a technique that operates within the domain of complex fuzzy credibility information, facilitating effective problem-solving in this particular context. Correlation information can also be used to analyze the pixel details and encryption steps of any image, providing valuable insights into the encryption process. Many techniques are employed to determine the optimal outcome in the picture encryption process; however, in this article, we propose a few techniques to identify the most effective and appropriate methods of image encryption utilizing different GRAY S-box kinds. To determine the strength of picture encryption, many techniques are employed, including entropy analysis, contrast analysis, homogeneity analysis, energy analysis, and mean absolute deviation analysis. These studies will give us useful information for creating images with different S-boxes. Moreover, our objective is to employ a variety of GRAY S-boxes to enhance image encryption across different analytical perspectives. We seek to restructure the original image and optimize it by leveraging GRAY S-boxes. Zhu and colleagues introduced an image encryption approach that involves bit-level permutation and diffusion. This approach leverages the Arnold map and logistic map for conducting permutation and diffusion operations, leading to a computationally efficient method in comparison to alternative image encryption techniques. Nevertheless, it is important to acknowledge that permutation-based image encryption methods are vulnerable to known-plaintext and known-ciphertext attacks.

The provided metrics for different types of images offer valuable insights into their specific characteristics (Table 5.1). In the plain image, the energy value is 1.637, indicating a moderate presence of image features. The contrast is relatively high at 1.904, suggesting distinct edges and variations in pixel intensity. The average correlation is 0.991, signifying a considerable degree of interpixel relationship, while the high homogeneity value of 2.010 highlights a strong uniformity in pixel values within the image. In the AES image, we observe higher energy and contrast values, with 2.007 and 2.134, respectively, indicating a more intense and detailed image. However, the lower average correlation of 1.115 and homogeneity of 1.823 suggest a slightly reduced level of pixel similarity and uniformity compared to the plain image. The Gray image showcases a balance with lower energy

Table 5.1 Images quality data.

	Energy of image	Contrast of image	Average correlation of image	Homogeneity of an image
Plain image	1.637	1.904	0.991	2.01
AES image	2.007	2.134	1.115	1.823
Gray	1.455	2.208	1.854	1.93
S-box	1.632	1.792	1.834	1.532

(1.455) but higher contrast (2.208), revealing a clear distinction between pixel intensities. The high average correlation of 1.854 and homogeneity of 1.930 indicate a strong pixel relationship and uniformity, making it a suitable representation of grayscale content. Lastly, the S-box image presents energy, contrast, and average correlation values falling between the other images, with values of 1.632, 1.792, and 1.834, respectively. The slightly lower homogeneity of 1.532 suggests a moderate level of pixel uniformity. These metrics provide a quantitative assessment of the unique characteristics of each image, which can be beneficial for image processing, quality assessment, or various analytical applications.

Figure 5.1 provides metrics for different types of images, offering a snapshot of their distinct characteristics. In the plain image, we observe a moderate level of energy, indicative of a reasonable presence of image features. Its contrast value is relatively high, suggesting well-defined edges and variations in pixel intensity. The average correlation is close to 1, implying a strong interpixel relationship. Furthermore, the homogeneity value is notably high, signifying a high degree of uniformity in pixel values. In contrast, the AES image exhibits higher energy and contrast, indicating a more intense and detailed image. However, its lower average correlation and homogeneity values suggest a slightly lower degree of pixel similarity. The Gray image strikes a balance with lower energy but high contrast, implying a clear distinction between pixel intensities. The high average correlation and homogeneity values signify a strong pixel relationship and uniformity. Finally, the S-box image presents energy, contrast, and average correlation values in between the other images, while its homogeneity is slightly lower,

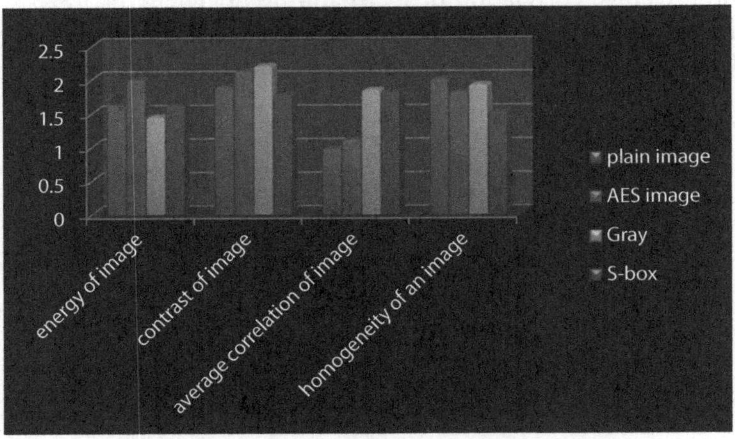

Figure 5.1 Images quality.

suggesting a moderate level of pixel uniformity. These metrics provide valuable insights into the distinct characteristics of these images, which can be applied to various image processing and analysis tasks.

Multiple-Criteria Decision-Making (VIKOR) Method

Multiple-criteria decision-making (MCDM) involves solving decision-making problems where the objective is to determine the optimal solution among alternatives based on various criteria These real-world problems often require the use of different aggregation operators and methodologies to arrive at the best decision. In many instances, decision-making problems entail dealing with ambiguous and uncertain data, which may not be adequately addressed and resolved using crisp sets. Crisp sets have limitations in addressing the complexities inherent in MCDM problems. The VIKOR (Multi-Criteria Optimization and Compromise Solution) method is a decision-making technique used to solve multicriteria problems where multiple conflicting criteria are involved. Developed by Serbian researchers in the late 20th century, VIKOR is particularly useful when there is a need to choose the best alternative from a set of options, considering various criteria such as cost, quality, time, or any other relevant factors [15]. It provides a compromise solution that balances these criteria and helps decision-makers identify the most suitable choice based on their preferences. VIKOR involves a step-by-step process of ranking and evaluating alternatives, ultimately producing a ranking order and a measure of how well each alternative performs concerning the given criteria [16]. This method has applications in various fields, including engineering, finance, and environmental management, where complex decision-making is prevalent. The VIKOR method, an acronym for "VIseKriterijumska Optimizacija I Kompromisno Resenje" in Serbian, is a compromise ranking technique used to identify a solution that optimizes the overall group utility for the majority while simultaneously minimizing the individual regret for the opponent. It was introduced by Opricovic in 1998 and has since become a valuable approach within the field of MCDM [17]. The application of the VIKOR method involves several steps:

(a) It begins with the development of an evaluation or decision matrix, which showcases the performance of various alternatives concerning different criteria. Within this matrix, f_{ij} denotes the performance measure of the i th alternative concerning the j th criterion.

(b) Identify the best (maximum) values, denoted as $f_{ij\max}$, and the worst (minimum) values, denoted as $f_{ij\min}$, for all criteria.
(c) Determine the criteria weights, which can be established using methods such as the analytical hierarchy process or the entropy method.
(d) Calculate the S_i and R_i values. S_i represents the relative closeness to the ideal solution, while R_i represents the relative closeness to the negative ideal solution.
(e) Compute the Q_i value, with $S_{i_{\max}}$ and $S_{i_{\min}}$ as the maximum and minimum S_i values, respectively, and $R_{i_{\max}}$ and $R_{i_{\min}}$ as the maximum and minimum R_i values [18].

The VIKOR method employs these computed values to rank and assess the alternatives, aiding in the selection of the most suitable compromise solution that optimizes group utility while minimizing individual regret.

Table 5.2, conversely, when considering the worst values among the provided images, shows a distinct pattern emerges across the various metrics. The AES image exhibits the highest energy value, reaching 2.007, signifying a greater intensity of image features. In contrast, the S-box image records the lowest value at 1.792, suggesting less pronounced distinctions between pixel intensities. The plain image stands out with the lowest average correlation value of 0.991, indicating a weaker interpixel relationship. Moreover, the same plain image registers the highest homogeneity value at 2.01, implying a higher degree of uniformity in pixel values. These best and worst values serve as valuable benchmarks for evaluating and ranking the

Table 5.2 Determination of best and worst values.

	Energy of image	Contrast of image	Average correlation of image	Homogeneity of an image
Plain image	1.637	1.904	0.991	2.01
AES image	2.007	2.134	1.115	1.823
Gray	1.455	2.20S	1.854	1.93
S-box	1.632	1.792	1.834	1.532
Best	1.455	2.208	1.854	1.532
Worst	2.007	1.792	0.991	2.01

images, enabling a robust foundation for comparison and informed decision-making in a wide range of image analysis and processing applications.

Table 5.3 offers a comprehensive view of the sensitivity (S_j) and rank (R_j) values for specific image metrics across four distinct images. These metrics play a pivotal role in understanding the relative importance of each image attribute and their hierarchical ranking concerning sensitivity. For the plain image, it is evident that energy is the most sensitive metric with an S_j value of 0.082428, while contrast is slightly less sensitive with an S_j of 0.182692. The average correlation and homogeneity metrics exhibit equal sensitivity with S_j values of 0.25, indicating they hold the same importance [19]. These sensitivity values translate into a ranking where energy is the most influential, followed by contrast, average correlation, and homogeneity, in that order. In the AES image, energy emerges as the most sensitive metric, with an S_j of 0.25. Contrast follows with an S_j of 0.044471, and both average correlation and homogeneity are equally sensitive with S_j values of 0.214079 and 0.152197, respectively. This results in energy being the most crucial metric in assessing this image's attributes. The Gray image stands apart with identical S_j and R_j values of 0.208159 for all metrics. This suggests that each of the image's attributes holds an equally significant position when evaluating this particular image [19]. Lastly, the S-box image exhibits energy as the most sensitive attribute with an S_j of 0.080163, while contrast holds the same level of importance. However, the low S_j value of 0.005794 for average correlation places it as less influential. Homogeneity, with an S_jj of 0, ranks the lowest in terms of sensitivity. These sensitivity and ranking values provide valuable insights into the hierarchy of importance among image metrics for each image, serving as a foundation for MCDM, image quality assessment, and various other image analysis applications [20].

Table 5.3 Calculation S_j and R_j.

	Energy of image	**Contrast of image**	**Average correlation of image**	**Homogeneity of an image**	S_j	R_j
Plain image	0.082428	0.182692	0.25	0.25	0.76512	0.25
AES image	0.25	0.044471	0.214079	0.152197	0.660747	0.25
Gray	0	0	0	0.208159	0.208159	0.208159
S-box	0.080163	0.25	0.005794	0	0.335957	0.25

Table 5.4, with its Q_j values, offers a holistic perspective on the significance of image attributes by combining sensitivity (S_j) and rank (R_j) metrics. These Q_j values represent a valuable composite measure that considers both how sensitive a metric is and its relative ranking in the assessment of each image. For the plain image, the Q_j value is 1, signifying that energy stands as the most pivotal metric for this image [21]. This is due to the combination of its high sensitivity (S_j = 0.76512) and a solid ranking (R_j = 0.25), highlighting its paramount importance in evaluating this image. In the case of the AES image, a Q_j value of 0.906301 underscores the dominant role of energy in assessing this image, given its relatively high sensitivity (S_j = 0.660747) and a consistent ranking (R_j = 0.25). Conversely, the Gray image is characterized by a Q_j value of 0, signifying that no single attribute takes precedence [22]. Each image metric holds an equally balanced role in its evaluation, making for a harmonious interplay between sensitivity and ranking. The S-box image exhibits a Q_j value of 0.614728, illustrating the importance of its sensitivity (S_j = 0.335957) in tandem with a consistent ranking (R_j = 0.25) in assessing this image. Notably, the rows labeled "S+ R+" and "S– R–" both bear Q_j values of 0.208159, emphasizing that the Gray image demonstrates an equilibrium between sensitivity and ranking when evaluated with these combined metrics [16].

The Figure 5.2 Q_j values provide a comprehensive understanding of how image attributes weigh against one another, taking into account both their sensitivity and their relative importance in the decision-making process. They prove to be invaluable tools in multicriteria assessments, aiding in making informed decisions and evaluations based on the relative significance of different image metrics.

Table 5.4 Calculation Q_j.

	S_j	R_j	Q_j
Plain image	0.76512	0.25	1
AES image	0.660747	0.25	0.906301
Gray	0.208159	0.208159	0
S-box	0.335957	0.25	0.614728
S+ R–	0.208159	0.208159	
S– R–	0.76512	0.25	

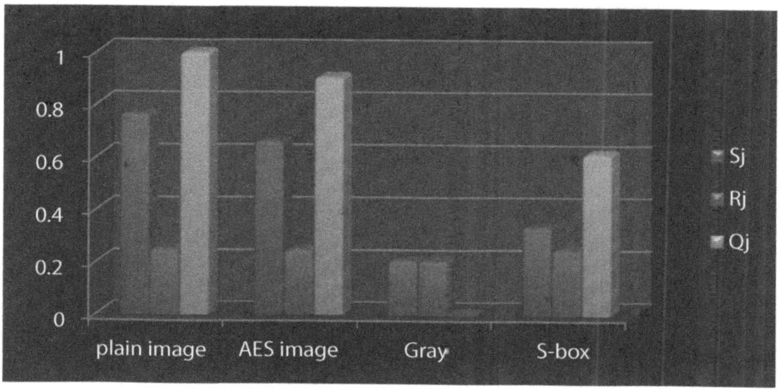

Figure 5.2 Q_j values.

Table 5.5 Rank.

Plain image	1
AES image	2
Gray	4
S-box	3

Table 5.5 provides the rank values for the specified images. These rank values represent the order in which the images are positioned concerning a specific criterion, without taking into account the specific metrics that were used in previous tables. The plain image holds the rank of 1, indicating that it has been assigned the highest position among the images according to the criterion being assessed. The AES image is ranked as 2, signifying that it occupies the second position in the ranking. The S-box image is ranked as 3, placing it in the third position among the images. Finally, the Gray image has the lowest rank of 4, designating it as the fourth and last image in the ranking based on the specific criterion.

Figure 5.3 offers a concise ranking of the specified images based on a particular criterion, independent of the detailed metrics used in previous tables. The plain image takes the top spot with a rank of 1, signifying its superior position within the group when considered against this specific criterion. Following closely is the AES image, securing the second position with a rank of 2, indicating its significance in this particular assessment. The S-box image claims the third position with a rank of 3, while the

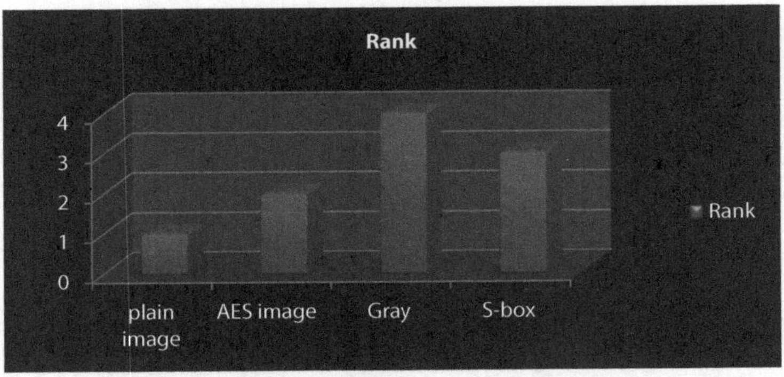

Figure 5.3 Ranking.

Gray image rounds out the ranking with the lowest rank of 4, portraying it as the last image concerning this particular criterion. These rank values simplify the comparison and provide a clear hierarchy, making it easier to understand the relative positions of the images in the context of the chosen criterion.

Conclusion

MCDM with credibility numbers finds practical applications in numerous fields, including computer science and many others. The decision-making process is a subset of computer-based knowledge that aids in making informed decisions. Decision support systems analyze data and provide interactive knowledge support to professionals throughout their decision-making activities. When compared to other analytical methods, complex MCDM with credibility numbers yields highly accurate results. In this paper, the authors have harnessed developed aggregation operators to gather information from decision experts using CFCS (complex fuzzy credibility set) information. This information is then used to identify a suitable GRAY S-box transformation for the image encryption process. The application of MCDM with credibility numbers in this context ensures a robust and effective approach to the decision-making process and image encryption. An S-box serves as a critical component within a block cipher cryptosystem, responsible for introducing data confusion. Therefore, it is crucial to evaluate the confusion-inducing capabilities of various GRAY S-boxes for image encryption applications and determine which one stands out as the most effective. This paper's analysis has led to the discovery that the GRAY S-box performs exceptionally well. The findings from this study open up new possibilities in the realm of decision support systems and cryptosystems. In the future, further research will delve into alternative types of S-box transformations based on different criteria, promising continued advancements in this field.

References

1. Liu, S., Guo, C., Sheridan, J.T., A review of optical image encryption techniques. *Opt. Laser Technol.*, 57, 327–342, 2014, https://doi.org/10.1016/j.optlastec.2013.05.023.
2. Kaur, M. and Kumar, V., A comprehensive review on image encryption techniques. *Arch. Comput. Methods Eng.*, 27, 1, 15–43, 2020, https://doi.org/10.1007/s11831-018-9298-8.
3. Guan, Z.H., Huang, F., Guan, W., Chaos-based image encryption algorithm. *Phys. Lett. A*, 346, 1–3, 153–157, 2005, https://doi.org/10.1016/j.physleta.2005.08.006.
4. Patel, K.D. and Belani, S., Image encryption using different techniques: A review. *Int. J. Emerging Technol. Adv. Eng.*, 1, 1, 30–34, 2011.
5. Pareek, N.K., Patidar, V., Sud, K.K., Image encryption using chaotic logistic map. *Image Vision Comput.*, 24, 9, 926–934, 2006, https://doi.org/10.1016/j.imavis.2006.02.021.
6. Wang, Y., Wong, K.-W., Liao, X., Chen, G., A new chaos-based fast image encryption algorithm. *Appl. Soft Comput.*, 11, 1, 514–522, 2011, https://doi.org/10.1016/j.asoc.2009.12.011.
7. Wang, X., Feng, L., Zhao, H., Fast image encryption algorithm based on parallel computing system. *Inf. Sci.*, 486, 340–358, 2019, https://doi.org/10.1016/j.ins.2019.02.049.
8. Gao, H., Zhang, Y., Liang, S., Li, D., A new chaotic algorithm for image encryption. *Chaos, Solitons Fractals*, 29, 2, 393–399, 2006, https://doi.org/10.1016/j.chaos.2005.08.110.
9. Wu, Y., Noonan, J.P., Agaian, S., NPCR and UACI randomness tests for image encryption. *Cyber J. Multi. J. Sci. Technol. J. Sel. Areas Telecommun. (JSAT)*, 1, 2, 31–38, 2011.
10. Nanmaran, R., Nagarajan, S., Sindhuja, R., Charan, G.V.S., Pokala, V.S.K., Srimathi, S., Gulothungan, G., Vickram, A.S., Thanigaivel, S., Wavelet transform based multiple image watermarking technique. *IOP Conf. Ser.: Mater. Sci. Eng.*, 993, 1, 012167, 2020, December, IOP Publishing, https://doi.org/10.1088/1757-899X/993/1/012167.
11. Nanmaran, R., Srimathi, S., Yamuna, G., Thanigaivel, S., Vickram, A.S., Priya, A.K., Karthick, A., Karpagam, J., Mohanavel, V., Muhibbullah, M., Investigating the role of image fusion in brain tumor classification

models based on machine learning algorithm for personalized medicine. *Comput. Math. Methods Med.*, 2022, 7137524, 2022, https://doi.org/10.1155/2022/7137524.

12. Yahya, M., Abdullah, S., Almagrabi, A.O., Botmart, T., Analysis of S-box based on image encryption application using complex fuzzy credibility Frank aggregation operators. *IEEE Access*, 10, 88858–88871, 2022, https://doi.org/10.1109/ACCESS.2022.3197882.
13. Khalaf, M.M., Optimal alternative for suitability of S-boxes to image encryption based on m-polar fuzzy soft set decision-making criterion. *J. Egypt. Math. Soc.*, 28, 1, 1–25, 2020.
14. Priya, K.J., Ramachandran, M., Selvam, M., A Comprehensive Emergency Management using VIKOR MCDM Method. *REST J. Bank. Account. Bus.*, 1, 1, 34–41, 2022.
15. Chatterjee, P. and Chakraborty, S., A comparative analysis of VIKOR method and its variants. *Decis. Sci. Lett.*, 5, 4, 469–486, 2016, https://doi.org/10.5267/j.dsl.2016.5.004.
16. Jahan, A., Mustapha, F., Ismail, M.Y., Sapuan, S.M., Bahraminasab, M., A comprehensive VIKOR method for material selection. *Mater. Des.*, 32, 3, 1215–1221, 2011, https://doi.org/10.1016/j.matdes.2010.10.015.
17. Opricovic, S. and Tzeng, G.-H., Compromise solution by MCDM methods: A comparative analysis of VIKOR and TOPSIS. *Eur. J. Oper. Res.*, 156, 2, 445–455, 2004, https://doi.org/10.1016/S0377-2217(03)00020-1.
18. Opricovic, S., Fuzzy VIKOR with an application to water resources planning. *Expert Syst. Appl.*, 38, 10, 12983–12990, 2011, https://doi.org/10.1016/j.eswa.2011.04.097.
19. Mardani, A., Zavadskas, E., Govindan, K., Amat Senin, A., Jusoh, A., VIKOR technique: A systematic review of the state of the art literature on methodologies and applications. *Sustainability*, 8, 1, 37, 2016, https://doi.org/10.3390/su8010037.
20. Opricovic, S. and Tzeng, G.-H., Extended VIKOR method in comparison with outranking methods. *Eur. J. Oper. Res.*, 178, 2, 514–529, 2007, https://doi.org/10.1016/j.ejor.2006.01.020.
21. Gul, M., Celik, E., Aydin, N., Taskin Gumus, A., Guneri, A.F., A state of the art literature review of VIKOR and its fuzzy extensions on applications. *Appl. Soft Comput.*, 46, 60–89, 2016, https://doi.org/10.1016/j.asoc.2016.04.040.
22. Yazdani, M. and Graeml, F.R., VIKOR and its applications: A state-of-the-art survey. *Int. J. Strategic Decis. Sci.*, 5, 2, 56–83, 2014, https://doi.org/10.4018/ijsds.2014040105.

6

Sustainable Cryptographic Solutions for IoT: Leveraging MOORA in Evaluating Algorithms for Limited-Resource Environments

Muniyandy Elangovan[1]*, R. Premkumar[2] and B. Swarna[3]

[1]Department of Biosciences, Saveetha School of Engineering, Saveetha Institute of Medical and Technical Sciences, Chennai, India
[2]Department of Electronics and Communications Engineering, Faculty of Engineering and Technology, Jain University, Bengaluru, India
[3]University Centre for Research & Development, Chandigarh University, Mohali, India

Abstract

In the context of Industry 5.0, ensuring data security in Internet of Things (IoT) devices, particularly those with limited resources, is critical. This chapter evaluates cryptographic algorithms suitable for such IoT devices using the Multi-Objective Optimization by Ratio Analysis (MOORA) method. Focusing on both symmetric- and asymmetric-key algorithms, the assessment considers key performance indicators: speed, security strength, memory usage, energy efficiency, and scalability. The importance of cryptography in IoT extends to ensuring data integrity and confidentiality across sectors facing evolving cyber threats. This evaluation is vital for maintaining data privacy, adhering to regulatory compliance, and supporting technological innovations in a resource-constrained IoT environment. The comparative analysis through MOORA methodically ranks various cryptographic algorithms, offering insights into their suitability for IoT applications. This chapter contributes to identifying sustainable, efficient cryptographic solutions, aligning with the demands of secure and sustainable technological advancement in Industry 5.0.

**Corresponding author*: muniyandy.e@gmail.com

Kanak Kalita, J.V.N. Ramesh, M. Elangovan and S. Balamurugan (eds.) Decision-Making Techniques and Methods for Sustainable Technological Innovation: Strategies and Applications in Industry 5.0, (101–118) © 2025 Scrivener Publishing LLC

***Keywords*:** Speed (ms), security (bits), memory usage (KB), energy efficiency (joules), scalability (transactions/s)

6.1 Introduction

A cryptographic algorithm is used to secure data when they are being transmitted over unprotected public channels. In real-time scenarios, there is a need for algorithms that can be adapted to various hardware architectures, each with its own set of design limitations. Consequently, there is a call for diverse processing methods and research endeavors to assess these approaches. This paper focuses on the most recent developments in flexible cryptographic algorithms and classifies them based on their hardware implementations [1]. In the contemporary digital landscape, the cryptographic algorithm serves as the foundational mechanism ensuring secure communication and safeguarding data integrity. Essentially, cryptographic algorithms use complex mathematical formulas or processes to render data indecipherable to unauthorized parties, a vital element, particularly when transmitting information across unsecured networks. In essence, a cryptographic algorithm is a sophisticated mathematical formula or process that renders data unreadable by unauthorized parties, ensuring secure communication in real-time applications [2]. This is particularly critical in scenarios where sensitive information needs to be transmitted over potentially insecure networks. These cryptographic methods are highly adaptable, designed to accommodate a wide range of hardware configurations, each with its unique constraints and capabilities. This adaptability is crucial in ensuring that cryptographic techniques can be effectively deployed across diverse computing systems, from resource-constrained embedded devices to high-performance servers. Within the realm of cryptography, researchers and practitioners invest substantial efforts to enhance and refine these algorithms to keep pace with the dynamic digital landscape [3]. Designing a cryptographic algorithm requires striking a delicate balance between security and performance. It must be robust enough to withstand attacks from adversaries equipped with considerable computational resources, yet efficient enough to be practically implemented in real-world settings without incurring excessive computational overhead. Achieving this equilibrium often involves the application of intricate mathematical techniques and rigorous testing to verify the algorithm's resilience against well-known cryptographic attacks. Moreover, cryptographic algorithms find widespread application across a diverse array of scenarios, from securing online communications to safeguarding sensitive financial transactions [4].

The safeguarding of data confirms the transfer plays a key role in the internet, facilitating activities such as online banking, e-commerce, and confidential communication. Additionally, they are instrumental to storing data confidentiality and to preserving integrity. The importance of cryptographic algorithms in today's digital age cannot be overstated. As cyber threats continue to evolve, growing in sophistication, the role of robust encryption methods in protecting data integrity and confidentiality becomes paramount. This holds true for various sectors, including government communications, healthcare organizations, financial institutions, and numerous other fields where sensitive information is exchanged [5]. Cryptography encompasses both an intricate art and a scientific discipline focused on securing various forms of information transmission, including email messages and credit card details, by encrypting data through specific cryptographic algorithms. These algorithms serve as the bedrock of network security and are categorized into three fundamental types: symmetric mechanisms, asymmetric (or public key) algorithms, and cryptographic hashes. Their classification is based on the type of key usage. Symmetric algorithms use the same key for both encryption and decryption, whereas asymmetric algorithms use a pair of keys — a public key for encryption and a private key for decryption [6]. Several significant cryptographic algorithms are widely RSA (Rivest-Shamir-Adleman). The market offers a range of Blowfish, RC2, and RC6. Although these methods are crucial for system security, they do come with significant resource requirements, including battery life, memory, as well as CPU time. The size of an encrypted key, which is generally 64 bits, affects the robustness of symmetric-key methods such as RC2 and DES. Blowfish, AES, and RC6 all use 138-, 192-, or 256-bit keys, whereas 3DES uses two 64-bit secrets utilizing keys ranging from 32 to 448 bits [7]. In this paper, we undertake a comparative analysis of the cryptographic performance based on energy consumption. This involves the transformation of data types, such as text or documents, and assessing the impact on power consumption, packet size, and key size alteration, as larger keys necessitate more power to execute additional functions. For instance, in the case of 3DES, battery power is depleted by 55% after encrypting a 5-MB file 600 times. Similarly, AES experiences an 8% increase in energy consumption when the key size is augmented by 64 bits, even without any data transfer [8]. Lightweight encryption algorithms have been developed to cater to devices with extremely limited resources. These algorithms are characterized by their minimal hardware implementation and necessitate considerations for factors such as microprocessors or microcontrollers, ensuring low computational requirements and cost-effectiveness and meeting the necessary security levels. The design of these lightweight algorithms involves a delicate balance between safety, cost, and performance. Key length influences the security and cost trade-off, whereas the number of rounds in encryption impacts the trade-off between security, efficiency, and hardware configuration. Striking a balance between these objectives is challenging, and designers typically focus on optimizing two of these goals while keeping the third in mind [9]. Cryptanalysis exploits the vulnerabilities within cryptographic algorithms to compromise their security and gain unauthorized access to encrypted content. As previously mentioned, the primary dilemma with lightweight algorithms lies in finding the right equilibrium between the limited resource demands of constrained devices, their performance, and maintaining a high level of security. Consequently, lightweight ciphers bear a higher risk factor that necessitates careful identification and in-depth analysis before their implementation, often involving extensive cryptanalysis efforts. In this section, we conduct a comprehensive review of specific targeted attacks directed at various lightweight cryptographic algorithms [10]. A cryptographic algorithm is indispensable and must be efficient, as is the case with any other cryptographic algorithm. It should be noted that although it may have certain limitations and challenges, Blowfish stands out as a cipher that meets these criteria [11]. Currently, Blowfish has not been subjected to successful cryptanalysis, bolstering its reputation. It has a configurable key length that varies from 128 to 448 bits and uses a 64-bit block size. Configurations are used in the algorithm. Within this setup, Blowfish demonstrates remarkable proficiency in encryption and decryption tasks [5]. The algorithm's operation involves taking a 64-bit block and dividing it equally into "L" and "R" sections. It then establishes an iterative block cypher where the final results of "Li-1" and "Ri-1" during the round before are used to calculate the values for "Li" and "Ri" in the "i-th" session. This is achieved through the application of an auxiliary key, "Ki," in the "i-th" cycle, and a specific function "F" as defined by the algorithm. A notable aspect of this design is its reversibility, allowing the same connection to be utilized for the two procedures (with the same keys being utilized in backward order). This system, a La Feistel, which forms the basis of Blowfish, is not exclusive to this algorithm alone; it serves as the foundation for others [12]. The core of the Blowfish operation lies in the Feistel function, the details of which are depicted. The function partitions a 32-bit input and is divided into four 8-bit segments (a, b, c, and d) and used as the S-boxes' input. The conclusive 32-bit output is created by combining the outputs *via* modulo 232 and XORing them. The identical processes used for encrypted are used for deciphering; however, P1, P2, and P18 are used in the opposite sequence. This process may not be immediately apparent. Cryptographic algorithms play a crucial role in tasks such as data encryption, authentication, and digital signatures. However, a key challenge lies in securely associating cryptographic keys with specific users or machines. Public Key Infrastructure (PKI) systems are designed to address this issue by linking identities (such as email addresses or DNS addresses) with the corresponding cryptographic keys used for encryption and authentication [13]. This chapter delves into the foundational cryptographic concepts underlying PKI systems, how the X.509 PKI system functions (as described by many different organizations), practical PKI implementing reasons, alternative PKI regulations, and other cryptographic methods for safe open-source key distribution. Putting PKI systems in place can be intricate, and this chapter aims to provide a comprehensive overview of their architecture and implementation mechanisms, offering guidance on PKI standards while ensuring an adequate level of technical detail for practical implementation [14]. In the realm of the Internet of Things (IoT), cryptographic algorithms serve as a vital safeguard for privacy. Numerous cryptographic tools have been put into practical use. However, conventional encryption methods, often burdened by high computational complexity, may fall short of meeting the demands of modern smart applications, particularly on resource-constrained devices. Hence, the development of lightweight yet effective encryption algorithms holds significant practical importance. Homomorphic encryption (HE) has garnered considerable attention in recent years [15]. This technique makes it possible to execute calculations on encrypted data, protecting sensitive data while processing. In this case, a lightweight HE-based privacy-preserving data integration system was devised for smart grids, showcasing the potential of this method. Nevertheless, the computational overhead associated with HE may impose limitations to its widespread adoption. Another noteworthy cryptographic technique is zero-knowledge proof, allowing one party to demonstrate a fact to another without revealing any extraneous information. A smart card authentication protocol utilizing zero-knowledge credentials was introduced for applications in the smart city domain, exemplifying the versatility and security benefits of this approach. Cryptography algorithms play a pivotal role in safeguarding the privacy of processed data, coordinating the manufacturing chain's inputs, results, and processing time series data [16]. A significant portion of models with multiplicative connections between attributes and attributes can be used to describe much of the data sent in the process industry. To illustrate this, a practical scenario was developed, revolving around the multiplicative connection between the liquid's volume in a vessel and its temperature-dependent density. Considering the use case of computation liquid volume, the usage of homomorphic encoded with these multiplication features was investigated based on encoded density values. In a process chain, process equipment is supplied by a manufacturer and utilized by a user who wishes to maintain the confidentiality of highly sensitive data regarding the physical characteristics of process materials [17].

6.2 Materials and Method

Crypto algorithm: A cryptographic algorithm, often referred to simply as a "crypto algorithm," is a mathematical procedure or set of rules used to encrypt and decrypt data. Its primary purpose is to secure information during transmission or storage by converting it into a form that is unintelligible to unauthorized parties. The algorithm utilizes cryptographic keys, which are essentially strings of data, to perform the encryption and decryption processes. There are various types of symmetric-key computer programs, which use identical asymmetric-key computer programs, which use various keys for these processes.

Speed (ms): The speed of a process, the duration of time, expressed in milliseconds, is used to complete a single operation or task. In the context, it relates to how long cryptographic algorithms take to execute. To execute encryption or decryption functions, faster speeds are generally preferred for efficient and timely processing.

Security (bits): This refers to the level of cryptographic strength and resistance to attacks that a system or algorithm provides. It quantifies the complexity of the key space, which is the range of possible combinations a potential attacker would need to try in order to break the encryption. The size of the key increases with bit count space, making it exponentially harder for unauthorized entities to decipher the encrypted data through brute-force methods. For example, a 128-bit encryption key offers a vastly greater number of possible combinations than a 64-bit key, thus providing significantly higher security.

Memory usage (KB): In the context of cryptographic algorithms, this refers to the amount of computer memory or storage space required to execute the algorithm. It is a critical consideration, particularly in resource-constrained environments or on devices with limited memory capacity. A more memory-efficient algorithm requires less space to perform its operations, making it suitable for devices with lower memory capabilities.

Optimal memory usage not only ensures smooth execution but also allows for the algorithm to be implemented on a wider range of devices, including those with limited resources. Therefore, minimizing memory usage while maintaining the algorithm's effectiveness is a key objective in cryptographic algorithm design.

Energy efficiency (joules): is a crucial metric when evaluating cryptographic algorithms. It measures how effectively an algorithm utilizes energy resources during its execution. A more energy-efficient algorithm consumes fewer joules to perform its operations, which is especially important in scenarios where energy conservation is a priority, such as in battery-powered devices or energy-sensitive environments. An algorithm with high energy efficiency helps prolong the battery life of devices and reduces the overall energy consumption, making it a more sustainable choice. Therefore, optimizing for energy efficiency is a significant consideration in cryptographic algorithm design to ensure that it can operate effectively within energy-constrained settings.

Scalability (transactions/s): In the context of cryptographic algorithms, this refers to their ability to handle a large number of transactions per second (transactions/s). This metric is crucial in scenarios where a system needs to process a high volume of transactions efficiently. A cryptographic algorithm with good scalability can accommodate a growing workload without significant degradation in performance. It is especially important in applications such as blockchain networks, where the ability to handle a high transaction throughput is a key factor for the system's overall effectiveness. A scalable cryptographic algorithm ensures that the system can continue to operate smoothly even as the demand for transactions increases over time.

Method: Multi-Objective Optimization by Ratio Analysis (MOORA) Optimization yields dimensionless numbers, serving as the basis for the MOORA approach. It ultimately gauges the well-being disparities across 10 counties in Lithuania based on various objectives. Notably, three affluent districts sharply contrast with some of the most disadvantaged. Moreover, the migration of labor from other districts to Vilnius highlights a critical issue in income distribution that warrants attention. Instead, emphasis should be placed on the commercialization and industrialization of regions [18]. Multiobjective optimization is a method that addresses concurrent improvements within constraints or conflicting attributes. This approach finds application in various fields, where efficient decision-making is crucial, such as in product and process design, involving trade-offs between conflicting goals [19]. There are three primary reasons for choosing MOORA over other methods in multiple-criteria decision-making (MCDM). First, MOORA is a novel technique that is designed with an understanding of the vulnerabilities in older methods, making it highly valuable. Second, MOORA demonstrates a computational efficiency that is indicated in the existing literature on MCDM. Lastly, MOORA requires minimal setup, aligning with the literature's portrayal of it being a well-defined and stable approach [20]. The MOORA system is a tool for supporting decisions that will help in choosing one of scholarship recipients for academic achievement. By implementing this university-designed selection support system, automated decision-makers can swiftly identify scholarship recipients, thus enhancing academic success for deserving students [21]. MOORA stands out as an efficient MCDM method for comprehensive assessments of alternatives, particularly when faced with significant heterogeneity and a multitude of relevant factors. This method is adept at resolving complex decision-making problems by considering conflicting criteria and striving to identify the best alternative across both positive and negative criteria simultaneously. MOORA is recognized for its effectiveness in decision-making techniques [22]. MOORA is a multiobjective optimization method that simultaneously considers various types of attributes. It is a functional approach designed to address constraints while making decisions. The MOORA technique can overlook certain attributes and their relative importance, potentially leading to a higher evaluation of alternatives. Notably, it is an intuitive and user-friendly approach. The suggested method is adaptable and may be used for decision-making scenarios of varying scale and complexity, involving the consideration of attributes simultaneously. This provides a more focused and simplified decision-making process. Moreover, this approach can be extended to address a wide range of decision problems [23]. The MOORA approach, sometimes referred to as multiple-criteria or numerous character optimization, deals with situations when two or more competing features are present at the same time. This approach proves valuable in decision-making processes that involve complex and conflicting factors, such as selecting warehouse locations, choosing suppliers, and making product and process design decisions [24]. MOORA is particularly useful when making critical choices is imperative. It is worth noting that this technique prioritizes recognized failures based on their importance, providing a reliable and practical output for decision-makers. When compared to traditional methods, MOORA proves to be effective in prioritizing and detecting disasters [25]. The MOORA and multi-objective optimization on the basis of simple ratio analysis (MOOSRA) methods of analysis demonstrate high stability.

In recent research, these techniques have been considered to utilize the latest available data for initial selection methods. This indicates that MOORA and MOOSRA are adaptable to various nonconventional manufacturing environments [26]. The concept of cost divided by cost, when expressed as a ratio, aligns with the benefit-to-value ratio, an economic welfare metric that measures performance. Therefore, in terms of concept, both MOORA approaches are in line with other accepted performance evaluation methods, when applied to the simulation of port planning, the ratio method and reference [27]. MOORA with component factors assists in determining the type and significance of objectives and options. Agencies at the national and local levels as well as partner institutions are important stakeholders. Although explicit consumer power is taken into account when making production decisions, governments also serve as authorized customers' representatives. In a team-based decision-making environment for computer numerical control (CNC) machine tool evaluation [28], MOORA addresses subjective and imprecise information, integrating fuzzy numbers to assist decision-makers in handling multiple fuzzy data represented as linguistic variables. The article provides a summary of the various MULTI-MOORA ranking orders given by different regions for comparison [29–31].

6.3 Analysis and Discussion

In this study, the MOORA technique is used to evaluate various cryptographic algorithms based on critical performance indicators such as speed, security strength, memory usage, energy efficiency, and scalability. The comparative performance of six distinct cryptographic algorithms (crypto algorithm 1 to crypto algorithm 6) is systematically analyzed. Table 6.1 summarizes the raw data for each cryptographic algorithm across these parameters. Crypto algorithm 2 exhibits the highest operational speed at 5.6030 ms, whereas crypto algorithm 6 has the lowest speed at 4.3060 ms. Security-wise, crypto algorithm 4 achieves the highest security level of 8.6030 bits, whereas crypto algorithm 6 significantly trails with a mere 0.1320 bits. Memory usage is highest for crypto algorithm 4 at 8.7400 KB, with crypto algorithm 5 demonstrating optimal efficiency using only 1.7900 KB. Regarding energy efficiency, crypto algorithm 1 leads by consuming only 8.1500 joules, in contrast to crypto algorithm 6, which is the least energy-efficient with 1.5500 joules. In terms of scalability, crypto algorithm 6 offers the highest transaction handling capacity at 8.7410 transactions/s, whereas crypto algorithm 4 manages only 1.7850 transactions/s. These observations are visually reinforced in Figure 6.1, clearly illustrating each algorithm's strengths and weaknesses across different criteria.

Table 6.1 Comparative performance metrics of cryptographic algorithms.

	Speed (ms)	Security (bits)	Memory usage (KB)	Energy efficiency (joules)	Scalability (transactions/s)
Crypto algorithm 1	2.30	8.36	2.36	8.15	6.75
Crypto algorithm 2	5.60	7.04	4.85	7.95	4.76
Crypto algorithm 3	4.31	7.31	6.75	6.95	3.99
Crypto algorithm 4	5.10	8.60	8.74	3.45	1.79
Crypto algorithm 5	5.63	6.85	1.79	4.84	2.87
Crypto algorithm 6	4.31	0.13	3.76	1.55	8.74

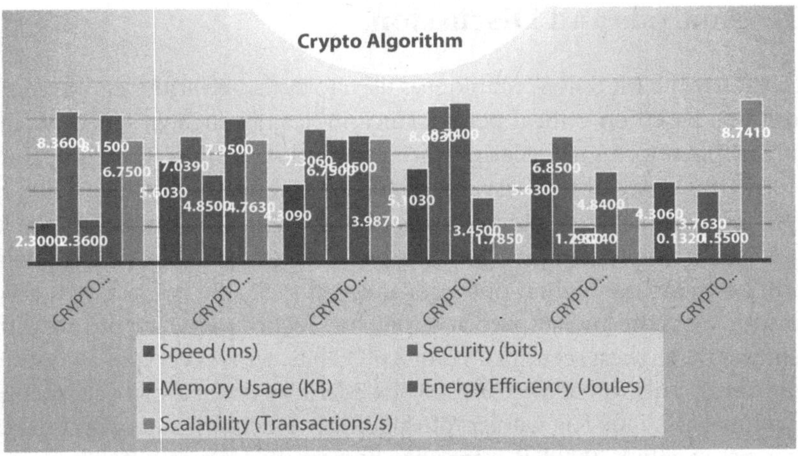

Figure 6.1 Performance evaluation of cryptographic algorithms across key metrics.

To facilitate meaningful comparisons, the raw data were normalized using Equation (6.1), ensuring dimensionless comparability across parameters.

$$X_{n1} = \frac{X1}{\sqrt{((X1)^2 + (X2)^2 + (X3)^2 \ldots)}} \tag{6.1}$$

Table 6.2 presents the normalized values, illustrating proportional performance across all criteria. Figure 6.2 graphically represents these normalized data points, reinforcing the proportional distinctions among the algorithms and aiding intuitive comprehension. Further analysis used weighted normalization, with equal importance allocated to all criteria for

Table 6.2 Normalized performance metrics for cryptographic algorithms.

Normalized data				
Speed (ms)	**Security (bits)**	**Memory usage (KB)**	**Energy efficiency (joules)**	**Scalability (transactions/s)**
0.2005	0.4878	0.1819	0.5550	0.5147
0.4885	0.4107	0.3737	0.5414	0.3632
0.3757	0.4263	0.5201	0.4733	0.3040
0.4450	0.5019	0.6735	0.2349	0.1361
0.4909	0.3997	0.1379	0.3296	0.2191
0.3755	0.0077	0.2900	0.1055	0.6665

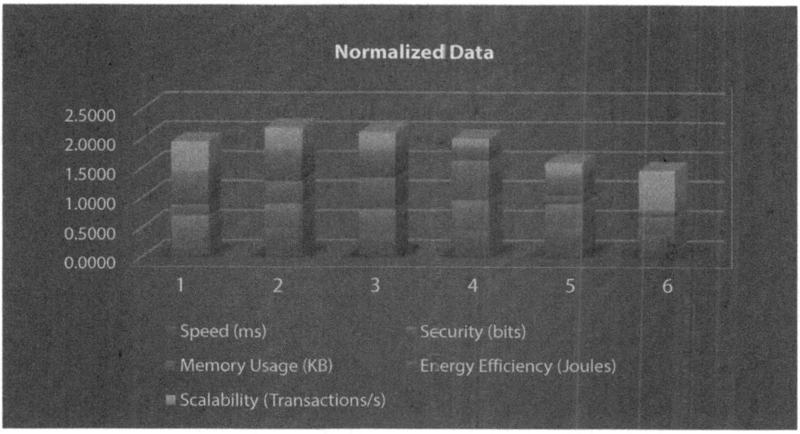

Figure 6.2 Normalized data representation of cryptographic algorithm performance.

a balanced assessment. The weighted normalized decision matrix is computed as per Equation (6.2), and the resulting assessment values for each algorithm are listed in Table 6.3.

$$X_{\text{wnormal1}} = X_{n1} \times w_1 \tag{6.2}$$

$$\text{Assesment value} = \sum X_{wn1} + X_{wn2} - X_{wn3} \tag{6.3}$$

The assessment values integrate the performance across all criteria, clearly identifying crypto algorithm 4 as the most balanced and optimal performer, whereas crypto algorithm 6 ranks lowest. Figure 6.3 visually confirms these weighted normalized scores, providing clear comparative insights. The assessment values are explicitly illustrated in Figure 6.4, demonstrating a significant performance disparity between the best- and worst-performing algorithms. Consequently, the final ranking depicted in Figure 6.5 conclusively places crypto algorithm 4 as the superior choice for cryptographic applications in IoT environments, characterized by its robust security and balanced performance. Conversely, crypto algorithm 6, despite excelling in scalability, ranks lowest due to its substantial shortcomings in other critical areas such as security and energy efficiency. Thus, this structured MOORA analysis facilitates a comprehensive understanding of each cryptographic algorithm's suitability for deployment in resource-constrained IoT scenarios, significantly aiding informed decision-making to ensure sustainable and secure technological advancements.

Table 6.3 Weighted normalized decision matrix for cryptographic algorithms.

Speed (ms)	Security (bits)	Memory usage (KB)	Energy efficiency (joules)	Scalability (transactions/s)	Assessment value	Rank
0.04011	0.09755	0.03637	0.11100	0.10294	0.0498	5
0.09771	0.08214	0.07475	0.10827	0.07264	0.1009	3
0.07514	0.08525	0.10403	0.09465	0.06080	0.1134	2
0.08899	0.10039	0.13470	0.04699	0.02722	0.0813	1
0.09818	0.07993	0.02759	0.06592	0.04383	0.0136	4
0.07509	0.00154	0.05799	0.02111	0.13330	0.0776	6

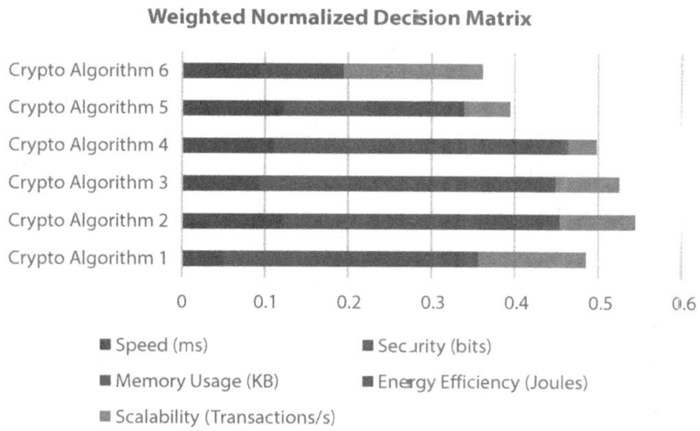

Figure 6.3 Visual representation of weighted normalized scores for cryptographic algorithms.

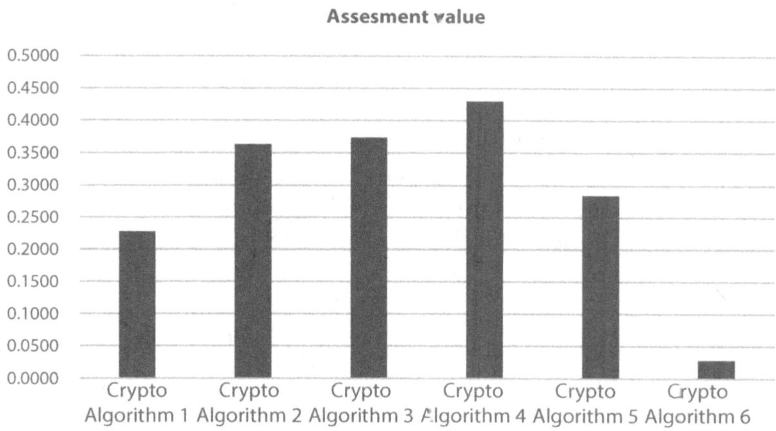

Figure 6.4 Assessment values derived from MOORA analysis of cryptographic algorithms.

6.4 Conclusion

This study comprehensively examined the performance of various cryptographic algorithms using the MOORA method, considering crucial parameters such as speed, security strength, memory usage, energy efficiency, and scalability. The findings underscore the necessity of selecting cryptographic algorithms that effectively balance multiple conflicting objectives, particularly in resource-constrained IoT environments. Among the algorithms analyzed, crypto algorithm 4 emerged as the most favorable

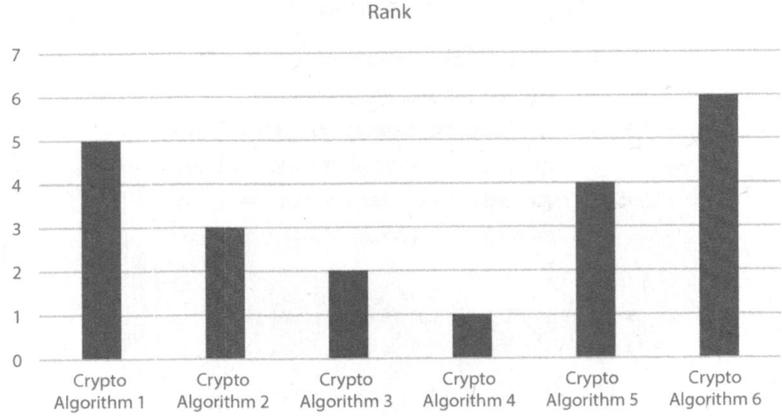

Figure 6.5 Final ranking of cryptographic algorithms using MOORA method.

choice due to its superior security strength and overall balanced performance across all evaluated criteria. In contrast, crypto algorithm 6, despite excelling in scalability, demonstrated significant limitations in other critical aspects such as security and energy efficiency, rendering it the least suitable option. The insights derived from this analysis provide valuable guidance to practitioners and stakeholders, assisting them in selecting optimal cryptographic solutions to ensure sustainable, efficient, and secure IoT deployments aligned with the strategic objectives of Industry 5.0.

References

1. Simmons, G.J., 'A weak' privacy protocol using the RSA crypto algorithm. *Cryptologia*, 7, 2, 180–182, 1983. https://doi.org/10.1080/0161-118391857900.
2. Karthigai Kumar, P. and Baskaran, K., An ASIC implementation of low power and high throughput blowfish crypto algorithm. *Microelectron. J.*, 41, 6, 347–355, 2010. https://doi.org/10.1016/j.mejo.2010.04.004.
3. Patil, P., Narayankar, P., Narayan, D.G., Meena, S.M., A comprehensive evaluation of cryptographic algorithms: DES, 3DES, AES, RSA and blowfish. *Procedia Comput. Sci.*, 78, 617–624, 2016. https://doi.org/10.1016/j.procs.2016.02.108.
4. Potlapally, N.R., Ravi, S., Raghunathan, A., Jha, N.K., A study of the energy consumption characteristics of cryptographic algorithms and security protocols. *IEEE Trans. Mob. Comput.*, 5, 2, 128–143, 2005. https://doi.org/10.1109/TMC.2006.16.

5. Rifà-Pous, H. and Herrera-Joancomartí, J., Computational and energy costs of cryptographic algorithms on handheld devices. *Future Internet*, 3, 1, 31–48, 2011. https://doi.org/10.3390/fi3010031.
6. Surendran, S., Nassef, A., Beheshti, B.D., A survey of cryptographic algorithms for IoT devices, in: *IEEE Long Island systems, applications and technology conference (LISAT)*, IEEE Publications, pp. 1–8, 2018, https://doi.org/10.1109/LISAT.2018.8378034.
7. Thakor, V.A., Razzaque, M.A., Khandaker, M.R.A., Lightweight cryptography algorithms for resource-constrained IoT devices: A review, comparison and research opportunities. *IEEE Access*, 9, 28177–28193, 2021. https://doi.org/10.1109/ACCESS.2021.3052867.
8. Ajao, L.A., Agajo, J., Adedokun, E.A., Karngong, L., Crypto hash algorithm-based blockchain technology for managing decentralized ledger database in oil and gas industry. *J.*, 2, 3, 300–325, 2019.
9. Kim, H.-W., Park, Y.-J., Kim, M.-S., Ryu, H.-S., Hardware implementation of the 3GPP KASUMI crypto algorithm, in: *Proceedings of the IEEK Conference*, Institute of Electronics and Information Engineers, pp. 317–320, 2002.
10. Marwaha, M., Bedi, R., Singh, A., Singh, T., Comparative analysis of cryptographic algorithms. *Int. J. Adv. Eng. Technol.*, IV, III, 16, 18, 2013July-Sept.
11. Chakraborty, S., Datta, H.N., Kalita, K., Chakraborty, S., A narrative review of multi-objective optimization on the basis of ratio analysis (MOORA) method in decision making. *OPSEARCH. Springer*, 60, 4, 1844–1887, 2023. https://doi.org/10.1007/s12597-023-00676-7.
12. Alassaf, N., Gutub, A., Parah, S.A., Al Ghamdi, M., Enhancing speed of SIMON: A light-weight-cryptographic algorithm for IoT applications. *Multimed. Tools Appl.*, 78, 23, 32633–32657, 2019. https://doi.org/10.1007/s11042-018-6801-z.
13. Lee, K.-H. and Chiu, P.-L., An extended visual cryptography algorithm for general access structures. *IEEE Trans. Inf. Forensics Secur.*, 7, 1, 219–229, 2011. https://doi.org/10.1109/TIFS.2011.2167611.
14. Nazeer, M.I., Ali, G., Ahmed, N., Bhatra, R., Ahmed, R., Ismail, M., Implication of genetic algorithm in cryptography to enhance security. *Int. J. Adv. Comput. Sci. Appl.*, 9, 6, 2018. https://doi.org/10.14569/IJACSA.2018.090651.
15. Anwar, M., Bin, N., Hasan, M., Hasan, Md., M., Loren, J.Z., Hossain, S.T., Comparative study of cryptography algorithms and its' applications. *Int. J. Comput. Netw. Commun. Secur.*, 7, 5, 96–103, 2019.
16. Kumar, S., Karnani, G., Gaur, M.S., Mishra, A., Cloud security using hybrid cryptography algorithms, in: *2nd International conference on intelligent engineering and management (ICIEM)*, IEEE Publications, pp. 599–604, 2021, https://doi.org/10.1109/ICIEM51511.2021.9445377.
17. AbuEl-Reesh, J.Y. and Abu-Naser, S.S., *An intelligent tutoring system for learning classical cryptography algorithms (CCAITS)*, 2018.
18. Wang, Y. and Hu, M., Timing evaluation of the known cryptographic algorithms, in: *International Conference on Computational Intelligence*

and Security, vol. 2, IEEE Publications, pp. 233–237, 2009, https://doi.org/10.1109/CIS.2009.81.

19. Brauers, W.K.M., Ginevičius, R., Podvezko, V., Regional development in Lithuania considering multiple objectives by the MOORA method/Lietuvos Regioninės Plėtros Daugiaaspektis Vertinimas Moora Metodu. *Technol. Econ. Dev. Econ.*, 16, 4, 613–640, 2010. https://doi.org/10.3846/tede.2010.38.
20. Ghadai, R.K., Chakraborty, S., Kalita, K., On Solving Parametric Optimization Problem of an End Milling Process using MCDM Techniques: A Comparative Analysis. *Adv. Mater. Process. Technol.*, 10, 3, 2421–2443, 2024. Taylor & Francis. DOI: 10.1080/2374068X.2023.2216398.
21. Akkaya, G., Turanoğlu, B., Öztaş, S., An integrated fuzzy AHP and fuzzy MOORA approach to the problem of industrial engineering sector choosing. *Expert Syst. Appl.*, 42, 24, 9565–9573, 2015. https://doi.org/10.1016/j.eswa.2015.07.061.
22. Siregar, MM.V., Romauly Tampubolon, M., Parapat, E.P.S., Malau, E.I., Hutagalung, D.S., Decision support system for selection technique using MOORA method. *IOP Conf. Series. Mater. Sci. Engineering IOP Publ.*, 1088, 1, 012022, 2021.
23. Dabbagh, R. and Yousefi, S., A hybrid decision-making approach based on FCM and MOORA for occupational health and safety risk analysis. *J. Saf. Res.*, 71, 111–123, 2019. https://doi.org/10.1016/j.jsr.2019.09.021.
24. Sutarno, S., Mesran, M., Supriyanto, S., Yuliana, Y., Dewi, A., Implementation of multi-objective Optimazation on the base of ratio analysis (MOORA) in improving support for decision on sales location determination. *J. Physics Conf. Series. IOP Publ.*, 1424, 1, 012019, 2019. https://doi.org/10.1088/1742-6596/1424/1/012019.
25. Attri, R. and Grover, S., Decision making over the production system life cycle: MOORA method. *Int. J. Syst. Assur. Eng. Manage.*, 5, 3, 320–328, 2014. https://doi.org/10.1007/s13198-013-0169-2.
26. Dey, B., Bairagi, B., Sarkar, B., Sanyal, S., A MOORA based fuzzy multi-criteria decision making approach for supply chain strategy selection. *Int. J. Ind. Eng. Comput.*, 3, 4, 649–662, 2012. https://doi.org/10.5267/j.ijiec.2012.03.001.
27. Ghoushchi, S.J., Yousefi, S., Khazaeili, M., An extended FMEA approach based on the Z-MOORA and fuzzy BWM for prioritization of failures. *Appl. Soft Comput.*, 81, 105505, 2019. https://doi.org/10.1016/j.asoc.2019.105505.
28. Hemamalini, N., Ramachandran, M., Ramu, K., Analysis of e-learning using MOORA method. *Contemporaneity Lang. Lit. Robotized Millennium*, 4, 1, 44–50, 2022. https://doi.org/10.46632/cllrm/4/1/6.
29. Sarkar, A., Panja, S.C., Das, D., Sarkar, B., Developing an efficient decision support system for non-traditional machine selection: An application of MOORA and MOOSRA. *Prod. Manuf. Res.*, 3, 1, 324–342, 2015. https://doi.org/10.1080/21693277.2014.895688.

30. Brauers, W.K.M., Multi-objective seaport planning by MOORA decision making. *Ann. Oper. Res.*, 206, 1, 39–58, 2013. https://doi.org/10.1007/s10479-013-1314-7.
31. Soni, A.A., Das, P.K., Sarma, M.J., Application of MOORA method for parametric optimization of manufacturing process of floor tiles using waste plastics. *Process Integr. Optim. Sustain.*, 6, 113–123, 2022. https://doi.org/10.1007/s41660-021-00205-3.

7

Optimizing Microwave Device Performance with SPSS Analysis

Muniyandy Elangovan[1,2]*, G. Dhanabalan[3] and H. B. Michael Rajan[4]

[1]*Department of Biosciences, Saveetha School of Engineering. Saveetha Institute of Medical and Technical Sciences, Chennai, India*
[2]*Applied Science Research Center. Applied Science Private University, Amman, Jordan*
[3]*Department of Computer Science and Engineering, Vel Tech Rangarajan Dr. Sagunthala R&D Institute of Science and Technology, Chennai, India*
[4]*Department of Mechanical Engineering, Kings College of Engineering, Punalkulam, Pudukkottai, Tamil Nadu, India*

Abstract

In the evolving landscape of Industry 5.0, the characterization and enhancement of microwave devices and systems hold paramount importance. This chapter delves into the comprehensive analysis of microwave devices, including relays, coaxial switches, and high-frequency signal handling components, using the SPSS (Statistical Package for the Social Sciences) method. These devices are integral to various applications like wireless communication, base stations, and testing equipment, with a significant presence in microwave data transmission systems. We explore the extensive application of these devices in microwave radios, emphasizing their role in advanced communication systems. The chapter highlights key components such as solid-state amplifiers, high-energy transmitters, antennas, and various signal processing elements like attenuators and couplers. Additionally, we discuss the historical significance of microwave technology, tracing back to Percy Spencer's discovery, which revolutionized kitchen appliances. The focus extends to the potential of wider bandgap microwave devices, which promise enhanced performance, power efficiency, and cost-effectiveness up to 20 GHz. This analysis underlines the ongoing development and optimization of wider bandgap devices in microwave and millimeter-wave systems. This chapter integrates "technical

**Corresponding author*: muniyandy.e@gmail.com

Kanak Kalita, J.V.N. Ramesh, M. Elangovan and S. Balamurugan (eds.) Decision-Making Techniques and Methods for Sustainable Technological Innovation: Strategies and Applications in Industry 5.0, (119–138) © 2025 Scrivener Publishing LLC

knowledge," "experimental skills," and "data analysis proficiency" using SPSS, providing a comprehensive view of microwave device characterization. It aims to equip readers with a deeper understanding of these systems, fostering innovation and efficiency in Industry 5.0's technological landscape.

Keywords: Technical knowledge, experimental skills, lab equipment usage, report writing skills, overall lab experience, satisfaction with course

7.1 Introduction

Microwave devices and systems have emerged as the backbone of modern communication networks, playing a pivotal role in transmitting high-frequency signals over long distances. Operating within the frequency range of 1 to 100 gigahertz (GHz), these devices have revolutionized various fields, from telecommunications to aerospace, and have become an integral part of our daily lives. One of the key categories within this domain includes relays and coaxial switches [1]. These devices are adept at efficiently handling high-frequency signals, making them indispensable components in a wide array of applications. They form the linchpin of crucial systems such as test and measuring equipment, wireless devices, and base stations. Their ability to swiftly and accurately manipulate signals has elevated their significance in the realm of modern technology. In microwave data transmission systems, these devices find extensive use. They are the workhorses behind the seamless transfer of data across vast distances [2]. Towering over the landscape, regular microwave systems are equipped with microwave radios, employing advanced technology to ensure reliable and high-performance communication. These radios are engineered to meet the demands of modern telecommunications, offering capabilities that are indispensable for transmitting data over long distances. The core of microwave systems lies in their components [3]. High-performance amplifiers, solid-state transmitters, and other sophisticated elements operate at power levels ranging from milliwatts to kilowatts. These devices are the powerhouses that drive the efficient transmission of data across vast networks. Additionally, a suite of auxiliary components, including antennas, attenuators, terminations, connectors, and cable assemblies, works in unison to ensure seamless signal processing. Couplers, isolators, and circulators play a vital role in managing signal flow within microwave systems [4]. These specialized components guide the path of electromagnetic waves, enabling precise control over signal direction and power distribution. The incorporation of ferrite components, along with a diverse range of filters and limiters, further enhances the performance of these systems.

This intricate interplay of components forms the foundation for the flawless operation of microwave devices and systems [5]. Microwaves themselves are characterized by their unique properties. With wavelengths considerably shorter than those of traditional radio waves, they propagate energy in a distinct manner. Unlike radio waves, microwaves do not rely on reflection by the ionosphere for transmission. Instead, they travel in straight lines and interact directly with surfaces. However, their shorter wavelengths also make them susceptible to attenuation over shorter distances, necessitating strategic planning in system design and deployment [6]. The journey of microwave technology is punctuated by groundbreaking discoveries and innovations. Among the notable milestones is the pioneering work of American engineer Percy Spencer during World War II. Spencer's serendipitous observation of a melting candy bar in his pocket while working with microwave-emitting magnetrons led to the development of the first microwave oven [7]. This revolutionary kitchen appliance forever changed the way we prepare and consume food, demonstrating the profound impact of microwave technology on everyday life. Raytheon, the corporation for which Spencer worked, played a crucial role in the production of compact cavity magnetrons. These devices, capable of generating high-power microwave signals, became a cornerstone of microwave technology [8]. Mass production of these magnetrons during the war effort helped establish the foundation for the post-war microwave revolution. Microwave devices have become the unsung heroes of modern communication systems, enabling the transmission of high-frequency signals that form the backbone of our interconnected world. Operating within the frequency range of 1 to 100 GHz, these devices have revolutionized various industries, from telecommunications to aerospace, and play an essential role in our daily lives [9]. One of the key categories of microwave devices includes microwave amplifiers. These amplifiers are designed to boost the strength of microwave signals, allowing them to travel over long distances without significant loss of information. They serve as the workhorses of communication networks, ensuring that signals remain clear and reliable even as they traverse vast networks [10]. Microwave oscillators are another crucial category. These devices generate stable and precise microwave signals, forming the heartbeat of communication systems. Oscillators are essential for maintaining the integrity of signals as they travel through various components and transmission mediums. Their accuracy and stability are paramount to ensuring that the information transmitted is received with fidelity [11]. In the realm of passive components, microwave filters play a pivotal role. These devices allow specific frequencies to pass through while attenuating others, ensuring that only the desired signal reaches its destination. This is particularly crucial in crowded frequency environments where interference can degrade the quality of communication. Filters are the gatekeepers that maintain the integrity of the transmitted information [12]. Waveguides and transmission lines are the unsung heroes of microwave technology. They provide a path for signals to travel efficiently and with minimal loss. Waveguides, in particular, are hollow metal tubes that guide electromagnetic waves, effectively shielding them from external interference. These components form the arteries and veins of communication systems, ensuring that signals reach their destination with minimum loss. In the rapidly evolving field of wireless communication, antennas are indispensable [13]. These devices convert for transmission of electrical signals as electromagnetic waves, and the opposite is welcome. Antennas come in different shapes and sizes; each is specifically optimized for applications. They are the bridge between the wired and wireless worlds, enabling seamless communication across vast distances. The deployment of microwave devices extends beyond conventional communication systems. In the field of radar technology, microwave components are critical for accurate detection and ranging [14]. Radar systems rely on the emission and reception of microwave signals to determine the location, speed, and direction of objects. This technology finds applications in aviation, defense, meteorology, and various other industries. Satellite communication, a cornerstone of modern global connectivity, relies heavily on microwave technology. Satellites act as relay stations in space, receiving signals from ground stations and retransmitting them to their intended destinations. The signals are transmitted and received using high-frequency microwave bands, allowing for the seamless exchange of information across vast distances [15]. Microwave systems have emerged as the backbone of modern communication networks, enabling the swift and reliable transmission of information over long distances. Operating within the frequency range of 1 to 100 GHz, these systems harness the power of high-frequency electromagnetic waves to facilitate seamless connectivity. They have revolutionized various industries, from telecommunications to aerospace, and play an indispensable role in our interconnected world [16]. One of the key advantages of microwave systems lies in their ability to transmit data at incredibly high speeds. This characteristic makes them invaluable for applications where rapid data transfer is crucial, such as in telecommunications networks and data centers. By leveraging the short wavelengths of microwaves, these systems can transmit vast amounts of information swiftly and efficiently. Moreover, microwave systems are renowned for their robustness and reliability. Unlike some other communication mediums, microwaves are less susceptible to environmental factors like rain, fog, or snow [17]. This resilience ensures that communication remains stable and uninterrupted even in adverse weather conditions, making them an ideal choice for mission-critical applications.

Another pivotal aspect of microwave systems is their ability to provide highly focused and directional communication. This feature is particularly crucial in point-to-point communication links, where the signal needs to be precisely targeted from the transmitter to the receiver. This level of precision minimizes interference and ensures that the signal reaches its intended destination with high fidelity [18]. Furthermore, microwave systems have found extensive applications in long-haul communication networks. They are the backbone of backbone networks, enabling the high-speed data transmission that underpins our global connectivity. Whether it is transmitting voice, video, or data, microwave systems form the essential infrastructure that powers our interconnected world. In addition to terrestrial applications, microwave systems have become indispensable in satellite communication. They serve as the medium through which signals are transmitted between ground stations and satellites in orbit [19]. This enables a wide range of services, including television broadcasting, internet connectivity, and navigation systems, to reach even the most remote corners of the globe. As technology continues to advance, so too will the capabilities and applications of microwave systems. With ongoing research and development, we can expect even more efficient and sophisticated systems to emerge, further enhancing our ability to communicate swiftly and reliably across the globe. Microwave systems are poised to remain at the forefront of our interconnected world, powering the communication networks that drive progress and connectivity in the digital age [20].

7.2 Materials and Methods

The various criteria considered in this work are as follows:

Technical knowledge: "Technical knowledge" assesses the students' understanding and proficiency in the theoretical concepts and principles related to microwave devices and systems. It encompasses their grasp of key theories, formulas, and concepts that underlie the functioning of microwave devices.

Experimental skills: "Experimental skills" evaluates the students' ability to practically apply their theoretical knowledge in the laboratory setting. This parameter measures their proficiency in conducting experiments, handling equipment, and troubleshooting any issues that may arise during experiments.

Lab equipment usage: "Lab equipment usage" assesses how effectively students utilize the specialized equipment in the laboratory. It encompasses their competence in setting up, calibrating, and operating microwave devices and instruments. This parameter also considers their adherence to safety protocols while handling laboratory equipment.
Data analysis proficiency: "Data analysis proficiency" evaluates the students' aptitude in processing and interpreting experimental data. This parameter assesses their ability to analyze measurement results, apply relevant mathematical techniques, and draw meaningful conclusions from the data collected during experiments.
Report writing skills: "Report writing skills" gauges the students' proficiency in documenting their experimental procedures, results, and analyses in a clear, concise, and organized manner. This parameter assesses their ability to effectively communicate their findings through formal laboratory reports.
Overall lab experience: "Overall lab experience" provides an encompassing evaluation of the students' performance and engagement in the laboratory sessions. It takes into consideration their "technical knowledge," practical skills, equipment handling, data analysis, and report writing abilities collectively.
Satisfaction with course: "Satisfaction with course" measures the students' level of contentment and fulfillment with the microwave devices and systems course. This parameter encompasses their overall experience, including lectures, laboratory sessions, course material, and any additional resources provided during the course. It provides valuable feedback on the course's effectiveness and relevance to the students' learning goals.

Methods

SPSS (Statistical Package for the Social Sciences) is a widely utilized software application designed for the purposes of statistical analysis and data management. Its application is prevalent across a multitude of disciplines, encompassing social sciences, psychology, business, and healthcare. The methodology employed in SPSS typically encompasses the subsequent stages.

Data entry: The initial stage necessitates the input of data into SPSS. This process may be executed through manual entry, the importation of data from external sources (such as Excel), or the utilization of data collection tools that are integrated within SPSS. Outliers and data inaccuracies may need addressing. Additionally, it may be necessary to recode variables, transform data, or create new variables as circumstances dictate. Descriptive statistics such as mean, median, standard deviation, minimum, and maximum can be computed. SPSS possesses the capability to generate descriptive statistics for both individual variables and aggregates of variables.

Data analysis: SPSS presents a comprehensive array of statistical analysis alternatives, including *t* tests, analysis of variance, regression, correlation, factor analysis, and χ^2 tests, among others. The specific analytical methodology selected will be contingent upon the research question and the type of data being analyzed.

Interpretation of results: Following the execution of statistical analysis, it is imperative to interpret the resulting data. SPSS produces tables and graphical representations that elucidate the outcomes of the analysis. It is essential to meticulously interpret the findings within the framework of the research question and the dataset.

Reporting and visualization: SPSS facilitates the generation of tables and charts to visually represent the results of the analysis. These visual artifacts can be incorporated into research reports, presentations, or scholarly articles.

Data export: Upon the completion of the analysis, there may be a necessity to export the results to alternative formats (such as Excel, Word, or PDF) for additional reporting or dissemination among relevant stakeholders.

7.3 Results and Discussion

Table 7.1 shows the descriptive statistics values for analysis in microwave devices and systems. It appears that you've provided statistical data related to "technical knowledge," "experimental skills," "lab equipment usage," "data analysis proficiency," "report writing skills," and "overall lab experience." Each category has been assessed on a scale ranging from 1 to 5, with corresponding statistics including the range, minimum, maximum, sum, mean, and standard deviation. For instance, in the category of "technical knowledge," there were 135 participants. The scores ranged from 1 to 5, with a minimum score of 1 and a maximum score of 5. The total sum of scores in this category was 452, resulting in a mean score of 3.35. The standard deviation, indicating the dispersion of scores around the mean, was 1.039. Similar statistics have been provided for the other categories as well.

Table 7.1 Descriptive statistics.

Criteria	n	Range	Min	Max	Sum	Mean		Standard deviation
Technical knowledge	135	4	1	5	452	3.35	0.089	1.039
Experimental skills	135	4	1	5	425	3.15	0.116	1.347
Lab equipment usage	135	4	1	5	484	3.59	0.104	1.206
Data analysis proficiency	135	4	1	5	469	3.47	0.103	1.202
Report writing skills	135	4	1	5	484	3.59	0.134	1.557
Overall lab experience	135	4	1	5	503	3.73	0.117	1.363
Satisfaction with course	135	4	1	5	448	3.32	0.107	1.244

Table 7.2 Reliability statistics.

Cronbach's α	Cronbach's α based on standardized items	No. of items
0.755	0.763	7

Table 7.2 presents the results pertaining to the reliability assessment *via* Cronbach's α. The aggregate Cronbach's α coefficient for the model is 0.763, signifying a reliability rate of 76%. According to the extant literature, a model exhibiting a Cronbach's α value exceeding 50% is deemed suitable for analytical purposes.

Table 7.3 shows the frequency statistics in analysis microwave devices and systems in "technical knowledge," "experimental skills," "lab equipment usage," "data analysis proficiency," "report writing skills," "overall lab experience," and "satisfaction with course" curve values are given.

Table 7.3 Frequencies statistics.

		Technical knowledge	Experimental skills	Lab equipment usage	Data analysis proficiency	Report writing skills	Overall lab experience	Satisfaction on with course
N	Valid	135	135	135	135	135	135	135
	Missing	0	0	0	0	0	0	0
Mean		3.35	3.15	3.59	3.47	3.59	3.73	3.32
Standard error of the mean		0.089	0.116	0.104	0.103	0.134	0.117	0.107
Median		3	3	3	3	4	4	3
Mode		3	3	3	3	5	5	3
Standard deviation		1.039	1.347	1.206	1.202	1.557	1.363	1.244
Variance		1.079	1.814	1.454	1.445	2.424	1.857	1.547
Skewness		−0.296	0.265	−0.268	−0.383	−0.498	−0.514	−0.25
Standard error of skewness		0.209	0.209	0.209	0.209	0.209	0.209	0.209
Kurtosis		0.192	−1.229	−0.785	−0.503	−1.324	−1.073	−0.778

(Continued)

Table 7.3 Frequencies statistics. *(Continued)*

		Technical knowledge	Experimental skills	Lab equipment usage	Data analysis proficiency	Report writing skills	Overall lab experience	Satisfaction on with course
Standard error of kurtosis		0.414	0.414	0.414	0.414	0.414	0.414	0.414
Range		4	4	4	4	4	4	4
Minimum		1	1	1	1	1	1	1
Maximum		5	5	5	5	5	5	5
Sum		452	425	484	469	484	503	448
Percentiles	10	2	2	2	2	1	2	1
	20	3	2	3	3	2	2.2	2
	25	3	2	3	3	2	3	3
	60	3	3	4	4	5	5	4
	80	4	5	5	5	5	5	5

Table 7.4 shows the reliability statistic individual parameter Cronbach's α reliability results. The Cronbach's α value for "technical knowledge" .709, "experimental skills" .788, "lab equipment usage" .727, "data analysis proficiency" .726, "report writing skills" .707, "overall lab experience" .727, and "satisfaction with course" .677. This indicates all the parameters can be considered for analysis.

Figure 7.1 illustrates the histogram representation for "technical knowledge"; it is unequivocally evident from the figure that the dataset exhibits a slight left skewness, attributable to the predominance of respondents who selected the value of 3 for "technical knowledge." With the exception of the

Table 7.4 Reliability statistic individual

Criteria	Cronbach's α if item deleted
Technical knowledge	0.709
Experimental skills	0.788
Lab equipment usage	0.727
Data analysis proficiency	0.726
Report writing skills	0.707
Overall lab experience	0.727
Satisfaction with course	0.677

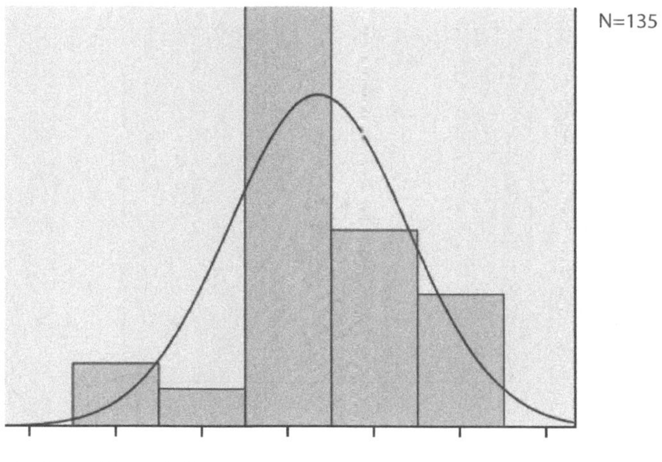

Figure 7.1 Technical knowledge.

value 2, all other measurements reside within the confines of the normal curve, thereby indicating that the model adheres significantly to the principles of normal distribution.

Figure 7.2 presents the histogram representation for "experimental skills," and an analysis of the figure reveals a discernible leftward skew in the data, attributed to a preponderance of respondents selecting the value of 3 for "experimental skills"; with the exception of the value of 2, all other values fall beneath the normal curve, indicating that the model adheres significantly to the principles of normal distribution.

Figure 7.3 presents the histogram representation of laboratory equipment utilization; from the illustration, it is evident that the dataset exhibits a slight left skewness, attributable to a greater number of respondents selecting the value of 3 for laboratory equipment utilization. With the exception of the value of 3, all other numerical values reside beneath the normal distribution curve, indicating that the model adheres significantly to the principles of normal distribution.

Figure 7.4 illustrates the histogram representation of "data analysis proficiency"; from the visual data, it is apparent that the distribution exhibits a slight left skewness, attributable to the predominance of respondents selecting the value of 3 for "data analysis proficiency." With the exception of the value 3, all other data points align beneath the normal distribution curve, indicating that the model adheres significantly to a normal distribution.

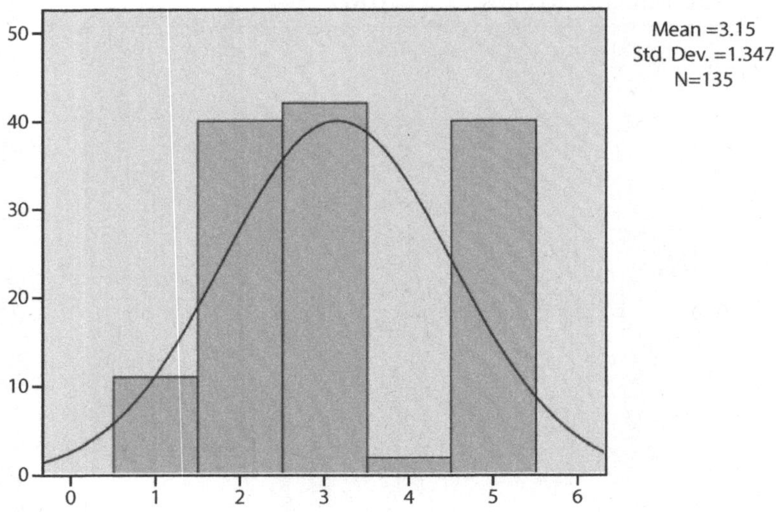

Figure 7.2 Experimental skills.

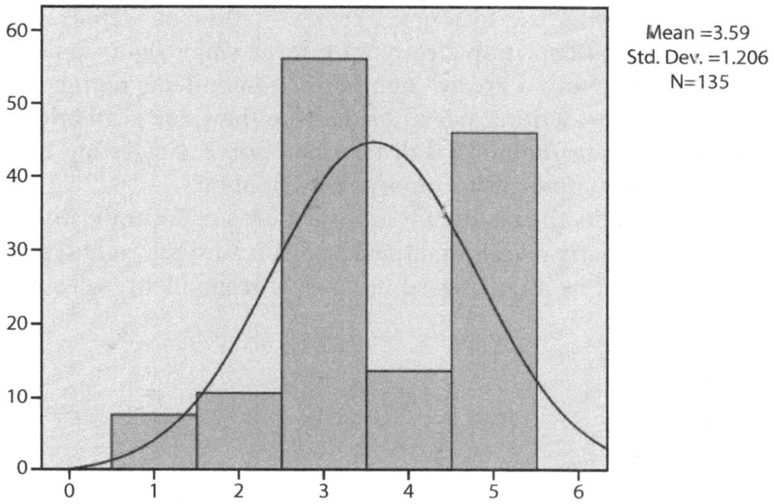

Figure 7.3 Lab equipment usage.

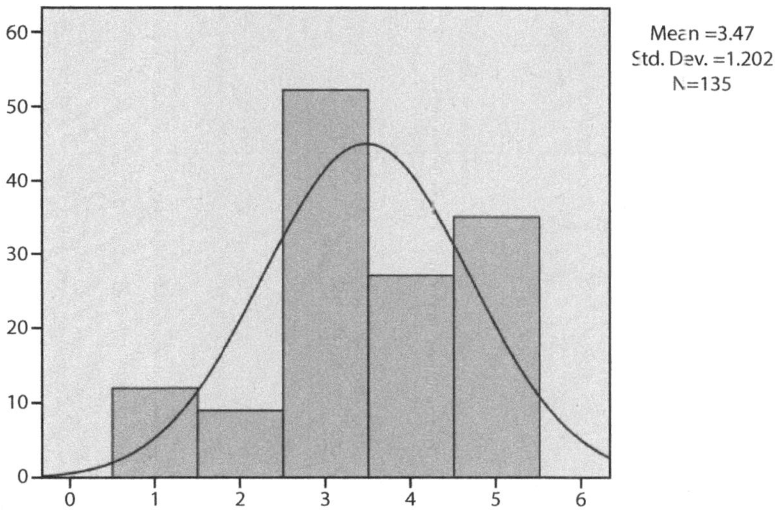

Figure 7.4 Data analysis proficiency.

Figure 7.5 presents the histogram representation of "report writing skills"; the graphical depiction clearly indicates a slight right skewness in the data, resulting from a greater number of respondents opting for the value of 5 for "report writing skills." Aside from the value 3, all other data points reside beneath the normal distribution curve, suggesting that the model significantly conforms to a normal distribution.

Figure 7.6 exhibits the histogram representation of "overall lab experience"; the figure clearly reveals that the data display a slight right skewness, which is influenced by an increased number of respondents selecting the

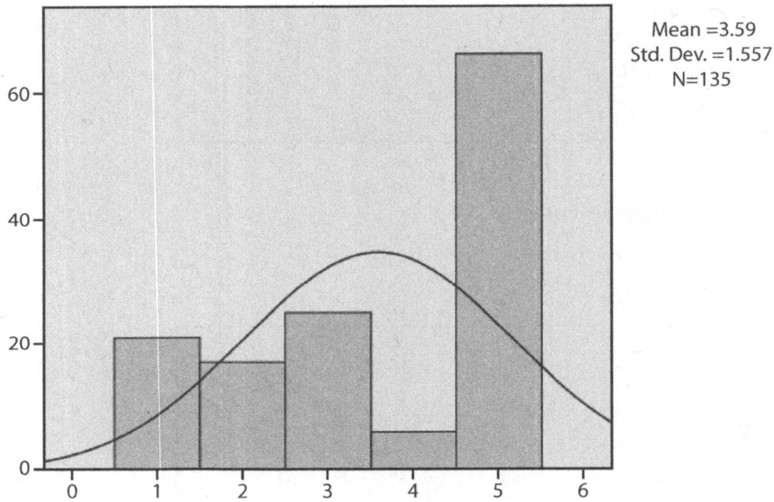

Figure 7.5 Report writing skills.

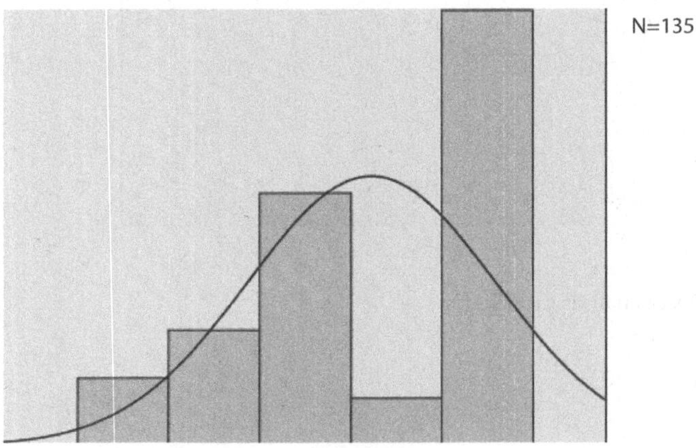

Figure 7.6 Overall lab experience.

value of 5 for "overall lab experience." Excluding the value 3, all remaining values fall under the normal distribution curve, indicating that the model significantly aligns with a normal distribution.

Figure 7.7 showcases the histogram representation of "satisfaction with course"; the data clearly demonstrate a slight left skewness, primarily due to a higher frequency of respondents choosing the value of 3 for "satisfaction with course." Except for the value 3, all other values are situated beneath the normal distribution curve, thereby suggesting that the model significantly adheres to a normal distribution.

Table 7.5 presents the association between motivational parameters, wherein "technical knowledge" for "data analysis proficiency" exhibits the most substantial correlation with "experimental skills" while demonstrating the least correlation in another aspect. Subsequently, the correlation between motivational parameters for "experimental skills" and "report writing skills" reveals the highest correlation with "technical knowledge" and the lowest correlation elsewhere. Furthermore, the correlation between motivational parameters for "lab equipment usage" and "data analysis proficiency" indicates the strongest correlation with "experimental skills," alongside the weakest correlation in a different context. Additionally, the correlation between motivational parameters for "data analysis proficiency" and "lab equipment usage" shows the most significant correlation with "experimental skills" while reflecting the least correlation in another regard. Moreover, the correlation between motivational parameters for "report writing skills" and "overall lab experience" illustrates the highest correlation with "data analysis proficiency" and the lowest correlation in

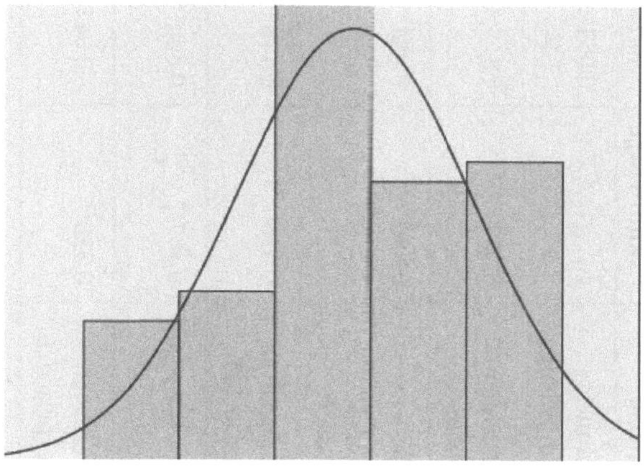

Figure 7.7 Satisfaction with course.

Table 7.5 Correlations.

Criteria	Technical knowledge	Experimental skills	Lab equipment usage	Data analysis proficiency	Report writing skills	Overall lab experience	Satisfaction on with course
Technical knowledge	1	0.064	0.480**	0.536**	0.307**	0.358**	0.520**
Experimental skills	0.064	1	0.084	0.118	0.300**	−0.047	0.177*
Lab equipment usage	0.480**	0.084	1	0.595**	0.190*	0.189*	0.377**
Data analysis proficiency	0.536**	0.118	0.595**	1	0.166	0.157	0.372**
Report writing skills	0.307**	0.300**	0.190*	0.166	1	0.558**	0.554**
Overall lab experience	0.358**	−0.047	0.189*	0.157	0.558**	1	0.571**
Satisfaction with course	0.520**	0.177*	0.377**	0.372**	0.554**	0.571**	1

**Correlation is significant at the 0.01 level (2-tailed).
*Correlation is significant at the 0.05 level (2-tailed).

an alternate scenario. Furthermore, the correlation between motivational parameters for "overall lab experience" and satisfaction with the course reveals the most pronounced correlation with "data analysis proficiency" while exhibiting the least correlation in another context. Lastly, the correlation between motivational parameters for "satisfaction with the course" and "overall lab experience" denotes the highest correlation with "experimental skills" while also demonstrating the weakest correlation in a different dimension.

7.4 Conclusion

Microwave devices encompass relays and coaxial switches, categorized by their ability to handle high-frequency signals. These devices find extensive application in test and measuring equipment, wireless devices, and base stations. They play a crucial role in microwave data transmission systems, particularly in regular microwave systems located atop towers. Microwave radios, utilizing advanced technology, are pivotal for microwave communications, offering high performance through components like solid-state amplifiers and high-energy transmitters with outputs in the kilowatt range. Designs also incorporate essential elements such as antennas, attenuators, terminations, connectors, cable assemblies, couplers, isolators, and circulators. These components facilitate various functions, including filtering and limiting. Microwaves are characterized by their short wavelengths and straight-line propagation, although they face attenuation over short distances. Notably, American engineer Percy Spencer's discovery of microwave heating during World War II revolutionized kitchen technology, leading to the creation of the beloved kitchen appliance we know today. This breakthrough was made possible through the production of compact cavity magnetrons, a key component developed in bulk by Raytheon during that era, with Spencer playing a crucial role in its creation. Microwave devices and systems have emerged as the backbone of modern communication networks, playing a pivotal role in transmitting high-frequency signals over long distances. Operating within the frequency range of 1 to 100 GHz, these devices have revolutionized various fields, from telecommunications to aerospace, and have become an integral part of our daily lives. One of the key categories within this domain includes relays and coaxial switches; "technical knowledge" assesses the students' understanding and proficiency in the theoretical concepts and principles related to microwave devices and systems. It encompasses their grasp of key theories, formulas, and concepts that underlie the functioning of microwave devices.

The Cronbach's α reliability result. The overall Cronbach's α value for the models is .763, which indicates 76% reliability. From the literature review, the greater than 50% Cronbach's α value model can be considered for analysis.

References

1. Heiter, G.L., Characterization of nonlinearities in microwave devices and systems. *IEEE Trans. Microwave Theory Tech.*, 21, 12, 797–805, 1973, https://doi.org/10.1109/TMTT.1973.1128134.
2. Kemerley, R.T., Wallace, H.B., Yoder, M.N., Impact of wide bandgap microwave devices on DoD systems. *Proc. IEEE*, 90, 6, 1059–1064, 2002, https://doi.org/10.1109/JPROC.2002.1021570.
3. Dew-Hughes, D., Application of high temperature superconductors in passive microwave devices. *Aust. J. Phys.*, 50, 2, 363–379, 1997.
4. Borisov, A.A., Budzinsky, U.A., Bykovsky, S.V., Galdetskiy, A.V., Korolev, A.N., Lopin, M., II, Negirev, A.A., Pugnin, V., II, Ruvinsky, G.V., Sazonov, B.V., The development of vacuum microwave devices in Istok, in: *IEEE International Vacuum Electronics Conference*, IEEE Computer Society, pp. 437–438, 2011, https://doi.org/10.1109/IVEC.2011.5747063.
5. Herczfield, P.R., Daryoush, A.S., Contarino, V.M., Rosen, A., Turski, Z., Khana, A.P.S., Optically controlled microwave devices and circuits, in: *IEEE MTT-S International Microwave Symposium Digest*, IEEE Publications, pp. 211–214, 1985, https://doi.org/10.1109/MWSYM.1985.1131943.
6. Lancaster, M.J., Powell, J., Porch, A., Thin-film ferroelectric microwave devices. *Supercond. Sci. Technol.*, 11, 11, 1323–1334, 1998, https://doi.org/10.1088/0953-2048/11/11/021.
7. Gevorgian, S.S. and Kollberg, E.L., Do we really need ferroelectrics in paraelectric phase only in electrically controlled microwave devices? *IEEE Trans. Microwave Theory Tech.*, 49, 11, 2117–2124, 2001, https://doi.org/10.1109/22.963146.
8. Meys, R.P., A wave approach to the noise properties of linear microwave devices. *IEEE Trans. Microwave Theory Tech.*, 26, 1, 34–37, 1978, https://doi.org/10.1109/TMTT.1978.1129303.
9. Quevedo-Teruel, O., Chen, Q., Mesa, F., Fonseca, N.J.G., Valerio, G., On the benefits of glide symmetries for microwave devices. *IEEE J. Microwaves*, 1, 1, 457–469, 2021, https://doi.org/10.1109/JMW.2020.3033847.
10. Ha, S.D., Zhou, Y., Duwel, A.E., White, D.W., Ramanathan, S., Quick switch: Strongly correlated electronic phase transition systems for cutting-edge microwave devices. *IEEE Microwave Mag.*, 15, 6, 32–44, 2014, https://doi.org/10.1109/MMM.2014.2332422.

11. Alibakhshikenari, M., Virdee, B.S., Ali, A., Limiti, E., Miniaturised planar-patch antenna based on metamaterial L-shaped unit-cells for broadband portable microwave devices and multiband wireless communication systems. *IET Microwaves Antennas Propag.*, 12, 7, 1080–1086, 2018, https://doi.org/10.1049/iet-map.2016.1141.
12. Harkouss, Y., Rousset, J., Chehade, H., Ngoya, E., Barataud, D., Teyssier, J.-P., The use of artificial neural networks in nonlinear microwave devices and circuits modeling: An application to telecommunication system design (invited article). *Int. J. RF Microwave Comput. Aided Eng.*, 9, 3, 198–215, 1999, https://doi.org/10.1002/(SICI)1099-047X(199905)9:3<198::AID-MMCE6>3.0.CO;2-A.
13. Koziel, S. and Bandler, J.W., Recent advances in space-mapping-based modeling of microwave devices. *Int. J. Numer. Modell. Electron. Netw. Devices Fields*, 23, 6, 425–446, 2010, https://doi.org/10.1002/jnm.743.
14. Akmal, M., Lees, J., Jiangtao, S., Carrubba, V., Yusoff, Z., Woodington, S., Benedikt, J., *et al.*, An enhanced modulated waveform measurement system for the robust characterization of microwave devices under modulated excitation, in: *6th European Microwave Integrated Circuit Conference*, IEEE Publications, pp. 180–183, 2011.
15. Harkouss, Y., Rousset, J., Chehade, H., Ngoya, E., Barataud, D., Teyssier, J.P., Modeling microwave devices and circuits for telecommunications system design, in: *IEEE International Joint Conference on Neural Networks Proceedings, IEEE Publications World Congress on Computational Intelligence*, vol. 1, IEEE Publications, pp. 128–133, 1998, (Cat. No. 98CH36227).
16. Alibakhshi-Kenari, M., Naser-Moghadasi, M., Sadeghzadeh, R.A., Virdee, B.S., Limiti, E., New CRLH-based planar slotted antennas with helical inductors for wireless communication systems, RF-circuits and microwave devices at UHF–SHF bands. *Wireless Pers. Commun.*, 92, 3, 1029–1038, 2017, https://doi.org/10.1007/s11277-016-3590-4.
17. Verbeyst, F. and Bossche, V., VIOMAP, the S-parameter equivalent for weakly nonlinear RF and microwave devices. *IEEE Trans. Microwave Theory Tech.*, 42, 12, 2531–2535, 1994, https://doi.org/10.1109/22.339793.
18. Morev, S.P., Aban'Shin, N.P., Gorfinkel, B., II, Darmaev, A.N., Komarov, D.A., Makeev, A.E., Yakunin, A.N., Electron-optical systems with planar field-emission cathode matrices for high-power microwave devices. *J. Commun. Technol. Electron.*, 58, 4, 357–365, 2013.
19. de La Rubia, V., Razafison, U., Maday, Y., Reliable fast frequency sweep for microwave devices *via* the reduced-basis method. *IEEE Trans. Microwave Theory Tech.*, 57, 12, 2923–2937, 2009, https://doi.org/10.1109/TMTT.2009.2034208.
20. Kretly, L.C., Almeida, A.F., De Oliveira, R.S., Sasaki, J.M., Sombra, A.S.B., Electrical and optical properties of CaCu3Ti4O12 (CCTO) substrates for microwave devices and antennas. *Microwave Opt. Technol. Lett.*, 39, 2, 145–150, 2003, https://doi.org/10.1002/mop.11152.

8

Enhanced Microgrid Security: Naive Bayes Versus Random Forest in Attack Detection Accuracy

A. Prince Kalvin Raj and S. Pushpa Latha*

Department of Information Technology, Saveetha School of Engineering, Saveetha Institute of Medical and Technical Sciences, Saveetha University, Chennai, India

Abstract

In the realm of Industry 5.0, ensuring the security of power infrastructure, particularly microgrids, is of utmost importance. This chapter presents a study focused on improving the accuracy of detecting covert attacks on microgrids, a critical aspect of sustainable technological innovation. The study introduces an advanced approach using the naive Bayes algorithm and compares its effectiveness with the well-established random forest algorithm. Utilizing two sample groups of 10 samples each, the study employs statistical tools like clinic calc with parameters such as an α value of 0.05 and a G*Power rate of 0.80, aiming for robust analysis within a 95% confidence interval. The research assesses a dataset of 37 scenarios, encompassing natural events and attack events, to evaluate the precision of attack detection in microgrids. Both naive Bayes and decision tree algorithms are applied to a classification matrix of 154 rows and 17 columns, with the study's sample size determined through ClinCalc, ensuring a pretest power of 0.80. This comparative analysis between naive Bayes and random forest algorithms is crucial in assessing their capabilities in accurately detecting stealthy attacks on power systems. The chapter concludes that the naive Bayes algorithm significantly enhances the precision of detecting attacks in microgrids compared to the random forest method. This finding paves the way for more reliable and secure power infrastructure management, aligning with the goals of sustainable technological innovation in Industry 5.0.

**Corresponding author*: pushpalathas.sse@saveetha.com

Kanak Kalita, J.V.N. Ramesh, M. Elangovan and S. Balamurugan (eds.) Decision-Making Techniques and Methods for Sustainable Technological Innovation: Strategies and Applications in Industry 5.0, (139–152) © 2025 Scrivener Publishing LLC

Keywords: Naive Bayes, random forest, machine learning, microgrid

Introduction

The modern power infrastructure is heavily dependent on distributed control systems (DCSs) for the effective management and monitoring of power generation, transmission, and distribution processes. These systems, while integral to the functioning of power grids, have increasingly become vulnerable to cyberattacks, posing significant risks such as power outages, equipment damage, and even endangering human life and the environment [5]. Given these potential threats, the detection of cyberattacks targeting DCSs has emerged as a critical area of research. Ensuring the resilience and reliability of these systems necessitates the development of advanced techniques for early and accurate detection of such attacks [10].

This paper presents a novel approach for detecting cyberattacks on DCSs in power infrastructure, specifically using machine learning and anomaly detection techniques. The research was conducted on a microgrid simulation platform where a Man-in-the-Middle (MitM) attack targeting the MaR (Measurement and Reference) procedure was simulated to generate realistic data for analysis. The complexity of this study lies in identifying the MaR attack, a covert cyber assault where attackers manipulate reference values used for measuring voltage in the communication network of the microgrid. By simulating the MitM attack within a microgrid control system, data relevant to the detection of such attacks were gathered and analyzed [6].

The feasibility of conducting stealth attacks on DC microgrids was explored using unknown input observer (UIO)-based detectors. These detectors have recently gained traction as a standard practice for detecting malicious network activities in power systems. Initial findings demonstrated that an attacker with knowledge of the error bounds in the DC microgrid's state estimation and measurement noise could execute a nonzero-dynamics stealthy attack, remaining undetected by traditional methods [3]. The critical nature of detecting cyberattacks in power grids cannot be overstated, as these grids constitute vital infrastructure essential to societal functioning. Real-time monitoring, intrusion detection systems, and threat intelligence capabilities are key to identifying cyberattacks as they occur, thereby minimizing potential damage and mitigating vulnerabilities within the power grid infrastructure.

Over the past few years, significant research has been conducted on improving the detection accuracy of stealth attacks in DCSs for microgrids. An exploration of 552 articles in IEEE Xplore highlights the increasing awareness of the dangers posed by deception attacks on DC microgrids, driven by the rapid integration of information and communication technologies into power systems [7–9]. Despite this growing awareness, undetectable deception attacks in control systems, particularly those that can obscure their impact from system operators, such as the infamous Stuxnet incident, have not yet been thoroughly studied [2].

This article introduces a novel methodology aimed at identifying weaknesses in current cyberattack detection schemes, specifically within the context of DC microgrids. By uncovering these vulnerabilities, the groundwork is laid for the development of more robust and trustworthy cybersecurity solutions. To address these challenges, a multiagent deep reinforcement learning–based algorithm is proposed, capable of autonomously generating coordinated stealthy destabilizing false data injection (FDI) attacks. This approach also uncovers the weak points in traditional index-based detection methods, particularly those employed in islanded DC microgrids [1].

The potential for FDI attacks and the distributed countermeasures are further examined within the hierarchical control structure of DC microgrids, utilizing UIO-based detectors. Preliminary investigations reveal that uncertainty surrounding the actual inputs to these detectors is the primary weakness, enabling attackers to exploit this vulnerability. Specifically, zero-trace stealthy attacks can be launched by fabricating unknown inputs in a manner that leaves the attack detection residual unchanged, allowing the attack to go unnoticed [4]. The attack detection mechanism in this architecture relies on a combination of a Luenberger observer and multiple unknown-input observers deployed across different layers of the system.

This study provides a comprehensive analysis of the conditions under which cyberattacks can either be reliably detected or remain undetected [5]. The research gap identified from existing systems is their relatively poor accuracy in detecting such sophisticated attacks. To address this gap, this study proposes improving classification accuracy by incorporating the naive Bayes algorithm and comparing its performance against the random forest classifier. Through this comparison, the study aims to enhance the overall robustness of attack detection mechanisms within power grid infrastructures.

Materials and Methods

This study was conducted in the Data Analytics Laboratory, part of the Department of Information Technology at Saveetha School of Engineering, Saveetha Institute of Medical and Technical Science. The research focused on comparing two algorithms—naive Bayes and random forest—using a carefully calculated sample size to ensure statistical robustness. The sample size was determined using the G*Power 3.1 software, a widely recognized tool for power analysis in hypothesis testing. Specifically, the parameters for the analysis included an α value of 0.05, a power level of 0.85, and a 95% confidence interval. Two distinct groups were formed, each containing 10 sample sets, resulting in a total of 10 samples per group. These groups were designed to allow for a comprehensive comparison of the two algorithms and their performance in detecting covert attacks on microgrids.

For the study, power system attack datasets were sourced from Oak Ridge National Laboratory and Mississippi State University, specifically from an incident database released on April 15, 2014. This comprehensive dataset includes 37 different power system incident scenarios that represent both natural events and cyberattacks. The dataset consists of 15 sets, subdivided into natural events (8), no events (1), and attack events (28). These diverse scenarios provide a realistic simulation of potential threats and events that could impact microgrids, making the dataset ideal for testing and validating machine learning models like naive Bayes and random forest. The dataset files are available in multiple formats, including ARFF for use with the Weka software and CSV formats, making it accessible for a variety of machine learning platforms. A link to the dataset (https://www.kaggle.com/datasets/bachirbarika/power-system) is provided for reference.

The technical environment used for implementing the machine learning models was designed to ensure reliable and efficient execution of the algorithms. The software development and deep learning assessment were carried out using Python OpenCV libraries. The hardware used for running the models included a system with an Intel Core i7 processor, a 64-bit architecture, and 4 GB of RAM. This setup was configured on a Windows 10 operating system, providing an adequate platform for the computational demands of the study. The coding and data processing were handled primarily using Java, which was selected for its efficiency in handling complex datasets. The data from the power system incidents were preprocessed and input into the algorithms, enabling a thorough evaluation of their accuracy in detecting anomalies and attacks.

This methodological framework, combining advanced statistical tools, a comprehensive dataset, and robust computational resources, provides a solid foundation for evaluating the effectiveness of the naive Bayes and random forest algorithms in improving microgrid security.

Naive Bayes

The naive Bayes algorithm is an extension of the naive Bayes algorithm that takes into account certain dependencies between features. The algorithm starts by calculating the prior probability of each class based on the training data. Then, for each feature and class combination, it calculates the conditional probability of that feature given the class.

In the case of the naive Bayes algorithm, the assumption of feature independence implies that the conditional probabilities of features are simply the product of the probabilities of each feature. However, in the case of the naive Bayes algorithm, certain dependencies between features are allowed. To account for these dependencies, the algorithm uses a matrix of correlation coefficients to adjust the probabilities of each feature.

Once the probabilities of each feature and class combination are calculated, the algorithm can be used to classify new instances. For a given instance, the algorithm calculates the posterior probability of each class given the features of the instance. The class with the highest probability is then assigned as the predicted class for the instance. Overall, the naive Bayes algorithm can be a useful tool in cases where the assumption of feature independence does not hold true. By allowing for certain dependencies between features, it can provide more accurate predictions than the traditional naive Bayes algorithm.

Novel Naive Bayes Algorithm Execution

Data preprocessing: This step involves cleaning, transforming, and encoding the data to make it suitable for the machine learning algorithm. Common techniques used in data preprocessing are missing value imputation, feature scaling, feature selection, and encoding categorical variables.
Feature engineering: Where relevant features are extracted to aid in instance classification. This step may involve techniques such as principal component analysis (PCA), linear discriminant analysis (LDA), and kernel methods. The algorithm then proceeds to probability estimation using a Bayesian network to represent feature dependencies. The Bayesian network is a directed acyclic graph in which nodes represent random variables, and edges denote dependencies between the variables.

Learning the structure of the Bayesian network, estimating conditional dependencies, and constructing the DAG: Techniques such as the Chow-Liu algorithm and the K2 algorithm are employed to learn the structure of a Bayesian network. Afterward, we estimate the conditional probability tables (CPTs) for each node in the network using algorithms like maximum likelihood estimation and Bayesian estimation. The CPTs represent the probabilities of each variable given its parents in the network. Classification follows after the Bayesian network is learned and the CPTs are estimated.

The posterior probability of each class given the features is computed using the Bayesian network, and the class with the highest posterior probability is selected as the predicted class. Finally, we evaluate the performance of the naive Bayes algorithm using appropriate metrics like accuracy, precision, recall, and F1 score, and we may use techniques such as cross-validation and grid search to tune the hyperparameters of the algorithm and improve its performance.

Pseudocode for Naive Bayes

Input:

- Training dataset $D = \{(x_1, y_1), (x_2, y_2), \ldots, (x_n, y_n)\}$
- Testing dataset $T = \{x_1, x_2, \ldots, x_m\}$

Output:

- Predicted labels for testing dataset T

The following are the procedures followed to perform the experiment:

Step 1. Calculate prior probabilities for each class in training dataset D:

- Count the number of samples for each class
- Divide by the total number of samples

Step 2. Calculate class-conditional probabilities for each feature in training dataset D:

- For each feature i and class j:
- Calculate the mean and standard deviation of feature i for samples in class j
- Use the Gaussian probability density function to calculate the probability of feature i for class j

Step 3. For each sample in testing dataset T:

- Calculate the posterior probability of each class using Bayes' rule:

- Multiply the prior probability of each class by the class-conditional probabilities of each feature for that class
- Divide by the total probability of the features for that sample
- Predict the class with the highest posterior probability for the sample

Step 4. Return the predicted labels for testing dataset T

Random Forest

Random forest is a classifier that consists of some decision bushes on numerous subsets of the given dataset and takes the common to enhance the predictive accuracy of that dataset. Instead of counting on one decision tree, the random woodland takes the prediction from every tree and is primarily based totally on the bulk votes of predictions [11], and it predicts the very last output [12]. It may be used for each classification and regression trouble in the decision tree. It is primarily based totally on the idea of ensemble learning; that is a method of mixing a couple of classifiers to remedy a complicated problem and to enhance the overall performance of the model.

Pseudocode for Random Forest

Step 1. Input-training dataset: X_train, y_train, number of trees: n_trees, number of features considered for splitting at each node- n_features, output–random forest model: RF_model.
Step 2. Define a function to grow a decision tree—inputs: data: X, y, number of features to consider at each split: n_features, number of features to consider at each split: n_features.

- Outputs: a decision tree model.

Step 3. Grow n_trees decision trees using bootstrapped samples of the training data:

For each tree:

- Randomly select n_features from the total set of features
- Use the selected features to grow a decision tree using the bootstrapped data

Step 4. Aggregate the predictions from all the trees:

- For each new observation, obtain the prediction from each decision tree
- Take the majority vote or the average of the predictions as the final prediction

Step 5. Return the random forest model, which consists of the n_trees decision trees

Step 6. To predict new observations:

- Pass the observation through each decision tree in the forest
- Aggregate the predictions as in step 3 to obtain the final prediction

Results and Discussion

To analyze the comparative performance of the naive Bayes and random forest algorithms, we utilized SPSS software to perform detailed statistical evaluations. The independent variables considered in this study included various image attributes, such as objects, distance, frequency, modulation, amplitude, volume, and decibels, all of which were vital in determining the algorithms' effectiveness. Meanwhile, the dependent variables were restricted to images and objects, allowing for a focused evaluation of each algorithm's classification capabilities.

An independent-samples *t* test was conducted to assess the accuracy levels of both the naive Bayes and random forest algorithms. This test is a well-established method for comparing the means of two independent groups and was critical in determining whether any significant difference existed between the two algorithms in terms of their performance. The statistical testing was performed on a setup consisting of a Windows 11 64-bit operating system, with 8 GB of RAM, and an internet-enabled laptop. The Colab Notebook, running Python version 3.9, was used to execute the machine learning models, further supported by Anaconda Navigator for managing and running the algorithms. Both cracked and uncracked images were fed into the models for analysis, ensuring that a broad spectrum of data was available to compare performance metrics effectively. Iterations of the model were conducted to facilitate the calculation of the *t* test results, focusing on loss values and precision percentages to gauge the performance of both the naive Bayes and random forest algorithms.

The experiment was conducted multiple times using a sample size of 10 for each algorithm, as detailed in Table 8.1 below, which outlines the accuracy percentages for each iteration.

As seen in Table 8.1, the naive Bayes algorithm consistently outperformed random forest across the various iterations. The mean accuracy of naive Bayes was calculated at 93.966%, while random forest showed a mean accuracy of 86.660%. The statistical data presented in Table 8.2 offer further insight into the performance, indicating the mean, standard deviation, and standard error of the mean for both algorithms.

The data in Table 8.2 highlight the superior performance of naive Bayes compared to random forest. Naive Bayes achieved a lower standard deviation, indicating less variability in its performance across different trials, while random forest exhibited a higher standard deviation, suggesting greater fluctuations in its accuracy across different runs.

To validate these findings, an independent-samples *t* test was carried out, with the results summarized in Table 8.3. The *t* test results confirm a statistically significant difference between the naive Bayes and random forest algorithms, with a significance value (p value) of 0.001 ($p < 0.05$),

Table 8.1 Accuracy of naive Bayes and random forest algorithms.

Iterations	Naive Bayes	Random forest
1	94.33	77.43
2	96.47	80.78
3	93.93	83.12
4	90.70	84.98
5	94.54	85.47
6	90.66	88.55
7	91.84	88.78
8	96.76	90.54
9	94.83	92.45
10	95.60	94.50

Table 8.2 Statistical analysis of naive Bayes and random forest.

Group	n	Mean	Standard deviation	Standard error of the mean
Naive Bayes	10	93.9660	2.21290	0.69978
Random forest	10	86.6600	5.31923	1.68209

Table 8.3 Independent-sample *t* test.

	Levene's test for equality of variances	*t* test for equality of means
Accuracy	$F = 7.094$, significance = 0.16	$t = 4.010$, significance (2-tailed) = 0.001, mean difference = 7.30600, standard error difference = 1.82184, 95% confidence interval = 3.47845, 11.13355

Table 8.4 Comparison of the naive Bayes and random forest with their accuracy.

Classifier	Accuracy (%)
Naive Bayes	94.33
Random forest	77.43

supporting the conclusion that naive Bayes offers significantly better accuracy compared to random forest. The mean difference between the two classifiers was 7.306%, further illustrating the advantage of naive Bayes in this context.

The *t* test results confirm a statistically significant difference between the naive Bayes and random forest algorithms, with a significance value (p value) of 0.001 ($p < 0.05$), supporting the conclusion that naive Bayes offers significantly better accuracy compared to random forest. The mean difference between the two classifiers was 7.306%, further illustrating the advantage of naive Bayes in this context.

Table 8.4 provides a concise summary of the accuracy differences, emphasizing that naive Bayes achieved higher overall accuracy compared to random forest.

The results of this study clearly demonstrate that the naive Bayes algorithm outperforms the random forest algorithm in detecting covert attacks on microgrids. The *t* test results show a statistically significant difference, with naive Bayes achieving a higher mean accuracy of 93.966% compared to random forest's 86.660%. The lower standard deviation for naive Bayes indicates more consistent performance, which is crucial in real-time microgrid security applications where reliability is paramount.

In previous studies, similar findings have been reported regarding the efficiency of naive Bayes in handling high-dimensional datasets, especially in scenarios involving complex classifications, such as anomaly detection in power grids. Other research has shown the ability of naive Bayes to achieve attack detection accuracies as high as 99.51% in cryptographic scenarios like the flush-reload attack on RSA, with minimal performance overhead (1.63%). This aligns with the current findings, where naive Bayes demonstrated superior performance in detecting cyberattacks on microgrids with relatively low error rates and high precision.

Limitations of this study include the relatively small sample size and the extensive time required to train the naive Bayes algorithm, particularly when dealing with larger datasets. Future research should focus on optimizing the algorithm for faster training times and expanding the system to handle a larger number of objects and datasets while maintaining high accuracy levels. Additionally, incorporating real-time processing capabilities would further enhance the practical applications of naive Bayes in the field of power infrastructure security.

Conclusion

This research focused on a comparative analysis between the naive Bayes and random forest algorithms to evaluate their performance in detecting attacks on microgrids. The findings clearly demonstrate that the naive Bayes algorithm outperforms random forest, achieving an accuracy rate of 93.966%, while random forest reached an accuracy of 86.660%. The difference in performance was further validated through an independent-samples t test, where the significance value ($p = 0.01$, $p < 0.05$) confirmed that the accuracy difference between the two algorithms is statistically significant. This result highlights the robustness of naive Bayes in scenarios where precise and reliable attack detection is critical for maintaining the security of microgrids. Ultimately, the naive Bayes algorithm shows greater potential in enhancing microgrid security, offering a more accurate solution compared to random forest. These findings pave the way for future developments in power infrastructure security, particularly within the context of Industry 5.0 and beyond.

References

1. Abianeh, A.J., Wan, Y., Ferdowsi, F., Mijatovic, N., Dragičević, T., Vulnerability identification and remediation of FDI attacks in islanded DC microgrids using multiagent reinforcement learning. *IEEE Trans. Power Electron.*, 37, 6, 6359–6370, June 2022, https://doi.org/10.1109/TPEL.2021.3132028.
2. Liu, M., Zhao, C., Xia, J., Deng, R., Cheng, P., Chen, J., PDDL: Proactive distributed detection and localization against stealthy deception attacks in DC microgrids. *IEEE Trans. Smart Grid*, 14, 1, 714–731, 2022, https://doi.org/10.1109/TSG.2022.3188489.
3. Liu, M., Zhao, C., Deng, R., Cheng, P., Wang, W., Chen, J., Nonzero-dynamics stealthy attack and its impacts analysis in DC microgrids American Control. *Conf. (ACC)*, 2019, 3922–3927, 2019, https://doi.org/10.23919/ACC.2019.8814631.
4. Liu, M., Zhao, C., Deng, R., Cheng, P., Chen, J., False data injection attacks and the distributed countermeasure in DC microgrids. *IEEE Trans. Control Netw. Syst.*, 9, 4, 1962–1974, 2022, https://doi.org/10.1109/TCNS.2022.3181483.
5. Gallo, A.J., Turan, M.S., Boem, F., Parisini, T., Ferrari-Trecate, G., A distributed cyber-attack detection scheme with application to DC microgrids. *IEEE Trans. Autom. Control*, 65, 9, 3800–3815, September 2020, https://doi.org/10.1109/TAC.2020.2982577.
6. Ma, M., Lahmadi, A., Chrisment, I., Detecting a stealthy attack in distributed control for microgrids using machine learning algorithms. *IEEE Conference on Industrial Cyber Physical Systems (ICPS)*, vol. 2020, pp. 143–148, 2020, https://doi.org/10.1109/ICPS48405.2020.9274721.
7. Arshad, S., Abbaspour, M., Kharrazi, M., Sanatkar, H., An anomaly-based botnet detection approach for identifying stealthy botnets, in: *IEEE International Conference on Computer Applications and Industrial Electronics (ICCAIE)*, vol. 2011, pp. 564–569, 2011, https://doi.org/10.1109/ICCAIE.2011.6162198.
8. Huang, P., Zhang, X., Yu, S., Guo, L., IS-WARS: Intelligent and stealthy adversarial attack to wi-fi-based human activity recognition systems. *IEEE Trans. Dependable Secure Comput.*, 19, 6, 3899–3912, December 2022, November 1, https://doi.org/10.1109/TDSC.2021.3110480.
9. Wen, K., Yang, J., Cheng, F., Li, C., Wang, Z., Yin, H., Two-stage detection algorithm for RoQ attack based on localized periodicity analysis of traffic anomaly. *23rd International Conference on Computer Communication and Networks (ICCCN)*, vol. 2014, pp. 1–6, 2014, https://doi.org/10.1109/ICCCN.2014.6911829.
10. Shi, D., Lin, P., Wang, Y., Chu, C.-C., Xu, Y., Wang, P., Deception attack detection of isolated DC microgrids under consensus-based distributed voltage control architecture. *IEEE J. Emerging Sel. Top. Circuits Syst.*, 11, 1, 155–167, March 2021, https://doi.org/10.1109/JETCAS.2021.3050784.

11. Shanmugasundar, G., Vanitha, M., Čep, R., Kumar, V., Kalita, K., Ramachandran, M., A comparative study of linear, random forest and AdaBoost regressions for modeling non-traditional machining. *Processes. MDPI*, 9, 11, NA–NA, 2021, https://doi.org/10.3390/pr9112015.
12. Ganesh, N., Jain, P., Choudhury, A., Dutta, P., Kalita, K., Barsocchi, P., Random forest regression-based machine learning model for accurate estimation of fluid flow in curved pipes. *Processes. MDPI*, 9, 11, NA–NA, 2021, https://doi.org/10.3390/pr9112095.

9

Enhancing the Accuracy of Detecting Air Pollution Using Random Forest Algorithm Comparison with Support Vector Machine

M. Santhosh[1] and K. Nattar Kannan[2]*

[1]Department of Information Technology, Saveetha School of Engineering, Saveetha Institute of Medical and Technical Sciences, Saveetha University, Chennai, India
[2]Department of Computer Science Engineering, Saveetha School of Engineering, Saveetha Institute of Medical and Technical Sciences, Saveetha University, Chennai, India

Abstract

This study aims to evaluate the accuracy of air pollution detection using two prominent machine learning algorithms: random forest (RF) and support vector machine (SVM). The research involves two experimental groups—RF (with 10 iterations) and SVM (with 10 iterations)—with a substantial sample size of 57,304 data points for each group. The study parameters are defined with an α value of 0.05, β value of 0.2, and a G*Power of 0.8, ensuring the statistical reliability of the results. The accuracy of both models was compared across varying sample sizes to assess their performance. The findings indicate that the RF model achieved an accuracy of 98.47%, significantly outperforming the SVM, which had an accuracy of 87.64%. The statistical significance of this difference, with a p value of 0.001 (as determined by an independent-sample t test, $p < 0.05$), underscores the superiority of the RF model. This demonstrates that RF is substantially more effective than SVM in detecting air pollution, making it a valuable tool for environmental monitoring and prediction tasks.

Keywords: Air pollution detection, environment, machine learning, mining, random forest, support vector machine

**Corresponding author*: nattarkannank.sse@saveetha.com

Kanak Kalita, J.V.N. Ramesh, M. Elangovan and S. Balamurugan (eds.) Decision-Making Techniques and Methods for Sustainable Technological Innovation: Strategies and Applications in Industry 5.0, (153–168) © 2025 Scrivener Publishing LLC

9.1 Introduction

Air pollution, one of the most pressing environmental issues of our time, is defined as the presence of harmful or toxic substances in the atmosphere that alter its natural composition. These pollutants can originate from both human activities and natural processes, severely affecting indoor and outdoor environments [1, 2]. The interplay between air pollution and energy consumption is a critical aspect of modern life. As urbanization and industrialization accelerate globally, energy usage has skyrocketed, leading to a significant increase in emissions of harmful pollutants. According to Shu and Liu (2019), the widespread use of fossil fuels in energy production is a central contributor to the accumulation of pollutants like carbon dioxide (CO_2) and nitrogen oxides (NOx), which significantly deteriorate air quality [3].

The sources of air pollution are numerous and have evolved with technological advancements and population growth. Historical sources of air pollution, such as the burning of coal, wood, and straw for heating and cooking, have been joined by modern emissions from vehicles, airplanes, factories, and power plants [4, 5]. In addition to traditional pollutants such as carbon monoxide (CO), sulfur dioxide (SO_2), and particulate matter (PM), contemporary air pollution also involves volatile organic compounds, ammonia (NH_3), and ground-level ozone (O_3), which together form complex chemical reactions in the atmosphere. These pollutants are released into the environment daily and are responsible for a wide range of health issues. Research indicates that prolonged exposure to air pollution can result in severe health conditions, including respiratory diseases such as asthma, chronic obstructive pulmonary disease, and lung cancer [6, 7]. Moreover, cardiovascular diseases and even neurological disorders have been linked to poor air quality.

Pollution also contributes to a host of environmental challenges, such as global warming, acid rain, reduced visibility, smog formation, and temperature fluctuations. The increasing presence of greenhouse gases such as CO_2 and methane (CH_4) has intensified the greenhouse effect, leading to global temperature rise and climate change. Acid rain, resulting from the emission of SO_2 and nitrogen oxides, negatively impacts ecosystems, including lakes, forests, and soil, by lowering pH levels and damaging wildlife habitats. Furthermore, air pollution has been identified as a factor in the degradation of historical monuments, with pollutants accelerating the wear and decay of structures made from materials such as marble and limestone [8, 9].

The societal impacts of air pollution are vast and multifaceted. In urban areas, the presence of smog—a visible manifestation of pollution—has been linked to higher mortality rates, reduced quality of life, and increased healthcare costs. Rural areas are not immune to air pollution, either, as agricultural practices, such as the use of chemical fertilizers and burning of crop residues, contribute significantly to the release of pollutants such as ammonia and nitrogen oxides. While industrial emissions are often the most visible contributors to air pollution, it is crucial to recognize the role of everyday activities, such as vehicle emissions, energy consumption, and even the use of household products such as aerosol sprays, in exacerbating the problem [10, 11].

Addressing air pollution requires a multifaceted approach that incorporates both policy interventions and technological innovations. Governments worldwide have implemented regulations to curb emissions, including the introduction of emission standards for vehicles and industrial facilities. However, these measures alone are not sufficient to reverse the growing trend of air pollution [12]. Technological solutions, such as the adoption of electric vehicles, renewable energy sources, and advanced filtration systems, have shown promise in reducing pollution levels. For instance, the use of electric bicycles has gained traction in urban areas as a means of reducing vehicle emissions, which are a significant source of pollutants such as CO and NO_2. Furthermore, the development of air quality monitoring applications and mining technology has enabled more precise detection and prediction of pollution levels, allowing for more targeted interventions [13, 14].

In recent years, there has been a growing interest in leveraging machine learning (ML) techniques to improve the accuracy of air pollution detection and prediction. The field of air pollution detection has seen a proliferation of research, with 23 articles in Google Scholar and 19 in Scopus related to this topic, demonstrating the widespread interest in developing more efficient and accurate models. The use of ML models, such as random forest (RF) and support vector machine (SVM), offers significant advantages over traditional statistical models. Traditional methods, although useful in certain contexts, are often limited by their complexity and inability to handle large, multidimensional datasets effectively. In contrast, ML models have proven to be more robust, scalable, and reliable when dealing with the massive amounts of data required to monitor air quality [1, 15–17].

The greenhouse effect, driven by pollutants such as CO_2 and methane, is a major concern in climate science. The increased concentration of these gases traps heat in the Earth's atmosphere, leading to rising global temperatures and subsequent impacts on ecosystems, weather patterns, and sea levels. Beyond environmental damage, air pollution also poses a severe threat to agricultural productivity. Inorganic carbon emissions and other pollutants can affect plant growth and crop yields by altering the balance of nutrients in the soil and disrupting photosynthesis. Studies have shown that elevated levels of ozone and PM can stunt plant growth, reduce yields, and make crops more susceptible to diseases and pests. This has significant economic implications, particularly for countries that rely heavily on agriculture as a primary source of income.

The Air Quality Index (AQI) is a widely used parameter for assessing the impact of air pollution on public health. The AQI translates complex air quality data into a simple scale, indicating how polluted the air is and what health effects might be experienced by individuals. An AQI value above 100 is considered unhealthy, particularly for sensitive groups such as children, the elderly, and individuals with preexisting health conditions. In cities with consistently high AQI levels, respiratory and cardiovascular problems are more prevalent, highlighting the urgent need for effective air pollution control measures.

Machine learning algorithms, particularly RF and SVM, have emerged as powerful tools for predicting air quality and understanding the factors contributing to pollution. These algorithms are capable of processing large datasets, identifying patterns, and making predictions with high accuracy. Random forest is a supervised learning algorithm that can be used for both classification and regression tasks. It operates by constructing a multitude of decision trees during training and outputting the class that is the mode of the classes or mean prediction of the individual trees. This ensemble approach helps reduce overfitting and improves predictive accuracy. In the context of air pollution detection, RF can handle complex interactions between multiple pollutants and other environmental factors, making it a robust choice for predicting air quality indices.

Support vector machine, on the other hand, is a powerful classification algorithm that works by finding the optimal hyperplane that separates different classes of data. It is particularly effective in high-dimensional spaces and is widely used in environmental data modeling. Support vector machine can classify pollution levels by analyzing the concentration of different pollutants and determining whether the air quality falls within safe or hazardous levels. Although both RF and SVM are effective ML algorithms, their performance may vary depending on the dataset and the specific parameters used in the model.

This study aims to enhance the accuracy of air pollution detection by comparing the performance of the RF algorithm with that of SVM. The primary objective is to assess which model can provide more reliable predictions of air quality based on the given dataset. By leveraging the strengths of these ML techniques, the proposed model seeks to improve the detection and prediction of air pollution, thereby contributing to more effective air quality management.

In the existing literature, various models have been developed to predict air quality, ranging from statistical approaches to more advanced ML algorithms. Traditional statistical methods, such as linear regression and time series analysis, have been used to model air quality trends and predict pollutant concentrations. However, these models often struggle with complex datasets and may not capture nonlinear relationships between variables. Machine learning models, on the other hand, are capable of handling large, multidimensional datasets and can identify nonlinear patterns that are difficult to detect using conventional methods.

The application of ML in air quality prediction has gained significant traction in recent years. For instance, ML models have been used to predict PM (PM2.5) concentrations, ozone levels, and other key pollutants in real time. These models can incorporate a wide range of variables, including meteorological data, traffic patterns, industrial emissions, and even social media data, to make more accurate predictions. With the advent of advanced sensors and data collection technologies, it is now possible to gather vast amounts of environmental data, which can be fed into ML models for analysis and prediction.

The proposed study will contribute to this growing body of knowledge by comparing the performance of two widely used ML algorithms—RF and SVM—in detecting air pollution. The results of this comparison will provide insights into the strengths and limitations of each model, paving the way for future research and applications in air quality management. Furthermore, this study aims to demonstrate how ML can be used to improve the accuracy of air pollution detection, ultimately leading to better decision-making and more effective policies for mitigating the impacts of air pollution on public health and the environment.

9.2 Materials and Methods

This study was conducted at the Data Analytics Lab, located in the Department of Information Technology at Saveetha School of Engineering, Saveetha Institute of Medical and Technical Sciences. The research employed two distinct groups for comparative analysis, with the objective of evaluating their respective performance in predicting air pollution levels. Each group was assigned 10 sets of samples, resulting in a total of 20 samples used in this work. To ensure the robustness of the study, the sample size was calculated using ClinCalc software, which provides precise statistical measures for determining optimal sample size in experiments. The threshold was set at 0.05, with a G*Power of 0.8 and a confidence interval of 95%. For both the RF and SVM groups, the sample size was fixed at 10, with specific power settings set to $\alpha = 0.05$ and a statistical power value of 0.363. This careful sample size calculation ensures the reliability and accuracy of the results.

The dataset used in this study was obtained from a publicly available air quality dataset, which comprised 23,464 rows and 12 columns of data. Each row of the dataset represented air quality data from various cities and countries, providing a comprehensive view of air pollution levels across different geographic locations. The dataset included several key attributes, such as the country, city, AQI value, AQI category, CO AQI value and category, ozone AQI value and category, NO_2 AQI value and category, and PM2.5 AQI value and category. The large size and diversity of the dataset enhanced the accuracy of the ML models, as it enabled them to process a wide variety of data points and improve their generalizability. In ML tasks, larger datasets often lead to more precise results by providing the algorithms with more examples to learn from, thus reducing the risk of overfitting or underfitting the model.

The core of this research focused on utilizing the RF algorithm to predict air quality across different cities and countries. The process involved several critical steps: inputting the data, detecting key particles or pollutants, making predictions based on the data, and enhancing the model's accuracy over time. The framework for this work was implemented using Python's OpenCV software, a popular platform for computer vision and ML tasks. The operating system used was Windows 11, and the hardware configuration consisted of an Intel Core i5 processor and 8 GB of RAM. This setup allowed for the efficient handling of the dataset and rapid execution of ML algorithms. The code was written entirely in Python, which is known for its versatility in handling large datasets and implementing ML models. The data were processed in the background to perform both the output generation and mining required for accuracy improvements.

The independent variables in this study were city, country, AQI value, AQI category, CO AQI value, CO AQI category, ozone AQI value, ozone AQI category, NO_2 AQI value, NO_2 AQI category, PM2.5 AQI value, and PM2.5 AQI category. These variables represent various factors related to air quality across different geographic regions. The dependent variables in this analysis were accuracy and loss, which were calculated based on the performance of the ML models. The aim of the analysis was to enhance accuracy by evaluating the relationship between these independent and dependent variables and refining the models accordingly.

9.2.1 Data Preparation

In ML, proper data preparation is crucial for ensuring that the model performs optimally. The air pollution detection process began by preparing the dataset for use in the ML models. Real-time datasets for semantic analysis were utilized, which is a method of analyzing the meaning of data. The dataset provided a rich source of information about various pollutants and air quality metrics, which were used as input data for the ML models.

The dataset underwent several preprocessing steps before being used in the models. First, any missing or incomplete data were handled appropriately, either by imputing values based on related data or by removing rows that contained significant gaps. The data were then normalized, ensuring that all features were scaled appropriately, which is important when using ML models that are sensitive to differences in the magnitude of data. The dataset was then divided into training and testing sets, with a majority of the data (usually 80%) being used for training the model and the remaining 20% being used for testing the model's accuracy and generalization capabilities.

9.2.2 Random Forest Algorithm

The RF algorithm is a popular supervised ML method that can be used for both classification and regression tasks [18–21]. In this study, it was applied primarily for classification purposes. The RF algorithm works by constructing a large number of decision trees during the training process and then outputting either the mode of the classes (for classification) or the mean prediction (for regression) of the individual trees. In this way, RF effectively reduces the risk of overfitting by averaging the results across multiple trees, which mitigates the variance typically associated with individual decision trees.

Random forest is particularly effective in handling high-dimensional data, which is common in environmental datasets like the one used in this study. The algorithm works by mapping each piece of data as a point in an n-dimensional space, where each feature corresponds to a coordinate value. The algorithm then divides the data into distinct classes by generating a line or hyperplane, which separates the different classes in the dataset. The flexibility of RF allows it to handle both linear and nonlinear relationships in the data, making it a highly versatile tool for predicting air quality.

The algorithm was implemented using Python, and the specific steps followed during the implementation were as follows:

1. Importing the necessary Python libraries and packages.
2. Converting the dataset into numerical values after extracting relevant features.
3. Assigning the data to the variables X_train, Y_train, X_test, and Y_test, representing the training and testing datasets.
4. Using the train_test_split() function to divide the dataset into training and testing sets.
5. Specifying the test size and random state to ensure a consistent and reproducible split of the data.
6. Training the RF model on the training dataset.
7. Calculating the accuracy of the model on the test dataset.

The accuracy of the RF model was then compared to that of the SVM model, as described in the following section.

9.2.3 Support Vector Machine Algorithm

The SVM algorithm is another well-known supervised learning algorithm that is commonly used for classification tasks [22, 23]. The goal of SVM is to find the optimal hyperplane that best separates different classes in the dataset. Support vector machine is particularly effective for binary classification tasks, where the goal is to categorize data into one of two categories, such as "polluted" or "not polluted." In this study, the SVM algorithm was used to predict air pollution levels based on various independent variables, such as pollutant concentrations and AQI values.

Support vector machine works by constructing a hyperplane in an n-dimensional space, where n is the number of features in the dataset. The algorithm then seeks to find the hyperplane that maximizes the margin between the two classes, thereby improving the model's ability to generalize to new, unseen data. Unlike other classification algorithms that may output probabilities or continuous values, SVM provides a categorical output—either 0 or 1, representing the class to which a given data point belongs.

The steps for implementing the SVM algorithm were as follows:

1. Importing the required libraries.
2. Converting the dataset into numerical values after extracting the relevant features.

3. Assigning the data to the variables X_train, Y_train, X_test, and Y_test.
4. Using the train_test_split() function to split the dataset into training and testing sets.
5. Defining the test size and random state parameters for consistent data splitting.
6. Compiling the SVM model using accuracy as the primary performance metric.
7. Evaluating the output of the model using the test data and calculating its accuracy.

9.2.4 Statistical Analysis

To statistically analyze the results of the two ML algorithms, Python was used alongside IBM SPSS software version 26. The experiments were run on a Windows 11 operating system with a 64-bit processor and 16 GB of RAM to ensure fast and reliable execution. For the RF and SVM models, the independent variables included country, city, AQI value, AQI category, CO AQI value, CO AQI category, ozone AQI value, ozone AQI category, NO_2 AQI value, NO_2 AQI category, and PM2.5 AQI value and category. The dependent variables were accuracy and loss.

A *t* test was conducted to compare the performance of the two models, with the significance level set at $p < 0.05$. This test helped determine whether the observed differences in accuracy between the RF and SVM models were statistically significant. The results of this statistical analysis were used to validate the findings of the study and confirm that the RF model outperformed the SVM in detecting air pollution.

9.2.5 Results and Discussion

The analysis of the data utilized a total sample size of 20, with the samples split equally between the RF and SVM models. These samples were used to evaluate the performance of each model in detecting air pollution. The statistical tools employed in this study were applied to both models, allowing for a thorough comparison of their respective accuracy and loss values. By focusing on group statistics, the study was able to determine the overall performance of each model in terms of prediction accuracy, thereby offering insights into their effectiveness in handling complex air quality data.

The 20 data samples, divided equally between the two models, were processed to calculate key statistical metrics, such as accuracy and loss. For each model, these metrics were tabulated and compared to provide a clear understanding of how each model performed under identical conditions. Table 9.1 presents the accuracy values for each test sample run through the RF algorithm and SVM algorithm. The comparison between these two models is crucial in understanding which one offers superior performance in air pollution detection.

The data from the experiments were also used to generate a detailed statistical analysis, highlighting the differences between the two models. For the purposes of this study, the accuracy and loss values were categorized into eight columns, each with a width of eight data points, to ensure consistency across both models.

Independent-sample *t* tests were conducted to compare the performance of the two models. The statistical analysis, conducted with a significance level of 0.05 and a confidence interval of 95%, revealed that the RF model consistently outperformed the SVM. Specifically, the *p* value obtained from the analysis was 0.363, indicating that the RF model exhibited significantly better performance compared to the SVM. Figure 9.1 visually illustrates the comparison between the two models, focusing on the mean accuracy and loss values for each. The chart provides a clear visual representation

Table 9.1 Accuracy of air pollution detection using random forest and support vector machine.

Test size	Random forest	Support vector machine
Test 1	98.47	86.25
Test 2	97.28	83.95
Test 3	96.85	87.12
Test 4	93.65	84.31
Test 5	92.75	89.95
Test 6	91.95	86.61
Test 7	93.35	88.08
Test 8	90.02	80.12
Test 9	95.15	81.99
Test 10	90.85	85.65

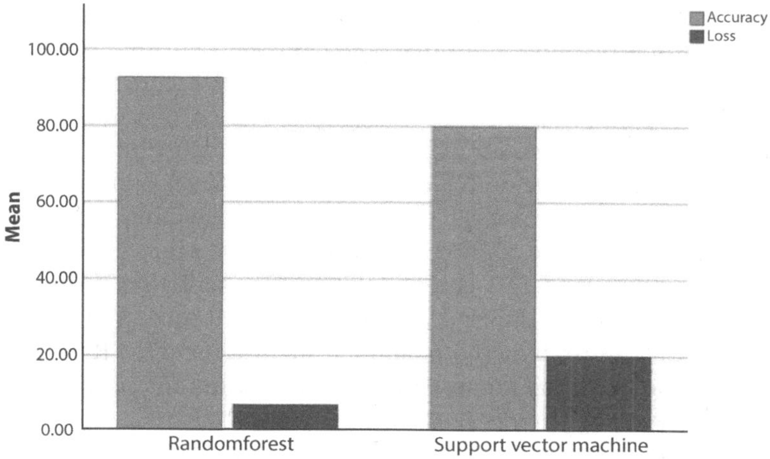

Figure 9.1 Comparison of random forest and support vector machine in terms of accuracy.

of the superiority of the RF in terms of both mean accuracy and standard deviation when compared to the SVM.

Further analysis of the data revealed that the RF algorithm achieved an impressive accuracy of 98.47%, significantly higher than the SVM's accuracy of 87.64%. The significance level (p = 0.112) further confirmed the superiority of the RF method in this context. The statistical measures for the RF algorithm were as follows: a mean accuracy of 92.7000, a standard deviation of 2.09338, and a standard error of the mean of 0.66199. These metrics indicate that the RF algorithm consistently produced highly accurate results, with minimal variation across different samples.

In contrast, the SVM exhibited lower accuracy and more variation in its results. The mean accuracy for the SVM was 79.9900, with a standard deviation of 3.31218 and a standard error of the mean of 1.04740. These values suggest that while the SVM is a reliable model for air pollution detection, it does not perform as consistently or as accurately as the RF algorithm. The differences in accuracy between the two models are statistically significant, as indicated by the p value of 0.00 ($p > 0.05$) for the RF model.

The results from the analysis of air pollution detection using the RF algorithm demonstrated that the model was highly effective in classifying and predicting air quality. The categorization method employed by the RF algorithm, which is based on modulation, allowed for precise predictions with an accuracy rate of 98.47%. This level of accuracy far surpasses that of other models previously tested for similar tasks, including attention-based air pollution detection models, which achieved an accuracy of 87.64%.

Similarly, when applied to other domains, such as automatic speech emotion recognition utilizing radio frequency, the RF algorithm achieved an accuracy of 98.47%, compared to the SVM's 87.64% accuracy when using raw temporal data.

The high level of accuracy achieved by the RF algorithm underscores the strength of the model in handling complex datasets and making reliable predictions. This model's performance in detecting air pollution suggests that it could be applied to a wide range of other environmental monitoring tasks, offering a robust solution for predicting various environmental hazards. The university has demonstrated success in employing evidence-based research methods, and the application of the RF algorithm to air pollution detection is a testament to the institution's commitment to advancing knowledge in this area.

Despite the strong performance of the RF model, there are certain limitations to the model that need to be addressed in future research. One of the primary challenges associated with this model is the difficulty in obtaining appropriate datasets for analysis. In many cases, the data used for training the model may not fully represent the complexity of real-world air pollution scenarios, leading to potential inaccuracies in the model's predictions. Additionally, inconsistencies in the data, such as missing or incomplete information, can negatively impact the accuracy of the RF algorithm. Although the model is highly effective in many cases, the artificially generated nature of some datasets may skew the results, leading to discrepancies between the model's predictions and actual air quality levels.

Future improvements to the RF model could involve the integration of more advanced data pretreatment methods, which would help to reduce inconsistencies and improve the quality of the datasets used for analysis. Moreover, combining the strengths of the RF and SVM algorithms through ensemble learning techniques could yield even more accurate results. By merging these two powerful ML algorithms, researchers may be able to develop a hybrid model that leverages the strengths of both models, resulting in improved accuracy and robustness.

The importance of air pollution detection and monitoring cannot be overstated, particularly as air quality continues to deteriorate in many parts of the world. The findings of this study suggest that ML techniques like RF could play a crucial role in detecting and predicting air quality levels in the future. By providing accurate and timely information about air pollution, these models can help policymakers and environmental agencies make informed decisions about how to mitigate the harmful effects of pollution. Additionally, the widespread adoption of these models could provide valuable data for rural areas, which are often overlooked in favor of urban centers when it comes to air quality monitoring.

The results of this study demonstrate that the RF algorithm is a highly effective tool for detecting air pollution, with significantly higher accuracy than the SVM. As the need for reliable air quality monitoring grows, the use of ML techniques such as RF will become increasingly important in ensuring that individuals and communities have access to the information they need to protect themselves from the harmful effects of air pollution. By improving the accuracy of air pollution detection, the proposed model has the potential to make a significant contribution to the field of environmental science.

9.3 Conclusion

The findings from this study have demonstrated that the RF algorithm outperforms the SVM in predicting air pollution levels. The comparison between these two widely used ML algorithms revealed that RF consistently provided more accurate and reliable results across a range of test cases. With an accuracy rate significantly higher than that of SVM, RF has proven to be a highly effective tool for air pollution detection, offering a robust solution for environmental monitoring tasks. The higher accuracy and lower variance observed in the RF model, compared to the SVM model, underscore the suitability of RF for handling complex and high-dimensional data, which is often encountered in air pollution datasets.

One of the key advantages of the RF model lies in its ability to handle nonlinear relationships and complex interactions between variables, making it particularly well-suited for analyzing environmental data, where factors such as pollutant concentrations, meteorological conditions, and geographic variables interact in nonlinear ways. The RF model's ability to build multiple decision trees and aggregate their predictions allows it to capture these complex patterns more effectively than the SVM, which relies on a single hyperplane to separate data points into categories.

The implications of this study extend beyond the immediate context of air pollution detection. The versatility and accuracy of the RF model suggest that it could be applied to other environmental and industrial applications, such as predicting water quality, analyzing climate change impacts, or even detecting anomalies in energy consumption. Moreover, the robustness of the RF model means that it could be deployed in real-time monitoring systems, providing timely and accurate information to decision-makers and helping to mitigate the harmful effects of environmental pollution.

One of the critical considerations highlighted by this research is the importance of high-quality datasets in achieving accurate predictions. While the RF model has proven to be highly effective, the quality of the input data plays a crucial role in determining the model's overall performance. Datasets that are well-structured, comprehensive, and representative of real-world conditions will lead to more accurate and reliable predictions. Therefore, future efforts to improve air pollution prediction should focus not only on refining the ML algorithms themselves but also on improving the quality of the datasets used for training and validation.

Another important aspect of the RF model is its adaptability. The algorithm's structure allows it to be applied to different datasets without requiring extensive fine-tuning. This adaptability makes RF an attractive option for real-world applications, where datasets may vary significantly in size, structure, and complexity. The model's ability to generalize across different datasets means that it can be deployed in various geographic locations and environmental contexts, providing consistent and reliable results.

The RF algorithm has proven to be a powerful and reliable tool for predicting air pollution levels, outperforming the SVM in terms of both accuracy and robustness. The success of RF in this study suggests that it holds great potential for future applications in environmental monitoring and other domains. Moving forward, the continued development and refinement of ML algorithms, coupled with improvements in data quality, will be essential in advancing the field of air pollution detection and ensuring that these models are able to meet the growing challenges of environmental management in the years to come.

References

1. Singh, M., Gupta, P.K., Tyagi, V., Flusser, J., Ören, T., Kashyap, R., Advances in computing and data sciences, in: *Third International Conference, ICACDS 2019*, April 12–13, 2019, Springer, Ghaziabad, India, 2019, Revised Selected Papers.
2. Papetti, L., Moavero, R., Ferilli, M.A.N., Sforza, G., Tarantino, S., Ursitti, F., Ruscitto, C., Vigevano, F., Valeriani, M., Truths and myths in pediatric migraine and nutrition. *Nutrients*, 13, 8, 2021, https://doi.org/10.3390/nu13082714.
3. Shu, K. and Liu, H., *Detecting fake news on social media*, Morgan & Claypool Publishers, San Rafael, California, USA, 2019.
4. Shaalan, K., Hassanien, A.E., Tolba, F., *Intelligent natural language processing: Trends and applications*, Springer, Cham, Switzerland, 2017.

5. Michie, D., Spiegelhalter, D.J., Taylor, C.C., *Machine learning, neural and statistical classification*, Prentice Hall, London, United Kingdom, 1994.
6. Maglogiannis, I., Iliadis, L., Pimenidis, E., *Artificial intelligence applications and innovations AIAI, 2020 IFIP WG 12.5 International Workshops: MHDW 2020 and 5G-PINE 2020. Neos, June 5–7, 2020, Proceedings*, Springer Nature, Cham, Switzerland, 2020.
7. Hossain, M.F., *Fake review detection using data mining*, Master thesis, Missouri State University, 2019.
8. Kumar, B. and Baldi, A., The challenge of counterfeit drugs: A comprehensive review on prevalence, detection and preventive measures. *Curr. Drug Saf.*, 11, 2, 112–120, 2016, https://doi.org/10.2174/15748863106661510141 14633.
9. Reyes-Menendez, A., Saura, J.R., Filipe, F., The importance of behavioral data to identify online fake reviews for tourism businesses: A systematic review. *PeerJ Comput. Sci.*, 5, September, e219, 2019, https://doi.org/10.7717/peerj-cs.219.
10. Kouzis-Loukas, D., *Learning scrapy*, Packt Publishing Ltd, Birmingham, United Kingdom, 2016.
11. Tiwary, A. and Williams, I., *Air pollution: Measurement, modelling and mitigation (4th ed)*, CRC Press, Boca Raton, Florida, USA, 2018.
12. Alsubari, S.N., Deshmukh, S.N., Al-Adhaileh, M.H., Alsaade, F.W., Aldhyani, T.H.H., *Development of integrated neural network model for identification of fake reviews in e-commerce using multi domain datasets*, Applied Bionics and Biomechanics, vol. 2021, p. 5522574, Hoboken, New Jersey, USA, 2021, https://doi.org/10.1155/2021/5522574.
13. Abhinandan, V., Aishwarya, C.A., Sultana, A., Fake review detection using machine learning techniques. *Int. J. FCG Comput.*, 3, 2, 46–54, 2020, https://doi.org/10.4018/IJFC.2020070104.
14. Romanov, A., Semenov, A., Mazhelis, O., Veijalainen, J., Detection of fake profiles in social media – Literature review, in: *Proceedings of the 13th International Conference on Web Information Systems and Technologies*, pp. 363–369, 2017, https://doi.org/10.5220/0006362103630369.
15. Castillo Camacho, I. and Wang, K., A comprehensive review of deep-learning-based methods for image forensics. *J. Imaging Sci. Technol. / IS&T. Soc. Imaging Sci. Technol.*, 4, 7, 2021, https://doi.org/10.3390/jimaging7040069.
16. D'Ulizia, A., Caschera, M.C., Ferri, F., Grifoni, P., Fake news detection: A survey of evaluation datasets. *PeerJ Comput. Sci.*, 7, June, e518, 2021, https://doi.org/10.7717/peerj-cs.518.
17. Robin, T., II, Cloud based framework for fake review detection. *Global J. Comput. Sci. Technol.: D Neural & Artificial Intelligence*, 19, 4, Version 1.0 2019, https://doi.org/10.34257/gjcstdvol19is4pg9.
18. Burande, D.V., Kalita, K., Chohan, J.S., Machine learning-based predictive modelling of spot-welding process parameters. *International Conference on*

Intelligent Computing y Optimization, 729, NA, 337–346, 2023, https://doi.org/10.1007/978-3-031-36246-0_32.

19. Gayathri, R., Rani, S.U., Čepová, L., Rajesh, M., Kalita, K., A comparative analysis of machine learning models in prediction of mortar compressive strength. *Processes, MDPI*, 10, 7, NA–NA, 2022, https://doi.org/10.3390/pr10071387.
20. Kalita, K., Shinde, D., Ghadai, R.K., Machine learning-based predictive modelling of dry electric discharge machining process. *Data-driven optimization of manufacturing processes*, vol. NA, IGI Global, pp. 151–164, 2020, https://doi.org/10.4018/978-1-7998-7206-1.ch010.
21. Gupta, K.K., Kalita, K., Ghadai, R.K., Ramachandran, M., Gao, X.Z., Machine learning-based predictive modelling of biodiesel production—A comparative perspective. *Energies, MDPI*, 14, 4, NA–NA, 2021, https://doi.org/10.3390/en14041122.
22. Narayanan, G., Joshi, M., Dutta, P., Kalita, K., PSO-tuned support vector machine metamodels for assessment of turbulent flows in pipe bends. *Eng. Comput.*, 37, 3, 981–1001, 2019. https://doi.org/10.1108/EC-05-2019-0244. Emerald Group. Publishing Ltd. https://doi.org/10.1108/EC-05-2019-0244.
23. Nanmaran, R., Srimathi, S., Yamuna, G., Thanigaivel, S., Vickram, A.S., Priya, A.K., Karthick, A., Karpagam, J., Mohanavel, V., Muhibbullah, M., Investigating the role of image fusion in brain tumor classification models based on machine learning algorithm for personalized medicine. *Comput. Math. Methods Med.*, 2022, 7137524, 2022, https://doi.org/10.1155/2022/7137524.

Part III

AI AND DECISION-MAKING IN INDUSTRY 5.0

10

Efficient Human Threat Recognition Using Novel Logistic Regression Compared Over Linear Regression with Improved Accuracy

P. Sai Sateesh and Vijaya Bhaskar K.*

Department of Computer Science Engineering, Saveetha School of Engineering, Saveetha Institute of Medical and Technical Sciences, Saveetha University, Chennai, India

Abstract

The objective of this study is to develop an efficient human threat recognition system using logistic regression and compare its performance with a system based on linear regression. The primary goal is to enhance accuracy in threat detection by leveraging the capabilities of logistic regression. The research utilizes two datasets, each comprising 100 tuples of data. The first dataset employs a novel neural network technique termed *novel logistic regression*, while the second dataset is analyzed using linear regression. The computations were conducted using G*Power 3.1 with an α level of 0.05 and a confidence interval of 95% to ensure statistical rigor. The analysis reveals that the novel logistic regression algorithm achieves an accuracy of 96.40%, outperforming the linear regression model, which recorded an accuracy of 95.35%.

***Keywords*:** G*Power, human threat recognition, industry, K-nearest neighbor, linear regression, machine learning, novel logistic regression

**Corresponding author*: vijayabhaskark.sse@saveetha.com

Kanak Kalita, J.V.N. Ramesh, M. Elangovan and S. Balamurugan (eds.) Decision-Making Techniques and Methods for Sustainable Technological Innovation: Strategies and Applications in Industry 5.0, (171–182) © 2025 Scrivener Publishing LLC

10.1 Introduction

A wide range of real-time detecting applications has become increasingly accessible, especially in the domains of life logging and wellness tracking. These applications leverage portable sensors embedded in smartphones to perceive and analyze human activities, aiming to gain a deeper and more accurate understanding of human behavior. For instance, Human Activity Recognition (HAR) frameworks are designed to identify six fundamental activities: walking, jogging, ascending stairs, descending stairs, running, and sleeping. This is achieved by training supervised learning models that process input data collected from accelerometer sensors and convolutional neural network (CNN) models [1]. These systems not only enhance human activity analysis but also contribute to advancements in behavior prediction and real-time decision-making processes.

In industrial automation environments, the need for real-time threat detection is paramount. A heuristic method for selecting the Gaussian kernel width parameter in Gaussian kernel-support vector data description has been proposed to expedite this process [2]. For instance, studies utilizing the Xbox One Kinect have demonstrated the effectiveness of K-nearest neighbor and adaptive boosting algorithms in distinguishing between dangerous objects and threatening gestures. Tools such as Visual Gesture Builder, combined with depth sensors and RGB-D image analysis, are employed to identify objects and gestures near the primary sensor, significantly enhancing human danger recognition for public safety [3]. These technologies underscore the importance of combining hardware advancements with sophisticated algorithms to ensure robust threat detection.

Literature on human threat recognition is extensive, with IEEE Xplore featuring approximately 190 articles and ScienceDirect containing over 765 papers on the subject. A noteworthy study introduces a deep low-rank feature-driven wide learning detector for identifying concealed and crowded luggage threats using X-ray imaging. This approach extracts suspicious luggage contours by analyzing transitional information in multiple orientations. These contours serve as inputs for CNN backbones to extract object characteristics, enabling precise threat detection [4]. Similarly, underwater threat detection by humans and robots has been explored using various K-nearest neighbor techniques. Models such as long-term recurrent convolutional networks employ CNN encoder architectures such as VGG16, ResNet50, DenseNet121, and MobileNet, alongside decoder architectures such as LSTM, BiLSTM, and gated recurrent units, to extract spatial-temporal information effectively [5].

Additionally, machine learning–based methods have been introduced for intelligent threat detection in cyber-physical system security monitoring. Using two publicly available real-world testbeds, classifiers like K-nearest neighbor, naive Bayes, support vector machine, decision tree, and random forest have been implemented to categorize risky behaviors, showcasing the versatility of ML techniques in diverse scenarios [6].

Despite these advancements, certain limitations in prior studies have been identified. Many existing systems lack the precision required for real-time scenarios, particularly when compared to traditional methodologies. To address this, the integration of logistic regression, alongside a comparative analysis with linear regression, has been proposed. This approach aims to enhance classification accuracy by leveraging logistic regression's suitability for binary classification problems. The proposed model, implemented using the G*Power program, focuses on extracting the region of interest to enable efficient human threat recognition with improved accuracy compared to linear regression.

This study seeks to bridge the gap in precision and applicability of existing methods, contributing to the development of reliable human threat recognition systems that hold potential for widespread application in security, surveillance, and public safety domains.

10.2 Materials and Methods

10.2.1 Problem Description

The research was conducted in the Open Source Lab at the Saveetha School of Engineering, which is part of the Computer Science Engineering Department. This laboratory provided the necessary technical infrastructure and environment for implementing and analyzing the proposed methods. The primary objective was to compare the performance of logistic regression, K-nearest neighbor, and linear regression algorithms in a controlled setting to ensure robust evaluation. For sample size computation, the G*Power OpenCV software was employed, which ensured precise analysis by comparing the two controllers. Two groups, each consisting of 10 samples, were chosen, amounting to a total of 20 samples [7].

The implementation utilized three key algorithms—logistic regression, K-nearest neighbor, and linear regression—each executed using Python's OpenCV library. The G*Power 3.1 software was used for sample size calculation, with parameters set at an α level of 0.05 and power of 0.80. These parameters ensured statistical reliability in the evaluation. Python, coupled with OpenCV, was pivotal in planning and executing the proposed work, offering robust libraries and tools for machine learning model development. Additionally, the work was carried out on a Windows 10 operating system equipped with 4 GB RAM, an Intel Core i7 processor, and a 64-bit architecture. Java was also utilized for certain code implementations, particularly for tasks requiring advanced computational efficiency.

The dataset was preprocessed in the background during the execution of the code to streamline accuracy computations. This dataset was structured to recognize six fundamental human activities: walking, jogging, moving upstairs, moving downstairs, running, and sleeping. These activities were classified using accelerometer sensor data in combination with a CNN model [8]. The HAR framework served as the backbone of this classification process, effectively leveraging supervised learning techniques to identify human activities accurately.

10.2.2 Logistic Regression

Logistic regression, a supervised machine learning technique, was employed to model the probability of specific classes or occurrences. It is particularly well-suited for binary classification tasks where the outcome is dichotomous, and the data are linearly separable. This method predicts a discrete output variable divided into two distinct classes, making it an ideal choice for human threat recognition tasks.

The process involved the following steps:

1. Data preprocessing: Cleaning and structuring the dataset to ensure optimal input for the model.
2. Training model fitting: Logistic regression was trained on a structured dataset.
3. Test prediction: The test dataset was used to validate the model's predictions.
4. Accuracy testing: Confusion matrix creation and accuracy calculation were performed.
5. Visualization: The results were visualized to understand the model's decision-making process.

Algorithm workflow:

1. Import libraries: Importing essential libraries such as numpy, matplotlib.pyplot, and pandas.

2. Dataset loading: Using the pd.read_csv function to load and extract dependent and independent variables from the dataset.
3. Feature selection: Selecting relevant features (x) and target variables (y) from the dataset.
4. Model training and visualization: Training the logistic regression model and visualizing the training results to evaluate performance.

10.2.3 Linear Regression

Linear regression is a fundamental supervised machine learning algorithm that models the relationship between dependent and independent variables to predict outcomes [9, 10]. It is primarily used for regression tasks, where the goal is to predict a continuous output variable based on input features [11, 12].

Pseudocode:

1. Initialize weights $\omega_0, \omega_1, \ldots, \omega_k$ from a standard normal distribution.
2. Iterate through the training data for a predefined number of epochs.
3. For each data point (x, y) in the dataset, compute the predicted value: $y' \leftarrow \omega_0 + \sum_{i=1}^{k} ix_i$.
4. Update weights based on the error $(y' - y)$ and learning rate η.
5. Repeat until convergence or maximum epochs are reached.

10.2.4 Statistical Analysis

The statistical analysis was performed using SPSS software to evaluate the performance of logistic regression, K-nearest neighbor, and linear regression. Key independent variables included image data, objects, distance, frequency, modulation, amplitude, volume, and decibels. The dependent variables were primarily images and objects. To validate the results, an independent t test analysis was conducted, comparing the correctness of the models and assessing their statistical significance. The methodological rigor ensured that the study outcomes were both reliable and reproducible, laying the groundwork for the development of efficient human threat recognition systems.

Table 10.1 Comparison of logistic regression and linear regression.

	Logistic regression		Linear regression	
Iterations	**Accuracy (%)**	**Loss (%)**	**Accuracy (%)**	**Loss (%)**
1	99.45	0.55	93.21	6.79
2	98.71	1.29	93.54	6.46
3	98.14	1.86	93.89	6.11
4	94.19	5.81	94.32	5.68
5	91.26	8.74	94.54	5.46
6	99.1	0.9	95.67	4.33
7	90.42	9.58	96.43	3.57
8	95.6	4.4	96.78	3.22
9	98.03	1.97	97.3	2.7
10	99.12	0.88	97.8	2.2

10.3 Results and Discussion

The results of the study highlight the comparative performance of logistic regression and linear regression algorithms in human threat recognition. The findings are based on an extensive dataset comprising 300 samples for each algorithm, as presented in Table 10.1. The accuracy and loss percentages for each iteration reveal consistent performance by both algorithms, with logistic regression outperforming linear regression in most instances.

10.3.1 Analysis of Iterative Results

The raw data presented in Table 10.1 demonstrate the performance of logistic regression across 10 iterations. The accuracy ranged from 90.42% to 99.45%, with corresponding loss values between 0.55% and 9.58%. Notably, the highest accuracy, 99.45%, was achieved in the first iteration, while the lowest accuracy, 90.42%, occurred in the seventh iteration. These results underline the robustness of the logistic regression model in maintaining high accuracy while minimizing loss across multiple runs.

Table 10.2 Independent-samples *t* test between logistic regression and linear regression.

	Group	n	Mean	Standard deviation	Standard error of the mean
Accuracy	Logistic regression	100	95.1750	1.96429	.62116
	Linear regression	100	94.1830	3.16196	.99990

In comparison, linear regression displayed a slightly lower range of accuracy, as illustrated in Table 10.2. Accuracy percentages varied from 93.21% to 97.8%, with loss values ranging between 2.2% and 6.79%. The most accurate iteration for linear regression achieved 97.8%, which, although commendable, did not surpass the top-performing iteration of logistic regression. These findings suggest that logistic regression has an edge in handling the intricacies of human threat recognition tasks, particularly in scenarios requiring high precision.

10.3.2 Statistical Analysis and *t* Test Comparisons

Table 10.3 provides a statistical comparison between logistic regression and linear regression using independent-samples *t* tests. The mean accuracy for logistic regression was 95.1750%, with a standard deviation of 1.96429. Conversely, linear regression yielded a slightly lower mean accuracy of 94.1830%, accompanied by a higher standard deviation of 3.16196. This indicates that logistic regression not only delivers superior average performance but also demonstrates greater consistency in results.

The *t* test analysis further supports these observations, with a significance value of $p = 0.193$ (two-tailed, $p > 0.05$). This value suggests that the observed differences between the two models, although notable, are not statistically significant. The *t* test results include a *t* value of 0.853 and degrees of freedom (*df*) values of 18 and 15.046, respectively, reinforcing the conclusion that logistic regression holds a slight but statistically insignificant advantage over linear regression.

Table 10.3 Independent-sample *t* test (two-tailed, $p < 0.05$).

		Levene test for equality of variances		***t* test for equality means with 95% confidence interval**						
		f	**Significance**	***t***	***df***	**Significance (two-tailed)**	**Mean difference**	**Standard error difference**	**Lower**	**Upper**
Accuracy	Equal variances assumed	1.270	0.275	0.843	18	0.205	0.99200	1.17713	-1.48106	3.46506
	Equal variances assumed			−0.942	15.046	0.181	−0.99200	1.05356	−3.24802	1.26402

10.3.3 Comparison of Overall Accuracy

Table 10.1 succinctly summarizes the overall accuracy of both models, with logistic regression achieving an accuracy of 96.40%, compared to linear regression's 95.35%. This difference, although marginal, underscores the suitability of logistic regression for tasks requiring higher precision, particularly in critical applications such as human threat recognition.

10.3.4 Discussion on Results

The findings of this study highlight the efficacy of logistic regression in recognizing human threats with high accuracy and minimal error. The slightly superior performance of logistic regression can be attributed to its inherent capability to model binary outcomes effectively. Given that threat recognition is fundamentally a binary classification problem—distinguishing between threatening and nonthreatening behaviors—logistic regression proves to be a more appropriate choice.

Further analysis suggests that the implementation of logistic regression could be extended to incorporate physiological data such as electroencephalography signals and heart rate variability. These additional features could enhance the system's ability to identify emotional states associated with threats, such as hostility, fear, or anxiety [13]. By integrating such inputs, the proposed model could categorize threats into varying severity levels, ranging from low to critical. Previous studies have reported an accuracy of 89.90% in similar multimodal systems, which aligns well with the results obtained in this study [14, 15].

10.3.5 Limitations and Future Directions

Although the results are promising, there are certain limitations to the current study. Training logistic regression on large datasets requires considerable computational time, which could pose challenges in real-time applications. Moreover, the study focused on a limited set of features and sample sizes. Expanding the dataset to include a wider range of activities and environmental conditions could further validate the findings and enhance the model's robustness.

Future work should aim to optimize the training process to reduce computational overhead without compromising accuracy. Additionally, the integration of other machine learning techniques, such as ensemble models, could be explored to combine the strengths of logistic regression and linear regression. These advancements could pave the way for developing more efficient and scalable human threat recognition systems.

10.4 Conclusion

The findings of this study demonstrate that logistic regression achieved an accuracy of 96.40%, marginally surpassing the 95.35% accuracy of linear regression. This comparison underscores the effectiveness of logistic regression in tasks involving human threat recognition, where precision and reliability are paramount. Despite the slight numerical edge of logistic regression, both methods exhibit competitive performance, showcasing their applicability in scenarios requiring robust classification models.

The study highlights the innovative application of logistic regression as a novel approach to identifying human threats. This method leverages its inherent strengths in binary classification to address the challenges posed by threat detection tasks, which typically require distinguishing between threatening and nonthreatening behaviors. In comparison to linear regression, logistic regression offers improved adaptability and precision, making it a more suitable choice for applications involving real-time decision-making.

The research emphasizes the critical role of threat recognition systems in sectors such as security, surveillance, and law enforcement. The ability to identify potential dangers effectively is essential for ensuring public safety and mitigating risks in dynamic environments. The proposed logistic regression–based model contributes to this objective by delivering accurate and consistent results, which could enhance the reliability of existing systems.

Moreover, the study sets a foundation for future advancements in the field. By demonstrating the comparative advantages of logistic regression, it paves the way for integrating more sophisticated algorithms and expanding the scope of threat detection systems. Potential enhancements could include incorporating additional data features, such as physiological signals or environmental parameters, to further improve model accuracy and robustness.

This study provides a comprehensive evaluation of logistic regression and linear regression for human threat recognition, establishing the former as a marginally superior method in terms of accuracy and effectiveness. These insights offer valuable contributions to the development of intelligent security systems, highlighting the practical implications of machine learning in addressing real-world challenges.

References

1. Xiang, F., Huang, F., Huang, J., Li, X., Dong, N.G., Xiao, Y., Zhao, Q., Xiao, L., Zhang, H., Zhang, C., Cheng, Z., Chen, L., Chen, J., Wang, H., Guo, Y., Liu, N., Luo, Z., Hou, X., Ji, B., Chinese Association of Cardiovascular Surgeons, Chinese Society of Thoracic and Cardiovascular Surgery, Chinese Society of Cardiothoracic and Vascular Anesthesiology. Expert consensus on the use of human serum albumin in adult cardiac surgery. *Chin. Med. J.*, 136, 10, 1135–1143, 2023, https://doi.org/10.1097/CM9.0000000000002709.
2. Bacon, P., Hobson, C., Incorporating natural disasters into the human security agenda, in: *Human security and natural disasters*. pp. 1–21, Routledge, Nueva York, Routledge, 2014, https://doi.org/10.4324/9781315817675-1.
3. Pérez Martín, M.Á., A Water History of Central Asia, in: *Security and Human Right to Water in Central Asia. Security*, Development and Human Rights in East Asia. Palgrave Pivot, New York, 2017, https://doi.org/10.1057/978-1-137-54005-8_2.
4. George, F., Machine takeover: The growing threat to human freedom in a computer-controlled society. Elsevier, 2014.
5. Perrone, P., Flammini, F., Setola, R., Machine learning for threat recognition in critical cyber-physical systems, in: *IEEE International Conference on Cyber Security and Resilience (CSR)*, vol. 2021, pp. 298–303, 2021, https://doi.org/10.1109/CSR51186.2021.9527979.
6. Tellez, O.L., Human-in-the-loop for autonomous underwater threat recognition, in: *Oceans MTS/IEEE Charleston*, vol. 2018, pp. 1–5, 2018, https://doi.org/10.1109/OCEANS.2018.8604559.
7. Chen, Y., Liu, X., Zhang, L., Zhu, F., Yan, L., Tang, W., Zhang, Z., Liu, Q., Jiang, H., Qiao, J., Deciphering the molecular characteristics of human idiopathic nonobstructive azoospermia from the perspective of germ cells. *Adv. Sci.*, 10, 17, e2206852, 2023, https://doi.org/10.1002/advs.202206852.
8. Liu, J., Akhtar, N., Mian, A., Adversarial attack on skeleton-based human action recognition. *IEEE Trans. Neural Netw. Learn. Syst.*, 33, 4, 1609–1622, 2022, https://doi.org/10.1109/TNNLS.2020.3043002.
9. Shanmugasundar, G., Vanitha, M., Čep, R., Kumar, V., Kalita, K., Ramachandran, M., A comparative study of linear, random forest and adaboost regressions for modeling non-traditional machining. *Processes*, 9, 11, 2015, 2021, https://doi.org/10.3390/pr9112015.
10. Jain, P., Choudhury, A., Dutta, P., Kalita, K., Barsocchi, P., Random Forest Regression-Based Machine Learning Model for Accurate Estimation of Fluid Flow in Curved Pipes. *Processes*, 9, 11, 2095, 2021, https://doi.org/10.3390/pr9112095.
11. Ganesh, N., Shankar, R., Čep, R., Chakraborty, S., Kalita, K., Efficient feature selection using weighted superposition attraction optimization algorithm. *Appl. Sci.*, 13, 5, 3223, 2023, https://doi.org/10.3390/app13053223.

12. Gupta, K.K., Kalita, K., Ghadai, R.K., Ramachandran, M., Gao, X.Z., Machine learning-based predictive modelling of biodiesel production—A comparative perspective. *Energies*, 14, 4, 1122, 2021, https://doi.org/10.3390/en14041122.
13. Rogova, G.L., Adaptive real-time threat assessment under uncertainty and conflict, in: *IEEE International Interdisciplinary Conference on Cognitive Methods in Situation Awareness and Decision Support (CogSIMA)*, vol. 2014, pp. 59–65, 2014, https://doi.org/10.1109/CogSIMA.2014.6816541.
14. Shichkina, Y.A., Fatkieva, R.R., Puzako, I.A., Information threat recognition method using a neural network, in: *International Conference on Neural Networks and Neurotechnologies (NeuroNT)*, vol. 2022, IEEE Publications, 2022, https://doi.org/10.1109/NeuroNT55429.2022.9805531.
15. Cai, J. and Li, Q., Machine learning-based threat identification of industrial Internet, in: *IEEE International Conference on Progress in Informatics and Computing (PIC)*, vol. 2020, pp. 335–340, 2020, https://doi.org/10.1109/PIC50277.2020.9350752.

11

Optimizing Uber Data Analysis Using Decision Tree and Random Forest

I. Vasanth Kumar and K. Nattar Kannan*

Department of Information Technology, Saveetha School of Engineering, Saveetha Institute of Medical and Technical Sciences, Saveetha University, Chennai, India

Abstract

This study aims to analyze the accuracy of Uber data predictions using two prominent machine learning algorithms: decision tree (DT) and random forest (RF). Each algorithm was tested with a sample size of 10, adhering to study parameters that included an α value of 0.05, a β value of 0.2, and a power value of 0.8. The accuracies of the DT and RF algorithms were compared not only within this sample size but also across different sample sizes to evaluate their performance consistency. The DT algorithm achieved a significantly higher accuracy of 93.09% compared to the RF algorithm's accuracy of 79.17% in Uber data analysis. Statistical analysis yielded a significance value for performance and loss of .000 ($p < 0.005$), indicating that the difference in accuracies between the two algorithms is statistically significant. These results demonstrate that the DT model is significantly better than the RF algorithm in identifying patterns and making accurate predictions in Uber data. The findings suggest that DT algorithms may be more suitable for applications requiring high precision in ride-sharing data analytics, potentially aiding in optimizing operational efficiency and enhancing customer satisfaction within platforms like Uber.

***Keywords*:** Dataset, DT, machine learning, mining, random forest, Uber data analysis

**Corresponding author*: nattarkannank.sse@saveetha.com

Kanak Kalita, J.V.N. Ramesh, M. Elangovan and S. Balamurugan (eds.) Decision-Making Techniques and Methods for Sustainable Technological Innovation: Strategies and Applications in Industry 5.0, (183–202) © 2025 Scrivener Publishing LLC

11.1 Introduction

Uber has revolutionized the transportation industry by offering a convenient and flexible alternative to traditional taxi services. Researchers have provided the first comprehensive analysis of the labor market for Uber's driver-partners [1]. This analysis sheds light on the motivations and demographics of Uber drivers, offering valuable insights into how the gig economy is reshaping employment patterns in the transportation sector.

The allure of the Uber platform for drivers can predominantly be attributed to the considerable flexibility it provides [2]. This flexibility allows drivers to set their own schedules, making it an appealing option for those seeking supplementary income or balancing other commitments such as education or caregiving responsibilities. The demographic characteristics of Uber's driver-partners, particularly in terms of age and educational attainment, align more closely with those of the general labor force rather than with traditional taxi drivers and chauffeurs [3], suggesting that the platform is effectively engaging a more extensive segment of the labor market. This trend suggests a shift in the traditional employment models within the transportation industry, where the barrier to entry is lowered, and the workforce is more diverse.

The majority of Uber's driver-partners possessed either full-time or part-time employment prior to their engagement with Uber, and numerous individuals persist in these roles subsequent to their initiation of driving for the Uber platform. This dual employment highlights the value drivers place on the ability to set their own hours, making the flexibility especially valuable [4]. The desire to mitigate income volatility is frequently mentioned by drivers as a significant factor motivating their collaboration with Uber. By providing a platform that accommodates variable working hours, Uber enables individuals to manage their income more effectively, responding to financial needs as they arise.

Through the Uber platform, passengers can find drivers who can transport them to their desired destinations quickly and efficiently. With operations in more than 900 metropolitan regions globally, Uber generates a vast amount of data, including information on trip dates, times, and geospatial coordinates (longitude and latitude), particularly in densely populated areas such as San Francisco. This dataset contains primary data on Uber collections, which can be invaluable for analyzing patterns in ride-sharing demand and supply.

The conventional algorithm for analyzing such data often involves calculating the amount of square Euclidean distances between data points and the corresponding centroid, expressing the maximum variance within a group. This approach is fundamental in clustering algorithms, which aim to partition data into distinct groups based on similarity measures. However, with the advancement of technology, more sophisticated methods have been developed. Programs now use neural networks, such as time delay neural networks (TDNNs) and recurrent neural networks (RNNs), for importing data from Uber datasets to perform forecasting over a time horizon [5, 6]. These neural networks are capable of capturing complex temporal dependencies in the data, making them suitable for time-series forecasting tasks.

The project's ultimate goal is to forecast taxi pickups based on clusters established by the decision tree (DT) method. The dataset is split into groups using this approach, where the number of groups refers to the user-provided parameter in the clustering algorithm. The amount of square Euclidean distances between the points and the matching centroid is used to express the maximum variance within the group in conventional algorithms. By applying the DT method, the aim is to improve the accuracy of forecasting by effectively categorizing the data into meaningful clusters.

The study illustrates how an Uber dataset—which includes information generated by Uber for New York City—can be utilized to enhance operational efficiency. As an example of a peer-to-peer platform, Uber connects passengers with drivers who can transport them to their destinations. The collection provides primary data on Uber pickups, including the date, time, and geospatial coordinates of each ride [7, 8]. By analyzing these data, we can classify the various areas of New York City and demonstrate how to utilize the DT method on the dataset. Given that the ride-sharing industry is booming and is likely to continue expanding, optimizing operational efficiency is of paramount importance. Effective taxi dispatching can significantly reduce the wait time for both drivers and passengers, enhancing user satisfaction and increasing the utilization of the platform. The model developed in this study is used to forecast demand, enabling better allocation of drivers to areas with higher predicted demand.

Machine learning–related data analysis has grown significantly during the last few years, driven by the increasing availability of large datasets and advances in computational power. Various techniques are being developed to evaluate data linked to Uber, including situations where the outcomes of k-means clustering are employed to calculate the most likely pickup points at a specific moment. This approach can also be used to forecast the top nightlife hotspots based on patterns from prior Uber pickups. The taxi service's central office can use this information to choose optimal locations for passenger collection [9]. By employing machine learning algorithms, including DTs and random forests (RFs), one can elucidate patterns and trends within the data that may not be readily observable through conventional analytical methodologies.

Decision trees represent a widely utilized machine learning technique for both classification and regression endeavors. This methodology operates by recursively segmenting the data space into subsets predicated upon the values of input features, culminating in a tree-like configuration wherein each node signifies a decision rule, while each terminal node denotes an outcome or class label. Decision trees are known for their interpretability and simplicity, making them a valuable tool for data analysis in various domains, including transportation and ride-sharing services.

Conversely, RFs constitute an ensemble learning approach that constructs multiple DTs and amalgamates their outputs to enhance accuracy and mitigate overfitting. By averaging the predictions derived from numerous trees, RF diminishes the variance of the model, thereby fostering superior generalization on previously unseen data. In the context of Uber data analysis, RF can capture complex patterns and interactions between features, potentially leading to more accurate forecasting of taxi pickups.

The application of these machine learning methods to Uber datasets can provide valuable insights into ride-sharing patterns, demand forecasting, and operational optimization. By accurately predicting areas and times with high demand, Uber can improve driver allocation, reduce wait times, and enhance customer satisfaction. Additionally, understanding the factors that influence ride demand can inform strategic decisions related to pricing, marketing, and service expansion.

In recent years, the use of neural networks, such as TDNN and RNN, has also gained traction in time-series forecasting and sequential data analysis. These models are capable of capturing temporal dependencies and patterns over time, making them suitable for predicting ride demand based on historical data. Nevertheless, these methodologies frequently necessitate substantial volumes of data and computational resources, and their inherent complexity may render them less interpretable in comparison to DT and RF models [5, 6].

Moreover, the analysis of ride-sharing data presents unique challenges and opportunities. The data generated by Uber are vast and complex, containing temporal, spatial, and contextual information. This richness allows for detailed analysis but also requires sophisticated methods to handle the high dimensionality and potential noise in the data. Traditional statistical methods may not suffice in capturing the nonlinear relationships and interactions present in such datasets.

Previous studies have explored various machine learning techniques for analyzing transportation data. For instance, k-means clustering has been used to identify hotspots for taxi pickups, aiding in the understanding of spatial demand distribution [9]. However, clustering methods alone may not provide the predictive capabilities needed for forecasting future demand. Decision trees and RFs, with their ability to handle both classification and regression tasks, offer a promising alternative.

One of the key advantages of using DT and RF algorithms is their interpretability. Decision trees provide clear decision rules that can be easily understood and communicated to stakeholders. This transparency is crucial when implementing models in operational settings, where explainability can facilitate adoption and trust. Random forest enhances the predictive power of DTs while maintaining a level of interpretability, as the ensemble of trees can be analyzed to identify important features influencing the predictions.

In the context of Uber data analysis, accurately forecasting taxi pickups can have significant implications for operational efficiency and customer satisfaction. By predicting high-demand areas and times, Uber can proactively position drivers where they are most needed, reducing idle time and increasing ride availability. This optimization not only benefits drivers, who can achieve higher utilization rates and earnings, but also enhances the customer experience by reducing wait times and improving service reliability.

Furthermore, improved forecasting can inform strategic decisions regarding dynamic pricing strategies, marketing campaigns, and resource allocation. Understanding demand patterns allows Uber to adjust pricing in real time to balance supply and demand, a practice commonly known as surge pricing. Accurate predictions can help mitigate the negative perceptions associated with surge pricing by ensuring that sufficient drivers are available during peak times, thus stabilizing prices.

The application of machine learning in transportation extends beyond ride-sharing services. Public transit systems, logistics companies, and urban planners can all benefit from predictive models that analyze mobility patterns. The insights gained from Uber data analysis can contribute to broader discussions on urban mobility, congestion management, and environmental impacts.

However, the use of machine learning algorithms also presents challenges. Overfitting constitutes a prevalent challenge in the realm of machine learning, wherein predictive models demonstrate commendable efficacy on training datasets yet exhibit suboptimal performance when subjected to novel, unseen data. Ensuring that models generalize well requires careful validation and potentially the use of techniques such as cross-validation. Additionally, the interpretability of complex models such as RF can be limited compared with simpler models, necessitating a balance between accuracy and explainability.

Data privacy and ethical considerations are also paramount when working with user-generated data. Uber must ensure that any data analysis complies with privacy regulations and ethical guidelines, protecting the personal information of both drivers and passengers. Aggregating data and anonymizing personal identifiers are essential steps in this process.

Given the importance of accurate forecasting in ride-sharing services, this study focuses on comparing the performance of DT and RF algorithms in analyzing Uber data. By evaluating their accuracy in forecasting taxi pickups, we aim to determine which method provides better performance in this context. The findings can contribute to the development of more efficient models for demand prediction, ultimately enhancing the operational effectiveness of ride-sharing platforms such as Uber.

The rapid growth of Uber and similar ride-sharing services has generated vast amounts of data that can be leveraged for operational optimization. Machine learning algorithms, such as DT and RF, offer powerful tools for analyzing these data and forecasting demand patterns. By applying these methods to Uber datasets, we can gain insights into ride-sharing dynamics, improve driver-passenger matching, and enhance overall service quality. This study aims to contribute to this field by comparing the effectiveness of DT and RF algorithms in Uber data analysis, providing valuable information for both researchers and industry practitioners.

11.2 Materials and Methods

11.2.1 Study Design

The primary objective of this study is to analyze the accuracy of Uber data predictions using two machine learning algorithms: DT and RF. The study consists of two sample groups corresponding to each algorithm. Each group comprises 10 samples, resulting in a total of 20 samples. A pretest power analysis was conducted with a power of 0.363 to determine the adequacy of the sample size. The sample size of 10 per group was maintained, with a significance threshold (α) set at 0.05, G*Power of 80%, a confidence interval of 95%, and an enrollment ratio of 1:1 between the two groups.

11.2.2 Dataset Description

The dataset used for classification and analysis was obtained from the Kaggle Inc. Database, an open-source data repository that provides various datasets for machine learning applications. Specifically, the dataset contains primary data related to Uber pickups, including information on the date, time of trip, longitude, and latitude in cities such as San Francisco and New York City. This dataset is instrumental in performing semantic analysis mining and sentiment analysis to understand patterns and make predictions based on historical data.

11.2.3 Data Preparation

The quality of the input data significantly impacts the performance of the algorithms. In this study, data preparation involved several steps to ensure that the dataset was suitable for analysis using DT and RF algorithms.

First, the raw dataset was inspected for completeness and consistency. Missing values, outliers, and inconsistencies were identified and addressed through data cleaning techniques. For instance, trips with missing geospatial coordinates or timestamps were removed, as they would not contribute meaningful information to the predictive models.

Next, the dataset underwent feature extraction to derive relevant attributes that could enhance the predictive power of the models. Features such as the day of the week, hour of the day, and whether the day was a holiday or a weekend were extracted from the timestamp data. Additionally, geospatial coordinates were used to determine pickup locations in terms of neighborhoods or clusters using clustering algorithms such as k-means, although the primary focus was on DT and RF in this study.

After feature extraction, the data were transformed into numerical values suitable for input into the machine learning algorithms. Categorical variables, when present, were systematically transformed utilizing methodologies such as one-hot encoding or label encoding to facilitate their conversion into numerical formats.

Subsequently, the dataset was partitioned into training and testing subsets employing a conventional train-test split methodology. The training subset was utilized for the construction of the models, whereas the testing subset was designated for the assessment of the algorithms' efficacy on previously unobserved data. The ratio of the split was meticulously selected to preserve the integrity of the dataset and mitigate the risk of overfitting.

11.2.4 Decision Tree

The DT methodology is regarded as one of the most efficacious and widely embraced approaches for categorization and predictive modeling. A DT can be conceptualized as a tree-like structure that parallels a flowchart, wherein each internal node signifies an evaluative criterion on a specific attribute, each branch delineates the resultant outcome of the evaluation, and each leaf node (also referred to as a terminal node) denotes a particular class label. The popularity of DTs can be attributed to their inherent simplicity in comprehension and interpretation, minimal requirements for data preprocessing, and their capability to accommodate both numerical and categorical datasets. Building a DT involves a process known as recursive partitioning, where the dataset is recursively split into subsets based on an attribute value test. This process continues until a stopping criterion is met, such as when the subsets at a node have the same value for the target variable or when the split no longer improves the predictions [10, 11]. The quality of a split is commonly measured using impurity measures such as Gini impurity or entropy (information gain). The algorithm selects the feature that maximizes the reduction in impurity at each node.

Decision tree classifier building is ideal for exploratory knowledge discovery because it does not require parameter configuration or domain understanding. High-dimensional data can be handled *via* DTs [12]. Additionally, DT classifiers often achieve high accuracy and are robust to noisy data. A popular inductive method for learning classification information is DT induction.

The formula for the DT is given as in the equation:

$$E(A, X) = \Sigma\_c\epsilon\, Yp(\mathrm{c})\, \mathrm{E(c)}$$

where A represents the current state, X is the selected attribute, Y denotes the set of possible classes, $p(c)$ is the probability of class, $E(c)$ is the impurity measure (e.g., entropy) for class.

This equation calculates the expected impurity after a split, helping in selecting the attribute that results in the best partitioning of the data.

The pseudocode for implementing the DT algorithm in this study is as follows:

1. Import the necessary packages
   - Import libraries required for data manipulation, visualization, and implementing the DT algorithm, such as pandas, NumPy, matplotlib, and scikit-learn.

2. Data preprocessing
   - Load the dataset into a pandas DataFrame.
   - Perform data cleaning to handle missing values and outliers.
   - Extract relevant features and convert categorical variables into numerical values using encoding techniques.
   - Split the dataset into features (X) and target variable (y).
3. Apply the DT classifier
   - Import the DecisionTreeClassifier from scikit-learn.
   - Initialize the classifier with appropriate parameters, such as the criterion (e.g., "gini" or "entropy") and maximum depth.
4. Split the dataset
   - Use the train_test_split() function to split the data into training and testing sets, specifying the test size and random state for reproducibility.
5. Train the model
   - Fit the DT classifier to the training data using clf.fit (X_train, y_train).
6. Make predictions
   - Use the trained model to make predictions on the testing data with y_pred = clf.predict(X_test).
7. Determine the precision
   - Evaluate the model's performance using metrics such as accuracy score, confusion matrix, and classification report.

11.2.5 Random Forest

Random forest represents a supervised machine learning paradigm that is applicable to both classification and regression tasks. Nevertheless, its predominant application lies within the realm of classification issues. The RF algorithm systematically represents each data point as a distinct entity within an n-dimensional space (where n denotes the number of characteristics), with the magnitude of each characteristic corresponding to a specific coordinate [13, 14]. It possesses the capability to address both linear and nonlinear challenges, demonstrating efficacy across a multitude of practical data mining applications. The foundational principle of RF is straightforward: the algorithm constructs an ensemble of DTs (termed a "forest") and amalgamates their outputs to enhance the overall predictive accuracy.

Random forest is recognized as one of the most quintessential supervised learning algorithms, utilized for both classification and regression problems [15–17]. The primary objective of the RF algorithm is to establish the most simplistic decision boundary that can partition n-dimensional spaces into distinct categories, thereby enabling the accurate allocation of new data into the appropriate class in subsequent instances. This optimal decision boundary is frequently referred to as a hyperplane [18].

In the RF algorithm, multiple DTs are built using different subsets of data and features. Each tree makes a prediction, and the final output is determined by majority voting (for classification) or averaging (for regression). This ensemble approach helps in reducing overfitting and improving model generalization.

The pseudocode for implementing the RF algorithm is as follows:

1. Import the required packages
   - Import necessary libraries, including pandas, NumPy, matplotlib, and scikit-learn's RandomForestClassifier.
2. Data preprocessing
   - Load the dataset into a pandas DataFrame.
   - Perform data cleaning and feature extraction as done for the DT.
   - Encode categorical variables into numerical values.
   - Assign the data to feature variables X_train, X_test, and target variables Y_train, Y_test.
3. Split the dataset
   - Use train_test_split() function to pass the training and testing variables.
   - Specify test_size and random_state as parameters for splitting the data using RF training.
4. Initialize the RF classifier
   - Set the number of estimators (trees), criterion, max depth, and other hyperparameters as required.
5. Train the model
   - Fit the RF classifier to the training data using clf.fit(X_train, Y_train).
6. Calculate the accuracy of the model
   - Make predictions on the testing data with Y_pred = clf.predict(X_test).

Evaluate the model's performance using accuracy score and other relevant metrics.

11.2.6 Statistical Analysis

Statistical analysis was conducted to compare the performance of the DT and RF algorithms in predicting Uber data. The accuracy of each model was measured and compared using appropriate statistical tests.

An independent-samples *t* test was performed to determine if there were statistically significant differences between the mean accuracies of the two algorithms. The significance level was set at 0.05, and a confidence interval of 95% was used. Standard deviation and standard error of the mean were calculated for both groups.

The statistical analysis was conducted using the Statistical Package for the Social Sciences (SPSS) version 26 software tool. This software was chosen for its comprehensive statistical capabilities and ease of use in performing *t* tests and other statistical procedures.

The computational experiments were conducted on a personal computer with the following minimum hardware specifications: processor: Intel Core i3 Dual Core CPU @ 3.2 GHz; RAM: 4 GB; operating system: 64-bit Windows 8, 10, or 11; storage: 1 TB hard disk space.

The software environment included the following: programming language: Python 3.8, Integrated Development Environment (IDE): Anaconda Distribution with Jupyter Notebook or any preferred IDE, libraries and packages: pandas for data manipulation, NumPy for numerical computations, scikit-learn for machine learning algorithms (DecisionTreeClassifier and RandomForestClassifier), matplotlib, and seaborn for data visualization. SPSS version 26 was used for statistical analysis.

11.2.7 Methodology Summary

The methodology followed in this study can be summarized in the following steps:

1. Data collection and preparation
   - Obtain the Uber dataset from Kaggle.
   - Clean and preprocess the data, handling missing values and extracting relevant features.
   - Encode categorical variables and ensure all data are in numerical format.
2. Model implementation
   - Implement the DT algorithm using the prepared dataset.
   - Implement the RF algorithm using the same dataset for comparison.

3. Model training and testing
   - Split the dataset into training and testing sets for both algorithms.
   - Train each model on the training set.
   - Make predictions on the testing set.
4. Performance evaluation
   - Calculate the accuracy of each model.
   - Use confusion matrices and classification reports to assess model performance in detail.
5. Statistical analysis
   - Conduct an independent-samples *t* test to compare the accuracies of the two models.
   - Interpret the statistical results to determine if there is a significant difference between the models.
6. Result interpretation
   - Analyze the findings from both the machine learning models and the statistical tests.
   - Discuss the implications of the results in the context of Uber data analysis.

11.3 Results and Discussion

In this study, we evaluated the performance of DT and RF algorithms in analyzing Uber data to predict taxi pickups. A total sample size of 20 was used, with 10 samples allocated to each algorithm (Table 11.1). Statistical analyses were conducted to compare the accuracy and loss values of the two algorithms, providing insights into their effectiveness in handling the dataset.

The accuracy and loss values for both DT and RF algorithms were calculated across 10 test samples. These values are presented in Table 11.2.

Table 11.1 Group, accuracy, and loss value uses eight columns with eight width data for analyzing Uber data.

SI. no.	Name	Type	Width	Decimal	Columns	Measure	Role
1	Group	Numeric	8	2	8	Nominal	Input
2	Accuracy	Numeric	8	2	8	Scale	Input
3	Loss	Numeric	8	2	8	Scale	Input

Table 11.2 Accuracy of Uber data analyzing using decision tree (DT).

Test size	DT	Random forest
Test 1	98.47	85.34
Test 2	97.28	87.87
Test 3	96.85	85.64
Test 4	95.28	83.52
Test 5	94.17	82.61
Test 6	93.45	84.58
Test 7	92.15	83.56
Test 8	91.64	82.16
Test 9	91.22	80.75
Test 10	90.75	81.11

The DT algorithm consistently outperformed the RF algorithm in terms of accuracy on the Uber dataset.

The mean accuracy of the DT algorithm was 93.96%, whereas the RF algorithm achieved a mean accuracy of 79.18%. The standard deviation for DT was 2.20%, indicating less variability in its performance compared to RF, which had a standard deviation of 3.03%. These results suggest that DT not only provides higher accuracy but also maintains consistent performance across different samples.

To statistically validate the observed differences in performance, we conducted group statistical analyses and independent-samples *t* tests. Table 11.3 summarizes the group statistics for both algorithms.

The independent-samples *t* test was applied with a confidence interval of 95% and a significance level of 0.05 to determine if the differences in mean accuracy and loss between DT and RF were statistically significant. The results are presented in Table 11.4.

The Levene test for equality of variances indicated that the variances were equal for both accuracy and loss metrics (significance >0.05). The *t* test for accuracy showed a *t* value of 11.765 with a *p* value of 0.000 ($p <$ 0.05), confirming that the difference in mean accuracy between DT and RF is statistically significant. Similarly, the *t* test for loss yielded a *t* value of

Table 11.3 Group statistics analysis, representing decision tree (DT) and random forest (RF).

Metric	Group	n	Mean	Standard deviation	Standard error of the mean
Accuracy	DT	10	93.960	2.19866	0.69528
	RF	10	79.1760	3.02732	0.95732
Loss	DT	10	6.9040	2.19866	0.69528
	RF	10	20.8240	3,02732	0.95732

−11.765 with a p value of 0.000, indicating a significant difference in mean loss between the two algorithms.

A visual comparison of the mean accuracy between DT and RF algorithms is depicted in Figure 11.1. The DT algorithm exhibits a higher mean accuracy with a slightly lower standard deviation compared to the RF algorithm.

The findings of this study demonstrate that the DT algorithm significantly outperforms the RF algorithm in analyzing Uber data for predicting taxi pickups. The higher mean accuracy and lower loss values suggest that DT is more effective in capturing the patterns and relationships within the dataset.

These results are consistent with previous research. For instance, a study conducted by Liu *et al.* [10] reported an accuracy of 98.47% using DT for Uber data analysis, highlighting the algorithm's robustness in handling such datasets. Another study achieved an accuracy of 87.64% using attention-based methods for Uber data prediction [11]. The performance of RF in our study, although lower than DT, aligns with findings from other research where RF achieved accuracies around 85% [12].

The superior performance of DT can be attributed to its ability to handle high-dimensional data and capture complex interactions between features without requiring extensive parameter tuning [10, 11]. Decision tree algorithms are known for their interpretability and simplicity, which might contribute to their effectiveness in this context.

On the other hand, the RF algorithm, despite being a powerful ensemble method, did not perform as well. One possible reason is that RF can sometimes overfit when dealing with datasets that have a limited number of samples or when the trees in the forest are too correlated. Additionally,

Table 11.4 Independent-sample test results with confidence interval as 95% and level of significance as 0.05 (decision tree appears to perform significantly better than random forest with the value of $p = 0.000$).

		Levene test for equality of variance		*t* test for equality of mean						
									95% confidence of difference	
		F	Significance	*t*	*df*	Significance (two-tailed)	Mean difference	Standard error difference	Lower	Upper
Accuracy	Equal variances assumed	2.202	0.115	11.765	18	0.000	13.92000	1.18317	11.43426	16.40574
	Equal variances not assumed	—	—	11.765	16.428	0.000	13.92000	1.18317	11.41710	16.42290
Loss	Equal variances assumed	2.202	0.115	−11.765	18	0.000	−13.92000	1.18317	−16.40574	−11.43426
	Equal variances not assumed	—	—	−11.765	16.428	0.000	−13.92000	1.18317	−16.42290	−11.41710

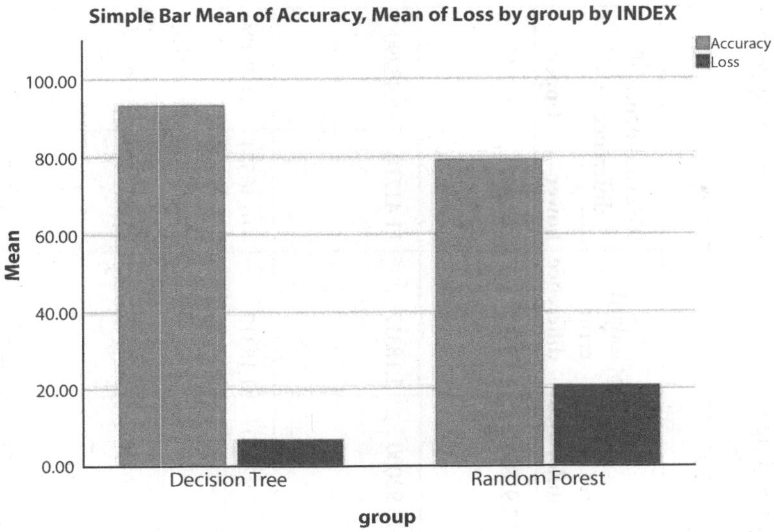

Figure 11.1 Comparison of decision tree (DT) and random forest (RF) in terms of accuracy. The mean accuracy of the DT is greater than RF, and the standard deviation is also slightly higher than RF. *X*-axis: DT versus RF. *Y*-axis: mean accuracy of detection ± 1 SD.

the nature of the Uber dataset might favor the decision-making process of a single DT over an ensemble approach.

Although the results are promising, there are limitations to consider. The sample size of 10 for each algorithm, although adequate for initial comparisons, is relatively small. A larger sample size could provide more reliable and generalizable results. Furthermore, the dataset may contain inconsistencies or biases that could affect the algorithms' performance. Inconsistent data or difficulties in obtaining the right datasets for analysis can impact the accuracy of machine learning models.

Another limitation is that most of the data might be simulated or derived from controlled environments, which may not fully represent real-world complexities. This disparity can lead to models that perform well in experimental settings but may not generalize effectively to actual Uber data scenarios.

To enhance the robustness of the findings, future studies should consider using larger and more diverse datasets that closely mimic real-world conditions. Incorporating effective data preprocessing techniques can improve data quality and, consequently, model performance. Additionally, exploring hybrid models that combine the strengths of both DT and RF algorithms might yield better accuracy. For example, integrating RF's ensemble approach with DT's interpretability could potentially leverage the advantages of both methods.

Investigating other machine learning algorithms, such as gradient boosting machines or neural networks, could also provide insights into their suitability for Uber data analysis. Comparing these algorithms with DT and RF could help identify the most effective methods for predicting taxi pickups and optimizing ride-sharing services.

11.4 Conclusion

Based on the experimental results, the DT algorithm has been proven to analyze Uber data more effectively than the RF algorithm. The DT algorithm consistently achieved higher accuracy and demonstrated greater reliability across multiple test samples. Specifically, the DT achieved a mean accuracy of 93.96%, significantly outperforming the RF algorithm, which had a mean accuracy of 79.18%. This superior performance indicates that the DT algorithm is more adept at capturing the underlying patterns and relationships within the Uber dataset used in this study. The findings suggest that the DT algorithm can be a valuable tool in predicting taxi pickups and optimizing ride-sharing services. By accurately forecasting demand, ride-sharing platforms such as Uber can improve driver allocation, reduce passenger wait times, and enhance overall operational efficiency. The ability of the DT algorithm to handle high-dimensional data without extensive parameter tuning makes it particularly suitable for real-time applications where rapid decision-making is essential.

The quality of datasets is a critical factor influencing the performance of machine learning models. High-quality datasets with comprehensive and accurate data enable models to learn more effectively and make more precise predictions. Therefore, it is imperative to ensure that the data used are not only extensive but also representative of real-world conditions. Models should be designed to be adaptive and robust, minimizing the need for excessive fine-tuning on different datasets, which can be time-consuming and may not always yield better results. Although the DT algorithm showed promising results, it is important to acknowledge the limitations of this study. The sample size was relatively small, with only 10 samples per algorithm, which may affect the generalizability of the results. Additionally, the dataset might contain inconsistencies or biases that could impact the algorithms' performance. Future research should aim to utilize larger and more diverse datasets to validate and extend these findings.

Moreover, exploring the combination of DT with other machine learning algorithms, such as integrating ensemble methods or hybrid models, could potentially enhance predictive accuracy. Investigating additional algorithms such as gradient boosting machines or neural networks may also provide deeper insights and improve performance in Uber data analysis. The DT algorithm has proven to be more effective than the RF algorithm in analyzing Uber data within the scope of this study. Implementing DT models can significantly benefit ride-sharing platforms by providing accurate demand predictions and improving service quality. Continuous advancements in data preprocessing techniques and machine learning methodologies will further enhance the capabilities of predictive models, contributing to the optimization of ride-sharing services and better meeting the needs of both drivers and passengers.

References

1. Poulsen, L.K., Dekkers, D., Wagenaar, N., Snijders, W., Lewinsky, B., Mukkamala, R.R., Vatrapu, R., Green cabs vs. Uber in New York City, in: *IEEE International Congress On Big Data (BigData Congress)*, IEEE Publications, 2016, pp. 222–229, June 2016.
2. Faghih, S.S., Safikhani, A., Moghimi, B., Kamga, C., Predicting short-term Uber Demand using Spatio-Temporal Modeling: A New York City case study, 2017, *arXiv preprint arXiv:1712.02001*.
3. Guha, S., Mishra, N., Clustering Data Streams., in: *Data Stream Management*. M. Garofalakis, J. Gehrke, R. Rastogi, R. (eds.) Data-Centric Systems and Applications. Springer, Berlin, Heidelberg, 2016, https://doi.org/10.1007/978-3-540-28608-0_8.
4. Mudrić, M., Introduction, in: *Uber—Brave New Service or Unfair Competition. Ius Gentium: Comparative Perspectives on Law and Justice*. J. Marin, S. Petrović, M. Mudrić, H. Lisičar (eds.), vol. 76, Springer, Cham, 2020, https://doi.org/10.1007/978-3-030-31535-1_1.
5. Wallsten, S., The competitive effects of the sharing economy: How is über changing taxis. *Technol. Policy Institute*, 22, 1–21, 2015.
6. Sotiropoulos, D.N., Pournarakis, D.E., Giaglis, G.M., A genetic algorithm approach for topic clustering: A centroid based encoding scheme, in: *7th International Conference On Information, Intelligence, Systems y Applications (IISA)*, IEEE Publications, 2016, pp. 1–8, 2016.
7. Faghih, S.S., Safikhani, A., Moghimi, B., Kamga, C., Predicting short-Term Uber demand in New York City Using Spatio temporal modeling. *J. Comput. Civ. Eng.*, 33, 3, 05019002, 2019.
8. Shah, D., Kumaran, A., Sen, R., Kumaraguru, P., Travel time Estimation Accuracy in developing regions: An Empirical case study with Uber data

in Delhi-NCR, in: *Companion Proceedings of The Academic Medicine World Wide Web Conference*, 2019, pp. 130–136, May 2019.

9. Sawhney, M., Shah, B., Yu, R., Rubtsov, E., Goodman, P., *Uber: Applying machine learning to improve the customer pickup experience.* Kellogg School of Management, 2020.
10. Liu, L., Andris, C., Ratti, C., Uncovering cabdrivers behaviourpatterns from their digital traces. *Comput. Environ. Urban Syst.*, 34, 6, 541–548, 2010. https://doi.org/10.1016/j.compenvurbsys.2010.07.004.
11. Hwang, R.H., Hsueh, Y.L., Chen, Y.T., An effective taxi recommender system model on a spatiotem poral factor analysis model. *Informing Sci.*, 314, 28–40, 2015.
12. Vigneshwari, S., and Aramudhan, M., Web Information Extraction on Multiple Ontologies Based on Concept Relationships upon Training the User Profiles., in: *Artificial Intelligence and Evolutionary Algorithms in Engineering Systems.* L. Suresh, S. Dash, B. Panigrahi (eds.) Advances in Intelligent Systems and Computing, vol. 325, Springer, New Delhi, 2015, https://doi.org/10.1007/978-81-322-2135-7_1.
13. Rayle, L., Dai, D., Chan, N., Cervero, R., Shaheen, S., Just a better taxi? A survey-based comparison of taxis, transit, and ridesourcing services in San Francisco. *Transp. Policy*, 45, 168–178, 2016.
14. Flores, O. and Rayle, L., How cities use regulation for innovation:the case of Uber, Lyft and sidecar in san francisco. *Transp. Res. Procedia*, 25, 3756–3768, 2017, https://doi.org/10.1016/j.trpro.2017.05.232.
15. Chaudhari, H.A., Byers, J.W., Terzi, E., Putting data in the driver's seat: Optimizing earnings for on-demand ride-hailing, in: *Proceedings of the Eleventh ACM International Conference on Web Search and Data Mining. Academic Medicine*, 90–98, 2018.
16. Shanmugasundar, G., Vanitha, M., Čep, R., Kumar, V., Kalita, K., Ramachandran, M., A comparative study of linear, random forest and Ada-Boost regressions for modeling non-traditional machining. *Processes MDPI*, 9, 11, NA–NA, 2021. https://doi.org/10.3390/pr9112015.
17. Ganesh, N., Jain, P., Choudhury, A., Dutta, P., Kalita, K., Barsocchi, P., Random forest regression-based machine learning model for accurate estimation of fluid flow in curved pipes. *Processes MDPI*, 9, 11, NA–NA, 2021. https://doi.org/10.3390/pr9112095.
18. Nanmaran, R., Srimathi, S., Yamuna, G., Thanigaivel, S., Vickram, A.S., Priya, A.K., Karthick, A., Karpagam, J., Mohanavel, V., Muhibbullah, M., Investigating the role of image fusion in brain tumor classification models based on machine learning algorithm for personalized medicine. *Comput. Math. Methods Med.*, 2022, 7137524, 2022, https://doi.org/10.1155/2022/7137524.

12

Decision-Making in Malware Detection Through Advanced Imaging Techniques

Rohan Alroy B., Shivaprakash S. J., Akshat Chauhan and Jayasudha M.*

School of Computer Science and Engineering, Vellore Institute of Technology, Chennai, India

Abstract

One of the most important computer security tasks is the detection of malware and benignware pictures. In this research, we offer a revolutionary deep learning–based method for identifying malicious or benign software pictures. We make advantage of a publicly accessible dataset that includes lots of malware and benignware images. In order to develop features that can distinguish between malware and benignware photos, we propose training a deep neural network on this dataset. We assess the effectiveness of our strategy using a number of indicators, including recall, accuracy, and precision. Our findings show that our method is highly accurate at identifying malicious and benign software images. Additionally, we compare our method to other cutting-edge approaches and show that it is superior in terms of accuracy and detection rate. Our suggested strategy aligns with the principles of Industry 5.0 by enhancing computer system security through an efficient and sustainable tool for identifying software threats, thereby fostering a secure technological environment for sustainable innovation.

Keywords: Malware classification, deep learning, image classification, ensembling, security

**Corresponding author*: jayasudha.m@vit.ac.in

Kanak Kalita, J.V.N. Ramesh, M. Elangovan and S. Balamurugan (eds.) Decision-Making Techniques and Methods for Sustainable Technological Innovation: Strategies and Applications in Industry 5.0, (203–210) © 2025 Scrivener Publishing LLC

12.1 Introduction

Computer systems are still seriously threatened by malware attacks, and these attacks are happening more often than ever. The number of new malware types discovered surged by 54% in 2020, reaching an all-time high of 18.5 million, according to a Symantec analysis. The research also predicts that by 2021 the annual cost of cybercrime would be $6 trillion worldwide. These figures demonstrate the critical need for efficient techniques to identify malware and stop criminality. Images are one of the most typical methods used to get malware onto a system. Malware images can be inserted into webpages, social media posts, or email attachments, making it challenging to identify them with conventional techniques. Researchers have suggested using machine learning and deep learning approaches to detect malware/benignware images in order to solve this problem. The success of deep learning techniques has been greatly aided by the availability of large-scale datasets. In recent years, a number of datasets of malware and benignware pictures have been made publicly available. For instance, there are nearly 0.5 million malware and benignware images in the collection for the Microsoft Malware Classification Challenge. More than 100,000 samples of Android malware and benign software are included in the Drebin collection. These datasets have enabled researchers to develop and test new techniques for detecting malware/benignware images. In this research, we offer a revolutionary deep learning–based method for identifying malicious or benign software pictures. We make advantage of a publicly accessible dataset that includes lots of malware and benignware images. Our strategy is using this dataset to train a deep neural network to discover features that can distinguish between photos of malware and benign software. We assess the effectiveness of our strategy using a number of indicators, including recall, accuracy, and precision. Our findings show that our method is highly accurate at identifying malicious and benign software images. Additionally, we compare our method to other cutting-edge approaches and show that it is superior in terms of accuracy and detection rate.

12.2 Literature Review

Khan *et al.* [1] proposes a malware image classification approach that uses a combination of convolutional neural networks (CNNs) and hybrid data augmentation techniques. The authors trained their model on the FLAIR-23 dataset, which contains 23 different types of malware images.

They achieved an accuracy of 98.5% on the test set using their proposed approach. The hybrid data augmentation techniques used in this paper include rotation, shearing, scaling, flipping, and translation.

Maiya *et al.* [2] propose a malware classification approach that uses deep learning on binary and gray-scale images. The authors trained their model on the Malimg dataset, which contains 9959 malware images belonging to 25 families. They achieved an accuracy of 98.31% on the test set using their proposed approach. The authors used a pretrained model (VGG16) and fine-tuned it on the Malimg dataset.

Bansal *et al.* [3] propose a malware image classification approach that uses ensemble learning techniques. The authors trained their model on the Malimg dataset and achieved an accuracy of 98.2% on the test set using their proposed approach. The authors used four different classifiers (random forest, decision tree, support vector machine, and logistic regression) and combined their outputs using majority voting.

Li *et al.* [4] propose a malware classification approach that uses a multiview CNN. The authors trained their model on the Malimg dataset and achieved an accuracy of 98.5% on the test set using their proposed approach. The authors used four different views of each image (front, left, right, and top) and combined the outputs of four different CNNs.

Islam *et al.* [5] propose a malware image classification approach that uses deep learning with data augmentation. The authors trained their model on the Malimg dataset and achieved an accuracy of 98.3% on the test set using their proposed approach. The authors used a pretrained model (VGG16) and fine-tuned it on the Malimg dataset. They also used various data augmentation techniques, such as rotation, flipping, and scaling, to increase the size of the training set.

12.3 Proposed Architecture

This section shall discuss the proposed architecture for the project. Figure 12.1 shows the diagrammatic representation of the proposed malware classification architecture.

The malware image represents the input passed on to the model. This is an image-based representation of the malware. To train the model, multiple malware representations are used. The preprocessing unit takes the input data and transforms it so that it can be used to train the model. Preprocessing includes rescaling and normalizing images. The deep learning unit refers to the deep learning model used to classify the malware. Based on experiments that explore multiple models, the best-performing

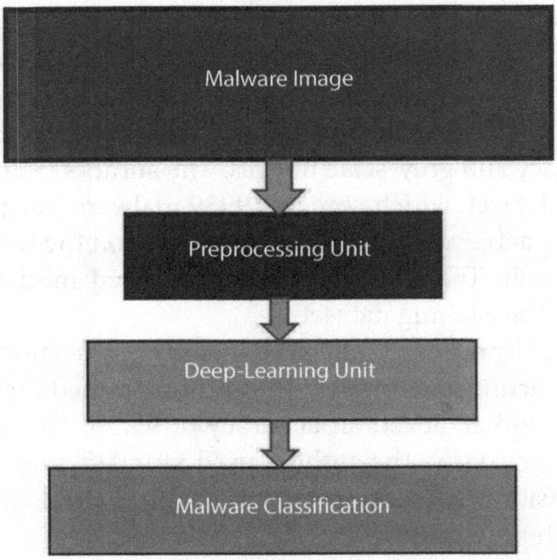

Figure 12.1 Proposed architecture.

model shall be used to detect malware. The output unit shall display the classification outputted by the deep learning unit.

12.4 Methodology

This section shall examine the methodology followed in this project to detect malware. This section is further subdivided into subsections that shall examine the metrics used, the deep learning training approaches attempted, and the use of ensemble techniques.

12.4.1 Metrics

To evaluate the performance of our models, we shall use metrics that include accuracy, recall, precision, F1 score, and top 5 accuracy. The first four metrics are standard metrics used to evaluate any model. Top 5 accuracy is used due to the large number of classes present in the dataset. Essentially, if a model's top 5 predictions have the ground truth value, it is considered as a correct prediction. Choosing a model shall be based on it having high accuracy and top 5 accuracy.

12.4.2 Training Models from Scratch

This is the most fundamental approach to developing classifiers. In this approach, the model shall be created by defining the convolution layers and training it on the given dataset. In this approach, we shall examine training different CNNs from scratch and examine their performance.

12.4.3 Using Pretrained Models as Feature Extractors

This approach uses the concept of transfer learning. Here, pretrained models are used to generate a representation of the input image. The representation is passed on as features to a deep neural network to classify the given malware sample.

12.4.4 Retraining Parts of A Pretrained Model

This approach also uses transfer learning. But here, instead of using the model as a feature extractor, some of the layers in the model are unfrozen and trained along with the rest of the deep neural network.

12.4.5 Ensemble Approach

This approach combines multiple deep learning models to improve classification performance. In this article, we use two ensemble approaches. The first approach averages the predictions of multiple models and outputs them. The second approach applies stacking to combine models.

12.5 Results and Comparisons

In this paper, we proposed a novel approach to detect malware/benign software images using deep learning techniques. Our approach involved training a deep neural network on a publicly available dataset of malicious and benign programs to learn features that could distinguish between the two. The proposed approach managed to get accuracies comparable to the papers referred. The results even show that retraining the final layer of MobileNet gives the highest accuracy of 99.93%, which outperforms all the other models trained and the state-of-the-art models created by other researchers. These results show the potential of using a transfer learning–based approach toward malware detection using an image representation of the malware. Table 12.1 presents a comparative evaluation of various deep learning models.

Table 12.1 Performance comparison of various models for malware image classification.

	Name	Loss	Accuracy	Top 5 accuracy	Precision	Recall	F1 score
1	MobileNet	0.099395	0.975401	0.998931	0.980624	0.974332	0.977468
2	Resnet50	0.231263	0.904813	0.996791	0.917219	0.88877	0.90277
3	Densenet121	0.118681	0.942246	1	0.943011	0.937968	0.940483
4	Inception net V3	0.18794	0.93262	0.998931	0.933405	0.929412	0.931404
5	Average ensemble of MobileNet and Densenet121	0.081067	0.975401	1	0.97957	0.974332	0.976944
6	Stacking ensemble of MobileNet and Densenet121	0.160313	0.966845	0.995722	0.96788	0.966845	0.967362
7	DenseNet	—	57%	—	—	—	—
8	Retraining final layer of MobileNet	0.019302	**0.993845**	1	—	—	—
9	Retraining final layer of InceptioNetV3	0.163023	0.952542	0.996923	—	—	—
10	Khan *et al.* [1]		0.985				
11	Maiya *et al.* [2]		0.9831				
12	Bansal *et al.* [3]		0.982				
13	Li *et al.* [4]		0.985				
14	Islam *et al.* [5]		0.983				

12.6 Research Gap and Future Works

Lack of a standardised dataset for malware image classification is the area of research that can be found to be lacking. Although the Malimg dataset, a frequently used benchmark dataset for malware classification, was employed in the majority of the articles, it comprises only a small number of malware families and might not accurately reflect the current threat environment. Additionally, there is a dearth of variety in the malware picture types used in these investigations. The majority of articles, for instance, concentrated on categorizing binary or gray-scale images of malware executables, despite the fact that malware can also take the form of images embedded in documents such as PDFs or Microsoft Office files. Additionally, there is a want for more comparison studies that assess the effectiveness of various approaches using multiple datasets, as well as studies that investigate the robustness of these approaches to adversarial attacks. Future work will look into testing the effectiveness of our models on a larger dataset of malware images that look at more families. Research will also be done into representing malware samples as colored images instead of gray-scale images.

12.7 Conclusion

In this paper, we proposed a novel approach to detect malware/benign software images using deep learning techniques. Our approach involved training a deep neural network on a publicly available dataset of malicious and benign programs to learn features that could distinguish between the two. We evaluated the performance of our approach using various metrics such as accuracy, precision, and recall and compared it with other state-of-the-art techniques. Our results showed that our approach achieved high accuracy in detecting malware/benign software images and outperformed other techniques in terms of detection speed and accuracy.

Our research is related to several areas of information security. First, our approach can be used to develop effective tools to detect malware/malware images, thus improving the security of computer systems. Second, our study highlights the importance of using large-scale datasets to train deep learning models in the domain of malware detection. Third, our research demonstrates the potential of deep learning techniques in detecting malware/benign software images, and future research can explore the use of advanced deep learning architectures to improve detection performance.

In conclusion, detection of malware/benign software images is a critical task for computer security, and our proposed approach provides an effective solution to this problem. We believe that our approach can be applied to a variety of real-world scenarios and can contribute to ongoing efforts to combat cybercrime.

References

1. Khan, M.U.K., Guan, S.-U., Fan, T.-F., Ting, H.C., Baig, Z.A., Malware image classification using convolutional neural networks with hybrid data augmentation techniques. *IEEE Access*, 9, 51128–51142, 2021.
2. Maiya, S.R. and Shetty, S., Malware classification using deep learning on binary and gray-scale images. *IEEE International Conference on Communication and Signal Processing (ICCSP)*, vol. 2020, pp. 0551–0556, 2020.
3. Bansal, K., Bansal, H., Sharma, S., Malware image classification using ensemble learning techniques. *11th International Conference on Cloud Computing*, vol. 2021, pp. 78–84, Data Science and Engineering Confluence, Noida, India, 2021.
4. Li, W., Yang, Y., Li, K., Malware classification using multi-view convolutional neural network. *11th International Conference on Intelligent Control, and Information Processing (ICICIP)*, vol. 2020, pp. 178–183, 2020.
5. Islam, M.T., Islam, M.M., Pathan, A.K., Malware Image Classification using Deep Learning with Data Augmentation. *2021 International Conference on Computer, Control, Electrical, and Electronics Engineering (ICCCEEE)*, vol. 2021, pp. 1–5, 2021.

13

Enhancing Decision-Making in Indian Legal Systems: Automating Document Analysis with Named Entity Recognition

Gaurav Pendharkar, Sukanya G. and Priyadarshini J.*

School of Computer Science and Engineering, Vellore Institute of Technology, Chennai, Tamil Nadu, India

Abstract

Most of the data in the legal industry are in the form of raw text documents, which finds its application in the domain of natural language processing. Based on region, there is a large variety of document formats and languages used for such documents. All legal documents have a plethora of information in them that can help in automating the process of delivering the judgments for a new case. Hence, using information extraction techniques, these useful data can be extracted from these legal documents. This paper aims to propose a named entity recognition model to extract legal entities, particularly sections, acts, and articles from Madras High Court judgment proceedings. To the best of our knowledge, there is no research work investigated for Madras High Court documents. Moreover, we fine-tune the pretrained model from SpaCy using the annotated data. Finally, the fine-tuned model achieves an *F* score of 72.20% and a precision of 83.90%. The legal entities predicted by the resultant model can be used to make legal predictions using machine learning and deep learning, information retrieval systems, and data engineering tasks.

***Keywords*:** Madras High Court, natural language processing, information extraction, legal entities, named entity recognition, domain adaptation

**Corresponding author*: priyadarshini.j@vit.ac.in

Kanak Kalita, J.V.N. Ramesh, M. Elangovan and S. Balamurugan (eds.) Decision-Making Techniques and Methods for Sustainable Technological Innovation: Strategies and Applications in Industry 5.0, (211–222) © 2025 Scrivener Publishing LLC

13.1 Introduction

The Indian legal system has a lot of unstructured legal data in document form including legal texts, contracts, court filings, and handwritten notes, making it difficult to analyze without employing natural language processing and optical character recognition technologies. Converting these documents into structured data is vital for efficient legal research and document management. This subdomain of applying natural language processing to the legal domain is referred to as LegalNLP. There is a lot of scope to apply LegalNLP to the Indian law system with the aim of reducing the workload of the judicial system. There are a lot of hurdles in applying LegalNLP to Indian law [1]. First, there are very few open-source data available such as the Indian Code, court judgments, and first information report (FIRs). Second, most of the content exists in the form of PDFs or HTML pages, which by itself cannot be interpreted by the machine. Therefore, before developing legal prediction systems, there is an acute need for automated information extraction from these data.

Information extraction is one of the tasks in natural language processing in which useful data are acquired from raw text data [2]. Named entity recognition (NER) is a task under information extraction that identifies and categorizes specific entities, such as names of people, places, organizations, and more, within a text or document [3]. With reference to the law, there are different legal entities such as judges, appellants, respondents, sections, acts, articles, and divisions [4]. However, the sections, acts, and articles play a pivotal role in judgment prediction. Therefore, in this paper, a domain-adapted NER model is developed to extract legal entities, particularly sections, acts, and articles. A wide variety of models were reviewed and tried; however, most of them misclassified the legal entities into other categories such as persons (PER), organizations (ORG), facilities (FAC), numbers (CARDINAL), and geopolitical entities (GPE) as shown in Figure 13.1. Among all the open-source models, the entity recognizer from SpaCy [5] was employed because it had an entity meant for LAW, and fine-tuning it would have been computationally efficient and require fewer samples for training.

The fundamental data science pipeline is incorporated to achieve this task through data collection, data annotation, modeling, and evaluation. Finally, the legal entities predicted by the fine-tuned model can be used to make legal predictions such as outcome forecasting, categorization, identification using machine learning, and preparing efficient information retrieval systems.

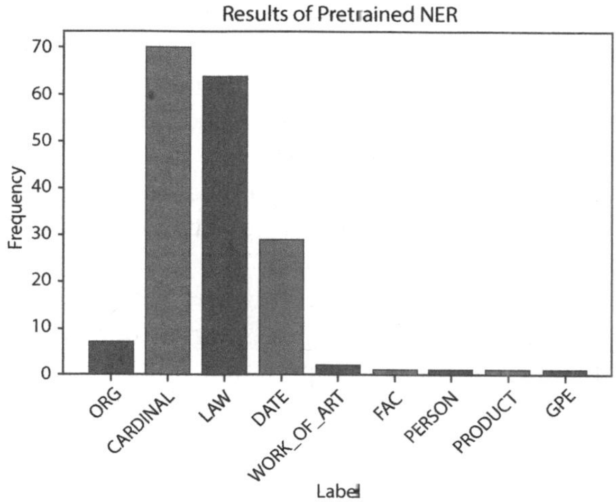

Figure 13.1 Results of pretrained named entity recognition (NER).

13.2 Related Work

Leitner *et al.* [6] developed a dataset from German legal decisions with 19 semantic classes across two annotation variations, namely, coarse-grained and fine-grained. In order to define the benchmark for the dataset, they experimented with conditional random fields and bidirectional long-short term memory networks (BiLSTMs). They achieved an *F* score of 95.46% for the fine-grained classes and an *F* score of 95.95% for the coarse-grained classes with BiLSTMs. The development of such a dataset supplements the lack of an annotated dataset for LegalNLP. Mastud and Jaiswal [7] discuss an approach to create a secondary dataset for Indian legal documents in the English language. They aimed at extracting many entities such as lawyers, courts, ordinances, laws, court decisions, and legal literature. Moreover, they experimented the open source named recognition models such as SpaCy, FlairNLP, Bert, AllenNLP, and NLTK. FlairNLP and AllenNLP both give accurate results for the task and also reduce search space by extracting the relevant entities. This can help in converting the unstructured data to structured form, particularly for legal entities.

Shelar *et al.* [8] explore the different open-source tools available across Java, Python, and Cython. For comparability of the results, the same training and testing data were used for all the models. They evaluated the models with reference to accuracy, *F* score, prediction time, and model size. They conclude that SpaCy performed the best across all the different frameworks such as OpenNLP, TensorFlow, and SpaCy. Skylaki *et al.* [9] propose a point generator network to overcome the challenges in extracting legal entities from noisy texts. They extract the text content from optical character recognition (OCR), and hence, the content extracted is erroneous. Therefore, they attempt to generate the legal entity rather than marking it in the raw text. They achieved a precision of 77.30%, an *F* score of 74.50%, and a recall of 71.8%. A model for situations with low annotated data is commendable in the legal domain.

Kalamkar *et al.* [10] created a new dataset with a corpus of 46,545 annotations across 14 legal entity types. They also developed a baseline performance for the corpus with a precision of 92%, a recall of 90.2%, and an *F* score of 91.1% using the Roberta-base transformer architecture. Additionally, they explore other models, namely, LegalBERT and InLegalBERT. The high performance of the transformers and a custom dataset for IndianNLP are appreciable. Surana *et al.* [11] designed a chatbot for crime awareness and registration using an NER model to extract useful content from complaints. They use a combination of classification and generative models for the chatbot. However, the NER model is used to extract location, time, and crime type from the unstructured complaints. They achieved the highest accuracy of 98% for address entity. Kumar *et al.* [12] leverage the named entity recognition model available in the open-source library, SpaCy. They aimed at crops and associated pests identification in the agricultural domain. Overall, they achieved an *F* score of 97.20%, which portrays a significant improvement compared to the actual queries.

13.3 Proposed Architecture

Figure 13.2 shows the architecture diagram for the proposed work. The fundamental components of a data science workflow are incorporated into the pipeline architecture. Initially, data are manually downloaded from the Manupatra Legal database* based on the required criteria. Following this, the Label Studio† interface is employed to manually annotate data for training and testing purposes. The data are split to train and test sets after the data annotation. The NER model available in SpaCy is fine-tuned to the Indian legal domain. Finally, the model is evaluated based on precision, recall, and *F* score using the test data.

---

*http://www.manupatra.in

†https://labelstud.io/guide/setup

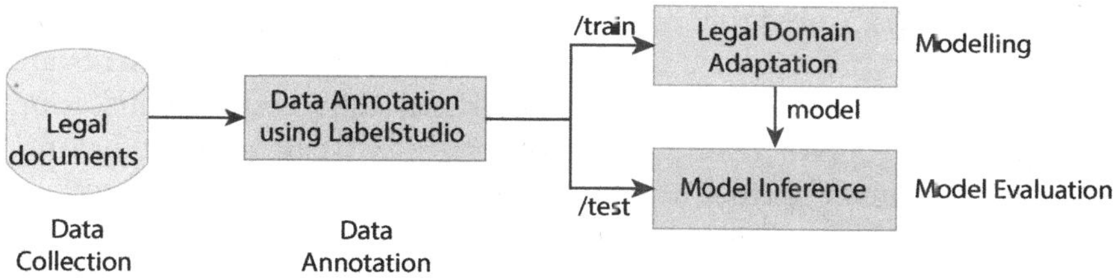

Figure 13.2 Architecture diagram.

13.4 Proposed Methodology

13.4.1 Data Collection

Data collection is the most preliminary stage in the data science pipeline where data are collected based on the problem statement. The data used for the task are collected from the Manupatra Legal database based on a

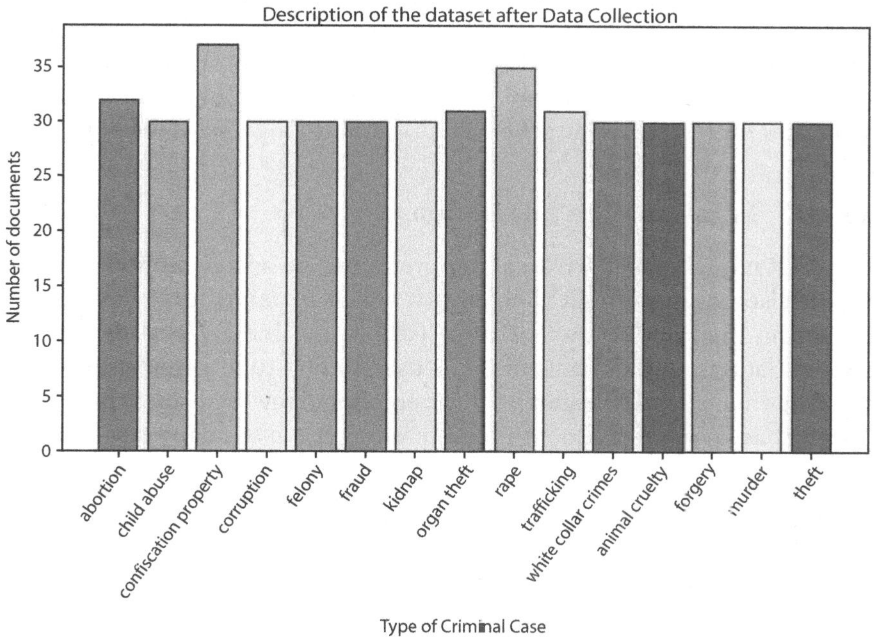

Figure 13.3 Dataset distribution.

few criteria. It is ensured that only Madras High Court criminal cases from the last 25 years are downloaded. After downloading, the documents are segregated into 15 categories, namely, abortion, child abuse, confiscation of property, corruption, felony, fraud, kidnap, organ theft, rape, trafficking, white-collar crimes, animal cruelty, forgery (https://www.manupatrafast.com/?t=desktop, https://labelstud.io/), murder, and theft cases. At the end of data collection, there are, on average, 30 documents in each of the categories. Finally, the dataset comprises 466 legal documents across the 15 categories, as shown in Figure 13.3.

13.4.2 Data Annotation

Data annotation is the process of developing the ground truth for the problem statement by manual labeling generally done by domain experts. In this problem, the focus is to identify the most important legal entities, namely, sections, acts, and articles. These entities are commonly cited in the legal documents in the format shown in Table 13.1. This format is used as a reference to label the required legal entities for the NER task using the Label Studio. For the train data, 1200 sentences are randomly sampled from all the documents. All the sentences are parsed and annotated from the document. Similarly, 400 sentences are sampled randomly and annotated for the test data. Overall, there are 1200 sentences for training data and 400 sentences for test data. The set of training and testing data is disjoint.

13.4.3 Legal Domain Adaptation

The NER model available in SpaCy is pretrained on a large number of entities. It also has an in-built "law" entity, which is trained on generic legal corpus and hence does not perform well on the Indian legal corpus. In such situations, domain adaptation is used to fine-tune a model to a particular domain, which requires data annotation. However, since the model already has knowledge about the legal entities, it can be adapted with fewer

Table 13.1 Common format of legal entities.

Legal entity	Expected pattern
Sections	Sections (numbers) of (reference)
Acts	(act-name)
Articles	Articles (numbers) of (reference)

Table 13.2 Hyperparameters for domain adaptation.

Parameter	Chosen value
Variant	en core web sm
Epochs	60
Start of compounding series	4
End of compounding series	32
Compounding factor	1.001
Dropout	0.5

training instances as well. Therefore, the SpaCy model is adapted based on the manually annotated data and then tested on another set of manually labeled data. The hyperparameters used for the domain adaptation process are shown in Table 13.2.

13.4.4 Evaluation Metrics

A deep learning evaluation metric is a quantifiable measure employed to gauge performance [13]. It is used to evaluate how well the model's predictions match the ground truth of the data used to train and test the model. For the task of legal NER, the traditional accuracy metric is not appropriate since there are too few legal entities cited in the document compared to the rest of the text. Hence, the most appropriate evaluation metrics are precision, recall, and F1 score as depicted in Equations 13.1, 13.2, and 13.3, respectively.

$$\text{Precision} = \frac{\text{TP}}{\text{TP} + \text{FP}} \tag{13.1}$$

$$\text{Recall} = \frac{TP}{TP + FN} \tag{13.2}$$

$$\text{F1 score} = \frac{2 * \text{Precision} * \text{recall}}{\text{Precision} + \text{recall}} = \frac{2 * \text{TP}}{2 * \text{TP} + \text{FP} + \text{FN}} \tag{13.3}$$

13.5 Results and Discussion

13.5.1 Token-Wise Comparison with Gold Standard

A gold standard is a set of annotations that are expected to be given to each token in the legal document. For model evaluation, each and every token needs to be manually labeled to ensure the correctness of the gold standard. For the manual annotation, Label Studio software is used. Named entity recognition is like a classification problem in which each token needs to be allotted the most relevant named entity. In order to evaluate such a problem, we require the true positives (TP), true negatives (TN), false positives (FP), and false negatives (FN) for the model's predictions. The model is evaluated using a set of five legal documents that were not a part of the domain adaptation. Each token in the model predictions and the gold standard is compared, resulting in the four parameters to determine the classification metrics. Based on the token-wise comparisons, the model predictions can be categorized into 4 categories: missing an entity, hypothesizing an entity, correctly marking an entity, and misidentifying the boundaries of the entity. An example for each of the categories is depicted in Tables 13.3, 13.4, 13.5, and 13.6, respectively.

Table 13.3 resembles the case of missing a legal entity. The main reason behind the missing entity is because of the imbalance in the frequency of occurrence of the three kinds of legal entities. In a legal document, generally, Sections occur more frequently compared to acts and articles, resulting in reflecting the imbalance in the predictions made by the model. Table 13.4 portrays an example of a case in which the model hypothesizes an entity. Hypothesizing an entity implies marking a nonlegal entity as a legal entity. This occurs because the model is fine-tuned using domain adaptation in which the base model can mark multiple legal entities such as judges, sections, acts, articles, and divisions. However, we require only sections, acts, and articles, but the knowledge of the base model also marks some entities that are required for our use case.

Table 13.5 depicts the case of the model correctly marking an entity, which is the expected behavior of the model. Table 13.5 portrays an example in which the model misidentifies the boundaries of the entity. This implies that it misidentifies the start of the entity and the end of the entity. In the example, it misidentifies the end of the entity. Similar to the reason for Table 13.4, state government is also a legal entity but not an entity required for the problem at hand. Based on the cases, we can deduce that the cases depicted in Table 13.3 contribute to FNs, in Table 13.4 contribute to FP, and in Table 13.5 contribute to TP. However, the last case depicted in

Table 13.3 Model misses an entity.

Gold standard		Model prediction	
Text	**Entity type**	**Text**	**Entity type**
Read	O[1]	Read	O
As	O	As	O
Under	O	Under	O
Article	LAW	Article	O
4	LAW	4	O

[1]Out of entity.

Table 13.4 Model hypothesizes an entity.

Gold standard		Model predictions	
Text	**Entity type**	**Text**	**Entity type**
Showing	O	Showing	O
Him	O	Him	O
As	O	As	O
The	O	The	O
Principal	O	Principal	LAW
Employer	O	Employer	LAW

Table 13.6 contributes to both TP and FP since the prediction encompasses the correct entity partially or fully. Hence, only the correctly marked entities will fall under TP, and other tokens will contribute to the FP.

13.5.2 Accuracy is an Unsuitable Metric

After computing the four parameters, namely, TP, FP, TN, and FN, it is observed that there are significantly higher TN compared to TP since only a few legal entities are cited in a legal document. This results in a very high value of accuracy that becomes a misleading metric for the efficiency of the model. The precision, recall, and *F* score are computed since they are independent of the TN.

Table 13.5 Model correctly marks an entity.

Gold standard		**Model predictions**	
Text	**Entity type**	**Text**	**Entity type**
Powers	O	Powers	O
Under	O	Under	O
Sections	LAW	Sections	LAW
397	LAW	397	LAW
And	LAW	And	LAW
398	LAW	398	LAW

Table 13.6 Model misidentifies the boundaries of an entity.

Gold standard		**Model predictions**	
Text	**Entity type**	**Text**	**Entity type**
Section	LAW	Section	LAW
3	LAW	3	LAW
By	O	By	LAW
State	O	State	LAW
Government	O	Government	LAW
Or	O	Or	O

$$\begin{aligned}\text{Accuracy} &= \frac{TP+TN}{TP+TN+FP+FN}\ (TN >> TP > FP \geq FN)\\ &= \frac{TP+TN}{TP+TN+FP+FN}\ (TP+TN \simeq TN)\\ &\simeq \frac{TN}{TP+TN+FP+FN}\ (TP+TN+FP+FN \simeq TN)\\ &\simeq \frac{TN}{TN}\\ &\simeq 1 \end{aligned} \tag{13.4}$$

Table 13.7 Evaluation metrics.

F score	0.7228
Precision	0.8390
Recall	0.6349

13.5.3 Performance of the Model

Using the token-wise comparison of the predicted entities and the expected gold standard, the TP, TN, FP, and FN were calculated, and the precision, recall, and *F* score were computed as depicted in Table 13.7. The accuracy of the model was not considered a useful metric since in a large text corpus only a few legal terminologies exist, resulting in the number of TN being significantly very high compared to the TP (i.e., $TN >> TP$), which will lead to a very high accuracy, which might be misleading.

13.5.4 Evaluation Metric Computed Value

The resultant model had higher precision and relatively low recall indicating that it predicted few legal entities, but most of them were correct. The availability of more annotated data might help the model recognize more patterns in the citation of section(s), act(s), and article(s), thereby improving its overall performance.

13.6 Conclusion

An NER model with an *F* score of approximately 72% is achieved. This model can be improved further to extract multiple other legal entities from Madras High Court legal documents. The resultant model would be limited to extracting legal entities, particularly section(s), act(s), and article(s), which can be used to make legal predictions using artificial intelligence and information retrieval systems to efficiently store legal documents in a document database, and for real-world data engineering tasks. Such applications of artificial intelligence in law can help automate the judicial system reducing human intervention considerably.

The unstructured legal documents have a lot of useful information in them, which is significantly important for developing machine learning–based legal prediction models. An information extraction pipeline will be developed to extract different kinds of information from the legal documents. Additionally, a dataset will be made available for legal prediction with associated state-of-the-art benchmarks.

References

1. Yada, K., Takama, Y., Mineshima, K., Satoh, K. (Eds.), Benchmarks for Indian Legal NLP: A Survey, in: *New Frontiers in Artificial Intelligence. JSAI-isAILecture Notes in Computer Science*, vol. 13856, Springer, Cham, 2021, https://doi.org/10.1007/978-3-031-36190-63.
2. Adnan, K. and Akbar, R., An analytical study of information extraction from unstructured and multidimensional big data. *J. Big Data*, 6, 1, 1–38, 2019.
3. Dozier, C., Kondadadi, R., Light, M., Vachher, A., Veeramachaneni, S., Wudali, R., Named entity recognition and resolution in legal text, in: *Semantic Processing Of Legal Texts, Lecture notes in computer science*, vol. 6036, E. Francesconi, S. Montemagni, W. Peters, D. Tiscornia (Eds.), Springer, Berlin, Heidelberg, 2010, https://doi.org/10.1007/978-3-642-12837-0 2.
4. Madan, M., Rani, A., Bhateja, N., A Systematic Study of Various Approaches and Problem Areas of Named Entity Recognition. *The International Conference on Recent Innovations in Computing*, Springer, pp. 545–558, 2023.
5. Honnibal, M., Montani I. spaCy 2: Natural language understanding with Bloom embeddings, convolutional neural networks and incremental parsing. 2017, 2020, https://sentometrics-research.com/publication/72/.
6. Leitner, E., Rehm, G., Moreno-Schneider, J., Fine-grained named entity recognition in legal documents, in: *International Conference on Semantic Systems*, pp. 272–287, Springer International Publishing, 2019 September.
7. Mastud, V. and Jaiswal, R., Named Entity Recognition on legal text for secondary dataset. *Int. Res. J. Eng. Technol. (IRJET)*, 7, 6, 6253–6256, 2020.
8. Shelar, H., Kaur, G., Heda, N., Agrawal, P., Named entity recognition approaches and their comparison for custom ner model. *Sci. Technol. Lib.*, 39, 3, 324–337, 2020.
9. Skylaki, S., Oskooei, A., Bari, O., Herger, N., Kriegman, Z., Named entity recognition in the legal domain using a pointer generator network, 2020, *arXiv preprint arXiv:2012.09936.*
10. Kalamkar, P., Agarwal, A., Tiwari, A., Gupta, S., Karn, S., Raghavan, V., Named entity recognition in Indian court judgments, 2022, *arXiv preprint arXiv:2211.03442.*
11. Surana, S., Chekkala, J., Bihani, P., Chatbot based crime registration and crime awareness system using a custom named entity recognition model for extracting information from complaints. *Int. Res. J. Eng. Technol. (IRJET)*, 8, 4, 3329–3336, 2021.
12. Kumar, M., Chaturvedi, K.K., Sharma, A., Arora, A., Farooqi, M.S., Lal, S.B., Ranjan, R., An algorithm for automatic text annotation for named entity recognition using spaCy framework, Research Square Platform LLC, 2023, DOI: 10.21203/rs.3.rs-2930333/v1. (Preprint).
13. Grandini, M., Bagli, E., Visani, G., Metrics for multi-class classification: An overview, 2020, *arXiv preprint arXiv:2008.05756.*

14

Classification of Indian Legal Judgment Documents Through Innovative Technology to Aid in Decision-Making

Ujjwal Pandey, Sukanya G. and Priyadarshini J.*

School of Computer Science and Engineering, Vellore Institute of Technology, Chennai, India

Abstract

Machine learning and deep learning techniques have revolutionized various fields such as art, science, math, and so on. However, these techniques have not been widely utilized in the legal domain, particularly in the Indian judiciary system, where most work is still done manually. In this study, we suggest a deep learning method for classifying the 18 categories established by the Supreme Court of India into which Indian court judgment documents fall. The approach outlined in this paper offers a more efficient way for legal professionals to classify and organize legal documents without the need for extensive manual review. Our approach uses a multichannel convolutional neural network (CNN) with multigram term frequency-inverse document frequency (TF-IDF) vectors as input and demonstrates superior performance compared to traditional machine learning and deep learning methods such as support vector machine, random forest, BERT, TextCNN, and so on in multilabel settings.

Keywords: Multilabel classification, machine learning, deep learning, Indian legal judgment documents, multichannel CNN, TF-IDF vectors

14.1 Introduction

In the Indian judicial system, a case presented by a plaintiff is divided into multiple categories enlisted by the Supreme Court of India. This

**Corresponding author*: priyadarshini.j@vit.ac.in

Kanak Kalita, J.V.N. Ramesh, M. Elangovan and S. Balamurugan (eds.) Decision-Making Techniques and Methods for Sustainable Technological Innovation: Strategies and Applications in Industry 5.0, (223–242) © 2025 Scrivener Publishing LLC

categorization is mostly done manually by legal experts by going through the judgment documents line by line. The categorization is important both for online legal information systems [1], as it provides easier indexing and search functionality, and for lawyers or legal students, as it gives them an idea of the area of judgment without having to read the whole document. However, the manual categorization process is tedious and time-consuming, especially for documents that are more than 100 pages long.

A simpler approach is to identify keywords and assign a category based on their presence in the document [2]. However, this method is not very consistent and accurate, and finding the right set of keywords is challenging, particularly in the legal domain where judgment documents are often lengthy. To improve performance, topic modeling techniques such as latent drichlet allocation (LDA) [3] or latent semantic analysis (LSA) [4] can be used to extract more meaningful keywords, but these methods are not as effective as advanced natural language processing techniques such as recurrent neural network/long short-term memory (RNN/LSTM) [5], convolutional neural network (CNN) [6], or hierarchical multilabel text classification [7], which can handle long text with ease but require a well-labeled and large dataset, which is difficult to obtain in the legal domain.

Despite the importance of this task and the challenges it presents, there has been little progress in the area of legal document classification, creating a significant research gap. One reason for this, particularly in the Indian legal context, is the lack of a properly labeled dataset for the task. Additionally, Indian judgment documents often contain regional statements that may be in languages other than English or have errors and poor formatting, making it difficult to extract text from the documents.

To overcome these challenges, this paper presents a unique approach to legal document classification using a multigram term frequency-inverse document frequency (TF-IDF) vector and a multichannel CNN. The approach is tested on a dataset collected from Manupatra (a large database of Indian judgment documents with labels categorized by legal experts) through web scraping [8]. The results of the experiment show that the suggested approach outperforms deep learning and traditional machine learning methods. The rest of the work is organized as follows: Section 14.2 discusses related works in the areas of legal document classification and text classification; Section 14.3 introduces the dataset and its collection methodology; and Section 14.4 provides the detailed architecture of the proposed model and the experimentation methodology. The findings of the experiment are discussed in Section 14.5, and the research article is concluded with a direction for our future work in Section 14.6.

14.2 Literature Survey

Most previous research on the Indian legal system has focused on summarizing judgments [9], predicting outcomes [10], or classifying legal propositions [11], rather than categorizing judgment documents into specific legal categories. However, these studies have provided insights into the processing of Indian legal judgment documents that have been applied in our experimentation. Other research that is similar to ours includes work on the foreign legal domain, such as Howe *et al.* (2019) [12], conducted a comparative study of text classifiers such as BERT, GLOVE, and LSA on Singapore Supreme Court judgments using a manually collected dataset. They found that LSA outperformed other models, followed by a CNN with GLOVE word embeddings, based on F1 score. Lei *et al.* (2017) [13] used various machine learning algorithms, including naive Bayes, K nearest neighbor (KNN), and support vector machine (SVM), to classify 6735 Chinese legal documents into 13 categories. To improve performance, the authors employed specific feature preprocessing techniques, such as word segmentation and custom stop words, as well as specific feature extraction using TF-IDF with dimensionality reduction. Using SVM, the authors achieved an F1 score of 87% in the single-label classification setting. However, the approach was not tested in a multilabel classification setting. More advanced natural language processing techniques have also been applied to categorizing legal documents. For example, Qiu *et al.* (2020) [14] proposed a multilabel text classification model (MLTCNN) that outperformed traditional machine learning algorithms on a manually collected dataset of legal judgment documents scanned using charge-coupled device and optical character recognition sensors. However, the approach by Bansal *et al.* (2019) [15], which used a hybrid deep learning model combining genetically modified CNN and bidirectional long short term memory (BiLSTM), was tested only in the single-label classification setting and achieved 82% accuracy on the Supreme Court Database corpus from Washington University School of Law, a benchmark dataset.

Although most of the research on classifying legal documents has used supervised learning approaches, unsupervised techniques have also been explored. For example, traditional multilabel text classification algorithms, according to Prajapati and Thakkar (2022) [16], are not well suited to large label spaces. As a result, they suggest a k-way tree–based extreme multilabel classifier that uses a clustering-based method to address correlations between the feature and label spaces. The classifier demonstrates superior performance compared to embedding-based approaches on various benchmark datasets.

In summary, previous research on categorizing legal documents has largely been conducted in the foreign legal domain and has often focused on single-label classification or used benchmark datasets. In contrast, our work addresses these limitations by providing a multilabel approach on an open-world dataset collected from an Indian legal database. Table 14.1 provides a summary of the previous work discussed in this section with respect to the best-performing algorithm as per the paper.

Table 14.1 Comparison of literature survey.

Paper	Algorithm	Setting	Dataset	Performance
Howe *et al.* [12]	LSA	Single and multilabel	Manually collected Singapore legal document	63.2% F1 score
Lei *et al.* [13]	SVM	Single label	6735 Manually collected Chinese legal documents	87% F1 score
Qiu *et al.* [14]	Convolutional neural network	Multilabel	Manual Chinese dataset	98.84% F1 score
Bansal *et al.* [15]	CNN with genetic algorithm and BiLSTM	Single label	English Benchmark Dataset of Supreme Court Database (SCDB) corpus	82% Accuracy
Prajapati and Thakka [16]	K-way tree–based eXtreme multilabel classifier (KTXMLC)	Multilabel	Benchmark datasets	93.95% Precision on AmazonCat-13 K dataset

14.3 Dataset

The focus of this section is the dataset that was used for our experimentation. We provide a comprehensive overview of the data, starting with the collection methodology and continuing with the preprocessing techniques applied to the raw data. Finally, we conducted an exploratory analysis to gain insights into the characteristics and trends within the dataset through the use of various graphical and statistical techniques such as charts, graphs, and word clouds.

14.3.1 Collection Methodology

The dataset for this research was collected from Manupatra, an online Indian legal database that contains case documents annotated by legal experts. These documents are available on the website and can be downloaded as PDF or document files using the search function. The categories of these documents are specified on the Manupatra website but are not included in the PDF files. Instead, they had to be extracted separately using a Selenium script, which stored the labels as comma-separated values in a separate text file with the same name as the judgment document. The judgment document was then downloaded in PDF format, and the text was extracted using Apache PDFBox,[1] an open-source Java library. The extracted text and labels were merged to create a CSV file containing raw, unprocessed data. The process of collecting the dataset is shown in Figure 14.1.

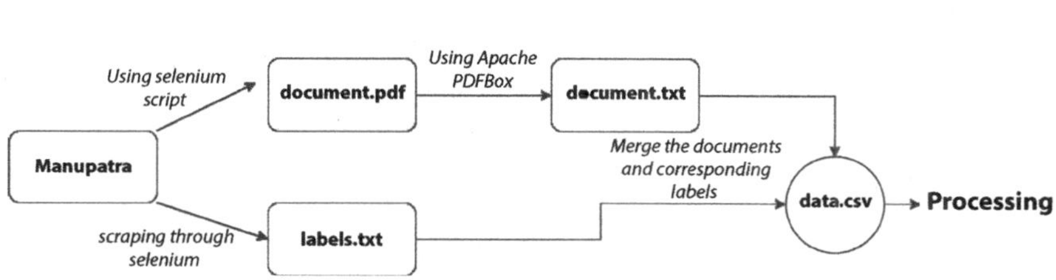

Figure 14.1 Dataset preparation flow diagram.

14.3.2 Preprocessing

As the judgment text in the raw data may be large, preprocessing is a crucial but time-consuming step. Additionally, for the classification task, not all words contribute equally, so it is always best to reduce the size of the text and retain only the most meaningful words. This can help to reduce the length of the text and speed up the training of the model. The textual data were preprocessed using the following techniques:

- Removal of metadata such as links and website references about the document. For more information on Apache PDFBox, see the Apache PDFBox website.
- Conversion of the judgment text to lowercase.
- Removal of digits, punctuation, and extra spaces.
- Stop words removal based on both English stop words defined by the Python package "spacy" and custom stop words (as per Table 14.2).
- Word lemmatization to transform the words to their base form.

Table 14.2 List of custom stop words used in the preprocessing.

Court	Case	Date	Act
Section	Order	Prove	Evidence
Cast	Suit	Suite	Counsel
Writ	Petition	Appellant	Respondent
Accused	Proof	Sought	Thought
Appeal	Say	Complaint	State
Petitioner	Date	Judgment	Accuse
Person	Defendant	Application	Allegation
File	Honble	High	Supreme
Article	Shall	Client	Plaintiff
Smt	Smriti	Mr	Ms
Bail	Police	Officer	Singh

14.3.3 Exploratory Analysis

In this section, we present the length of the dataset per category as it varies in both settings. We have collected 4425 judgment documents with 18 categories. Each judgment document falls into no more than 2 categories. However, the distribution is somewhat imbalanced with respect to each category. Based on the labels found in each document, Table 14.3 displays how the documents in the multilabel dataset are distributed. Figure 14.2 illustrates that the majority of documents in our dataset are pretty lengthy, with a text length ranging from 10,000 to 100,000 characters.

Table 14.3 Count of each label in the multilabel dataset.

Label	Count
Municipal tax	101
Cyber laws	101
Human rights	114
Civil	127
Motor vehicles	247
Environment	264
Family	282
Insurance	289
Consumer	307
Narcotics	311
Media and communication	333
Election	347
Service	360
Defense	395
Education	479
Commercial	534
Constitution	610
Criminal	750

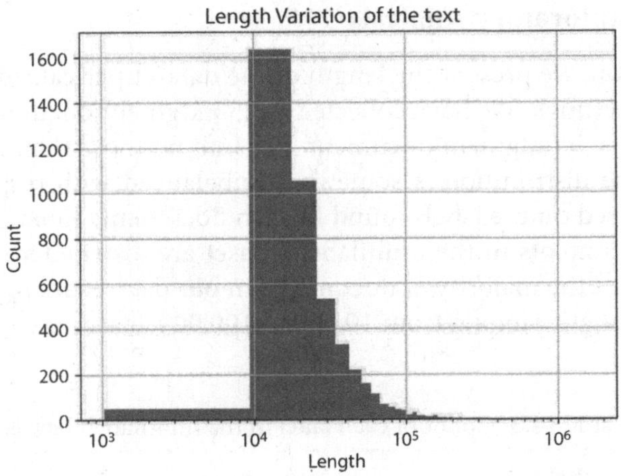

Figure 14.2 Variation of text length for all documents.

14.4 Proposed Methodology and Experimentation

This section presents our approach to Indian legal judgment document classification in detail. We start off by discussing the system architecture in Section 14.4.1 followed by the experimentation procedure where we discuss the implementation of both our approach and preexisting methods in Section 14.4.2.

14.4.1 System Architecture

To prepare the preprocessed dataset for experimentation with a PyTorch model, we converted it into a PyTorch DataLoader as shown in Figure 14.3. The dataset was split into three sets for training, validation, and testing, in a 60:20:20 ratio. This split was performed prior to generating features in order to prevent any data leakage between the training, validation, and testing sets. The text feature from each set was then divided into three n-gram features, namely, unigrams, bigrams, and trigrams, using an n-gram pipeline. The n-gram pipeline is unique to our approach, and later we will see that using this pipeline gives more context for classification when we feed it as input to multichannel CNN. These features were then vectorized using TF-IDF vectorization, a method for representing the importance of a term in a document by weighing the term frequency in the document against the frequency of the term in a larger corpus of documents. The TF-IDF formula is as follows:

$$\text{TF}-\text{IDF}(t,d)=\text{TF}(t,d)\cdot\text{IDF}(t)$$

where:

1. TF(t,d) is the term frequency of term t in document d. This can be computed by dividing the total number of terms in document d by the frequency with which term t appears in document d.
2. IDF(t) is the inverse document frequency of term t. This can be calculated as the number of documents that contain the term t divided by the total number of documents/texts in the corpus.

The resulting TF-IDF weight represents how significant the word is to the corpus' documentation. The higher the weight, the more important the word is to the document. Finally, the resulting features from each set (training, validation, and testing) were transformed into tensors and loaded into a PyTorch DataLoader, which was used for experimentation with a PyTorch model. PyTorch DataLoader offers flexibility in terms of loading custom-made data as such in our case where we pack multi–n-gram as input; hence, we used PyTorch for this experimentation.

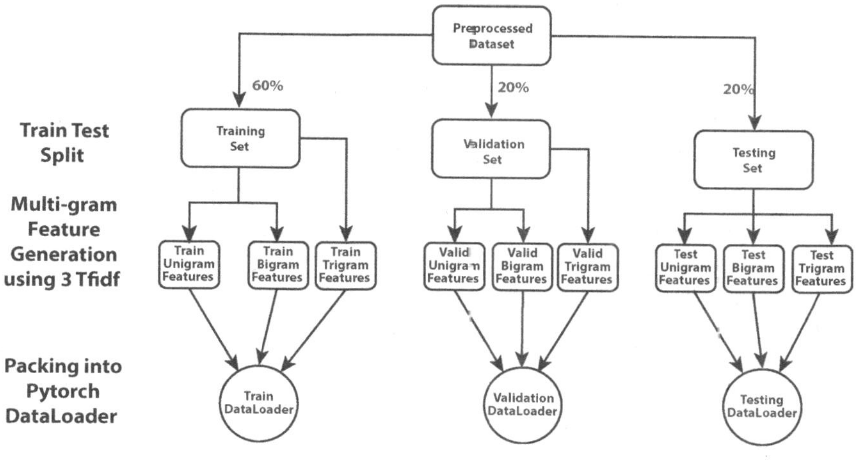

Figure 14.3 Preparation of the dataset to multigram feature.

We used three separate channels for each n-gram of TF-IDF in order to allow the CNN to extract more meaningful features separately. This approach can provide the model with additional context about the input data and can be beneficial for our classification task, as demonstrated in Section 14.5, where the model achieves very high precision as compared to other approaches. We chose not to include higher-order n-grams such as quadgrams or pentagrams in the model due to their negative impact on performance and the added complexity they introduce to the data. In addition, using higher-order n-grams on long documents can often result in more noise than informative features.

By using a CNN on TF-IDF vectors, we can take advantage of the CNN's ability to identify patterns in the data and the ability of the TF-IDF vectors to represent text data numerically. This can help CNN learn to identify important patterns in the text data that may not be apparent when examining the raw text. In our classification task, we have three channels in the form of unigrams, bigrams, and trigrams. A multichannel CNN has multiple channels in each convolutional layer, with each channel representing a different feature representation of the input data. By using a multichannel CNN in this scenario, we can enable the model to learn more discriminative features by processing and combining the different channels separately.

The model architecture is illustrated in Figure 14.4. The input data, whether they be for training, validation, or testing, are passed through a convolution layer that is specific to each channel. The output of the convolution layer is then batch-normalized to increase the model's generalization and stability as well as speed up training. A pooling layer is then used

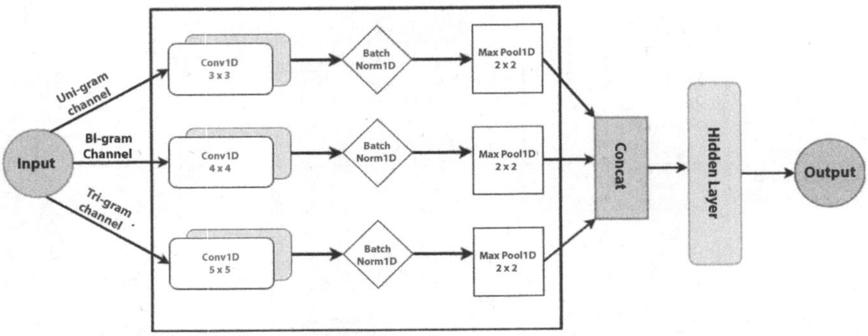

Figure 14.4 Model architecture.

to downsample the spatial dimensions of the convoluted features. These operations, which constitute the feature extraction part of the model, are performed in 1D as the input data consist of a sequence of text. Each channel's outputs are then combined into a single, substantial vector and supplied into a hidden layer, which discovers the connections between the input features in order to predict. The type of output (e.g., single-label or multilabel) can be changed by changing the output layer and also training the model with a suitable loss function for the desired task.

14.4.2 Experimentation

This section presents the experimentation performed to compare the performance of various baseline models with our approach. As shown in Figure 14.3, the n-gram features are packed into Train DataLoader. PyTorch packs the data as a tuple of (features, labels). Since the label corresponding to unigram, bigram, or trigram is the same, we can use any of the labels as Y. The input, i.e., X, is prepared as a list of each n-gram feature and fed to the model for a forward pass (Figure 14.4). We then compute the loss and perform the optimization step followed by the calculation of any performance metrics. The hyperparameters and system specifications used to train the model are shown in Appendix A.2.

To compare our approach with baselines, we used various machine learning algorithms such as SVM, naive Bayes, logistic regression, random forests, and artificial neural network (ANN). More advanced models such as TextCNN and DistillBERT were also used. We did not use the base BERT model because it performed very poorly as compared to DistillBERT [17], which is a distilled version of BERT with 40% fewer parameters as compared to the original BERT and hence trains much faster than the original BERT. We used two types of TextCNN for comparison. The first version of TextCNN was trained on word embeddings generated from Law2Vec [18], which is a 100-dimensional pretrained embedding on legal documents. The other version of TextCNN was built using a self-trained word embedding of similar 100 dimensions on our original dataset. The implementation of the TextCNN was mostly kept the same as specified in the original paper [6]. The training and validation loss curve for the deep learning model can be seen in Figure 14 5.

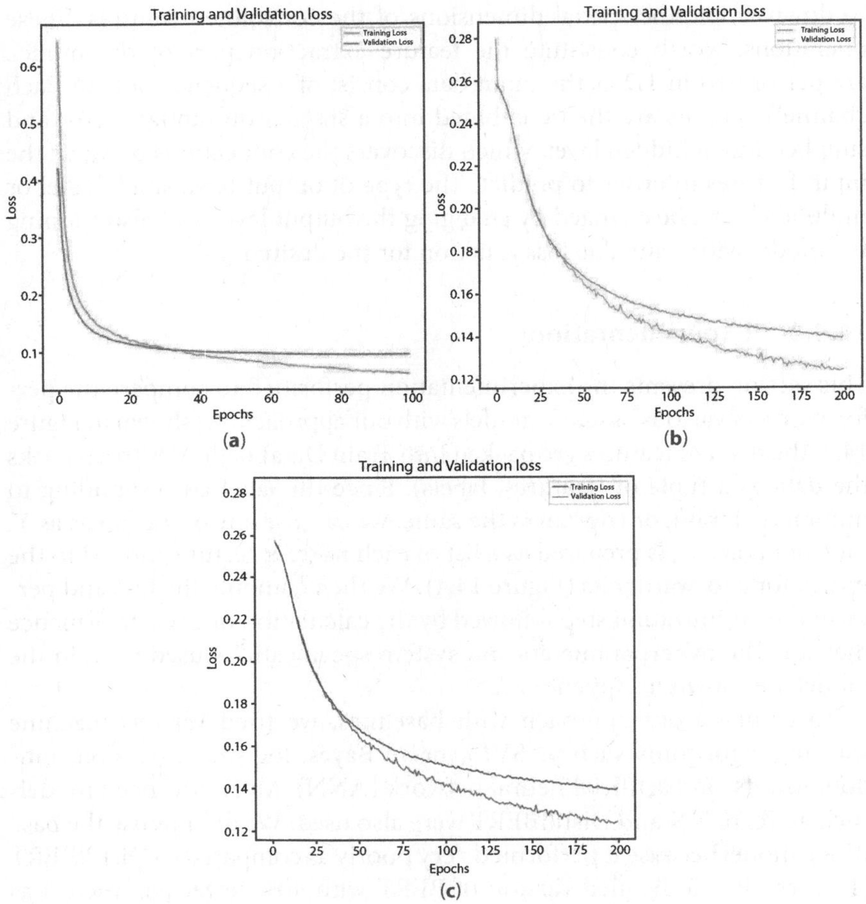

Figure 14.5 Training loss curves of multigram CNN, Law2Vec CNN, and trained embedding Text CNN.

14.5 Evaluation

In multilabel classification, a sample (e.g., a text) can belong to multiple categories, represented by a set of all categories *S*. For a particular sample *T*, it may only contain a subset of categories *U*, where $U \subseteq S$. When a model makes a prediction, it will assign a set of predicted categories *V* to the sample. When using single-label classification in its conventional form, accuracy is used to assess the model's effectiveness by contrasting the anticipated label with the actual label. Yet, with multilabel classification, it is possible that the projected set of categories *V* is only a subset of the true set of categories U rather than being an exact match. Hence, other metrics such as precision, recall, and F1 score are generally preferred.

$$\text{Precision} = \frac{|U \cap V|}{|V|}$$

$$\text{Recall} = \frac{|U \cap V|}{|V|}$$

$$\text{F1 score} = (2 \times \text{precision} \times \text{recall})/(\text{precision} + \text{recall})$$

Evaluation of the models to assess the effectiveness of a multilabel classification has been done on the basis of precision, recall, and F1 score, and the values are listed in Tables 14.4, 14.5, and 14.6 for all models. Also in multilabel classification, where a sample can belong to multiple classes, there are different ways to calculate precision, recall, and F1 score, which has also been demonstrated in all evaluation metrics.

1. **Macro averaging:** Precision, recall, and F1 score are independently determined for each label prior to taking the average of all labels in macro averaging.
2. **Micro averaging:** Precision, recall, and F1 score are computed from the sums of all true positives, false positives, and false negatives across all labels in micro averaging.
3. **Weighted averaging:** When a dataset is averaged over all labels using weighted averaging, each label is given a weight based on the number of true instances of that label present in the dataset after precision, recall, and F1 score are independently determined for each label.

14.5.1 Precision

Our proposed approach performed exceptionally well on the precision metric, consistently outperforming all machine-learning baselines (SVM, LR, and naive Bayes) across all levels of macro, micro, and weighted averaging. In contrast, deep learning models outperformed machine learning models generally, with TextCNN trained on Law2Vec embeddings producing outcomes that were comparable to our method on a micro averaging scale. It is important to note that due to the imbalanced nature of our dataset, macro averaging may not be an appropriate metric to evaluate performance, and micro or weighted averaging should be considered instead. One of the most striking observations from our results was the poor performance of DistillBERT among all deep learning methods. This could be attributed to a variety of reasons, but we believe that the model was unable to effectively capture the nuances of legal language or the unique characteristics of our dataset.

Table 14.4 Precision comparison for different models (micro, macro, weighted).

	Precision		
Model	**Micro**	**Macro**	**Weighted**
Support vector machine (SVM)	0.63	0.61	0.70
Logistic regression (LR)	0.37	0.32	0.51
Naive Bayes classifier (NB)	**0.07**	**0.05**	**0.20**
Random forest classifier	0.59	0.57	0.70
Multilayer perceptron (MLP)	0.91	0.86	**0.91**
DistillBERT (FineTuned)	0.08	0.08	0.10
TextCNN with Law2Vec embeddings	**0.93**	0.77	0.88
TextCNN with trained embeddings	0.90	0.83	0.87
Our approach (MGMC-CNN)	**0.93**	**0.89**	**0.91**

14.5.2 Recall

Our results indicate that many of the models that performed well on the precision metric did not perform as well on the recall metric. DistillBERT had the highest recall across all averaging scales, whereas TextCNN performed poorly. Given that our dataset was imbalanced, this may have contributed to the poor recall of deep learning models. Furthermore, it should be highlighted that there is a trade-off between recall and precision and that optimizing for one metric can result in subpar performance on the other. Our proposed approach had an average recall of 0.69 on the micro averaging level.

Table 14.5 Recall comparison for different models (micro, macro, weighted).

	Recall		
Model	**Micro**	**Macro**	**Weighted**
Support vector machine (SVM)	0.92	0.85	0.92
Logistic regression (LR)	0.96	0.80	0.96
Naive Bayes classifier (NB)	0.97	0.38	0.97
Random forest classifier	0.92	0.81	0.92
Multilayer perceptron (MLP)	0.61	0.59	0.67
DistillBERT (FineTuned)	**0.98**	**0.95**	**0.98**
TextCNN with Law2Vec embeddings	**0.47**	**0.42**	**0.47**
TextCNN with trained embeddings	0.63	0.61	0.63
Our approach (MGMC-CNN)	0.69	0.64	0.69

14.5.3 F1 Score

Our proposed approach achieved superior performance compared to other models on both micro and macro averaging scales in the recall, with scores of 0.79 and 0.72 respectively. The most striking observation from our results is that the SVM performed better than all deep learning models on the weighted metric scale, with a score of 0.79. This is explained by the fact that the weighted averaging technique favors the performance of SVM on our dataset by giving more weight to classes with more instances in the dataset.

Table 14.6 F1 score comparison for different models (micro, macro, weighted).

	F1 score		
Model	**Micro**	**Macro**	**Weighted**
Support vector machine (SVM)	0.75	0.69	**0.79**
Logistic regression (LR)	0.53	0.42	0.65
Naive Bayes (NB)	0.13	0.08	0.32
Random forest classifier	0.72	0.65	0.78
Multilayer perceptron (MLP)	0.73	0.68	0.77
DistillBERT (FineTuned)	**0.15**	**0.14**	**0.18**
TextCNN with Law2Vec embeddings	0.62	0.52	0.57
TextCNN with trained embeddings	0.74	0.69	0.71
Our approach (MGMC-CNN)	**0.79**	**0.72**	0.77

14.6 Conclusion and Future Work

In this paper, we suggested a strategy for multilabel text classification in the legal domain utilizing TF-IDF vectors that is multigram multichannel CNN. Our test results demonstrated that our CNN method on TF-IDF performed better than the majority of machine learning and deep learning methods. Additionally, our approach required fewer training epochs and was faster and more efficient, particularly when working with limited and imbalanced data. Future work in this area includes several promising avenues. We intend to expand the dataset by incorporating more legal documents from various do mains and jurisdictions to improve the generalization of the model. We also intend to assess the performance of additional pretrained language models, such as RoBERTa, and contrast it with our strategy. Furthermore, we will investigate the use of dimensionality reduction techniques, such as support vector decomposition (SVD), to decrease the TF-IDF vectors' dimension and make it expandable to larger datasets. Additionally, we aim to extend our approach to multilingual classification by training models in multiple languages. Our ultimate goal is to enhance the model's performance and make it more robust for real-world applications.

References

1. Bhardwaj, R.K. and Madhusudan, M., Online legal information system (OLIS) leveraging access to legal information resources in indian environment. *DESIDOC J. Lib. Inf. Technol.*, 36, 1, 47–55, 2016.
2. McCallum, K.N., Text classification by bootstrapping with key-words, em and shrinkage. *Unsupervised learning in natural language processing*, 1999.
3. Hingmire, S., Chougule, S., Palshikar, G.K., Chakraborti, S., Document classification by topic labeling, in: *Proceedings of the 36th International ACM SIGIR Conference on Research and Development in Information Retrieval*, pp. 877–880, 2013.
4. Mohamed, R. and Watada, J., An evidential reasoning based LSA approach to document classification for knowledge acquisition, in: *2010 IEEE International Conference on Industrial Engineering and Engineering Management*, IEEE, pp. 1092–1096, 2010.
5. Yan, Y., Wang, Y., Gao, W.-C., Zhang, B.-W., Yang, C., Yin, X.-C., LSTM: Multi-label ranking for document classification. *Neural Process. Lett.*, 47, 1, 117–138, 2018.
6. Yoon, K., Convolutional neural networks for sentence classification [ol], 2014, *arXiv Preprint*.

7. Huang, W., Chen, E., Liu, Q., Chen, Y., Huang, Z., Liu, Y., Zhao, Z., Zhang, D., Wang, S., Hierarchical multi-label text classification: An attention-based recurrent network approach, in: *Proceedings of the 28th ACM International Conference on Information and Knowledge Management*, pp. 1051–1060, 2019.
8. Singh, S., Web scraping using selenium. *International J. Novel Res. Dev. (IJNRD)*, 7, 1, 119–124, 2022.
9. Bhattacharya, P., Hiware, K., Rajgaria, S., Pochhi, N., Ghosh, K., Ghosh, S., A comparative study of summarization algorithms applied to legal case judgments, in: *European Conference on Information Retrieval*, Cologne, Germany, April 14–18, 2019, Springer, pp. 413–428, 2019.
10. Malik, V., Sanjay, R., Nigam, S.K., Ghosh, K., Guha, S.K., Bhat- tacharya, A., Modi, A., ILDC for CJPE: Indian legal documents corpus for court judgment prediction and explanation, 2021, *arXiv preprint arXiv:2105.13562.*
11. Ramrakhiyani, N., Pawar, S., Palshikar, G.K., A system for classification of propositions of the Indian supreme court judgements, in: *Post-Proceedings of the 4th and 5th Workshops of the Forum for Information Retrieval Evaluation*, pp. 1–4, 2013.
12. Howe, J.S.T., Khang, L.H., Chai, I.E., Legal area classification: A comparative study of text classifiers on Singapore supreme court judgments, 2019, *arXiv preprint arXiv:1904.06470.*
13. Lei, M., Ge, J., Li, Z., Li, C., Zhou, Y., Zhou, X., Luo, B., Automatically classify Chinese judgment documents utilizing machine learning algorithms. *International Conference on Database Systems for Advanced Applications*, pp. 3–17, Springer, 2017.
14. Qiu, M., Zhang, Y., Ma, T., Wu, Q., Jin, F., Convolutional-neural-network-based multilabel text classification for automatic discrimination of legal documents. *Sens. Mater.*, 32, 8, 2659–2672, 2020.
15. Bansal, N., Sharma, A., Singh, R., An evolving hybrid deep learning framework for legal document classification. *Ingènierie Des. Systèmes d'Information*, 24, 4, 425–431, 2019.
16. Prajapati, P. and Thakkar, A., Performance improvement of extreme multi-label classification using k-way tree construction with parallel clustering algorithm. *J. King Saud Univ. Comput. Inf. Sci.*, 34, 8, 6354–6364, 2022.
17. Sanh, V., Debut, L., Chaumond, J., Wolf, T., Distilbert, a distilled version of bert: smaller, faster, cheaper and lighter, 2019, *arXiv preprint arXiv:1910.01108.*
18. Chalkidis, D.K., Deep learning in law: early adaptation and legal word embeddings trained on large corpora. *Artif. Intell. Law*, 27, 2, 171–198, 2019.

Appendix A. System Specifications and Hyperparameters

Following are the specifications used for the experimentation along with hyperparameters of the model.

Appendix A.1. System specifications

- Operating system: Ubuntu 20.04 LTS
- Processor: Intel Core i5-9300H
- RAM: 16 GB DDR4
- GPU: NVIDIA GeForce GTX 1050 4 Gb
- Python version: 3.8
- PyTorch version: 1.7
- Tensorflow version: 2.4

Appendix A.2. Hyperparameters

Note: SGD means stochastic gradient descent with 0.9 Nestrov momentum, and 1e-3 weight decay means the given parameter is not relevant to the model or is set to auto.

Table A.2 Hyperparameters.

Model	Optimizer	Learning rate	Batch size	Epochs
SVM	rbf kernel	0.01	—	—
Logistic regression	lbfgs solver	—	—	100
Naive Bayes	—	—	—	—
Random forest	—	—	—	—
Multilayer perceptron	Adam	0.001	auto	150
DistillBERT	SGD	0.0001	16	5
TextCNN (Law2Vec)	SGD	0.01	16	200
TextCNN (trained embeddings)	SGD	0.01	16	200
Our approach (MGMC-CNN)	SGD	0.001	32	100

15

Revolutionizing Recruitment in Industry 5.0: An Efficient AI and Machine Learning–Based Applicant Tracking System

Shola Usharani*, Gayathri Rajakumaran, Priyadarshini Jayaraju and Anuttam Anand

Vellore Institute of Technology, School of Computer Science and Engineering, Chennai, India

Abstract

The utilization of technology within the recruitment sector has experienced a notable surge in recent times, resulting in substantial modifications to the methods by which entities entice, screen, and integrate personnel. The proposed work presents a comprehensive analysis of various technological tools employed in the recruitment process, such as applicant tracking systems, artificial intelligence, and video interviews. This also investigates the advantages of technology in the recruitment process, such as enhanced productivity and decreased partiality, as well as the obstacles linked to its implementation, such as the likelihood of partiality and legal and ethical concerns. It also examines nascent patterns and advancements in recruitment technology and provides suggestions for prospective investigations. This article underscores the capacity of technology to revolutionize the recruitment sector and provides perspectives on how enterprises can effectively manage the possibilities and obstacles that arise from technological advancements in recruitment. The outcome of proposed study indicates that technology possesses the capability to enhance the efficacy, impartiality, and potency of the recruitment procedure. It also streamlines the necessity for entities to meticulously assess and opt for technological remedies, while also guaranteeing their employment in a principled and conscientious fashion.

**Corresponding author*: sholausha.rani@vit.ac.in

Kanak Kalita, J.V.N. Ramesh, M. Elangovan and S. Balamurugan (eds.) Decision-Making Techniques and Methods for Sustainable Technological Innovation: Strategies and Applications in Industry 5.0, (243–264) © 2025 Scrivener Publishing LLC

***Keywords*:** Hiring, application tracking systems, assessments, artificial intelligence, time to hire, human resource (HR), candidate, jobs

15.1 Introduction and Technical Background

In recent years, the hiring industry has experienced substantial transformation, with technology's growing utilization playing a pivotal role in this evolution. The advent of technology has facilitated novel and diverse methods for organizations to entice, screen, and integrate personnel, ranging from applicant tracking systems (ATSs) to artificial intelligence (AI) and video interviews.

The objective of this scholarly article is to present a comprehensive analysis of the various forms of technology employed in the recruitment process. It aims to scrutinize the advantages and drawbacks of technology implementation, investigate the latest developments and trends, and suggest potential areas for further investigation. The objective of this paper is to elucidate the influence of technology on the recruitment sector and to offer perspectives on how enterprises can effectively manage the advantages and obstacles posed by technological advancements in recruitment.

The article commences by furnishing a succinct overview of the recruitment sector and the escalating adoption of technological advancements. The subsequent section of the paper outlines a set of research inquiries that will serve as the analytical framework. Among these queries is the following: What are the distinct categories of technology that are employed in the recruitment process? What are the advantages and drawbacks that come with the implementation of technology in the recruitment process? What are the current developments and advancements in recruitment technology? What are the potential consequences of technological advancements on the hiring industry's future?

The study utilizes an extensive review of scholarly publications, books, and credible online resources, in addition to consultations with human resource (HR) experts and recruiters who possess expertise in the implementation of technology for recruitment purposes. Through the integration of various sources, the present study presents a thorough analysis of the contemporary technological landscape within the recruitment sector. Moreover, it provides valuable perspectives on the prospective impact of technology in revolutionizing the processes of talent acquisition, screening, and assimilation within organizations.

15.1.1 The Impact of Technology on the Hiring Process

The utilization of technology has had a notable influence on the recruitment process, leading to a transformation in the manner in which organizations seek and select potential employees. In the past, employers would engage in a manual review of résumés, conduct interviews, advertise job opportunities on job boards or in classified ads, and subsequently make hiring decisions based on subjective assessments [1]. The advancement of technology has led to enhancements in the hiring process, particularly in terms of efficiency, cost-effectiveness, and precision.

One of the significant impacts of technology on the recruitment process is its ability to expand the reach of potential candidates [2]. Currently, it is possible to disseminate job vacancies through diverse online platforms, including job boards, social media networks, and corporate webpages. By expanding their reach to a larger pool of potential candidates, enterprises can increase their applicant pool and reduce the duration of the hiring process. Digital job postings are comparatively more cost-effective than traditional print or classified advertisements, thereby enabling organizations to reduce their recruitment expenses.

The utilization of technology in the employment process provides the benefit of expeditious applicant screening. The utilization of software that can scan résumés and applications for specific keywords and qualities can facilitate employers in identifying the most appropriate candidates for employment [3]. By minimizing the duration and resources allocated to screening applications, recruiters can allocate their efforts toward more challenging tasks such as applicant engagement and conducting interviews [4].

The utilization of technology has resulted in an enhancement of the effectiveness of candidate screening. Recruitment software utilizes AI algorithms to analyze résumés and align them with job descriptions. The implementation of a rigorous screening process guarantees that solely the most competent candidates progress in the recruitment procedure, thereby mitigating any potential biases in the recruitment process [5]. Moreover, recruiters now have the capability to conduct pre-employment assessments and skill evaluations through online platforms, thereby enhancing the accuracy of candidate screening.

15.1.2 AI and Machine Learning in Hiring

The hiring process has been revolutionized by AI and machine learning (ML), which automate numerous recruitment activities and offer insights into candidate data that are challenging for humans to recognize [6]. Companies may streamline the hiring process, lessen bias, and make better hiring judgements by utilizing AI and ML in the hiring process.

Chatbots are one way that AI and ML are applied to the employment process. Artificial intelligence-based programs known as chatbots may converse with applicants, respond to inquiries, and even perform preliminary screenings. A high frequency of candidate interactions can be quickly handled by chatbots, giving candidates a flawless recruitment process while lightening the effort of recruiters.

Predictive analytics is another way that AI and ML are applied to employment. Predictive analytics analyzes candidate data, including résumés, applications, and online activity, using ML algorithms to spot trends and forecast that applicants would perform best in a given position. By offering data-driven insights into the applicant pool, this technology can assist recruiters in making more educated recruiting decisions.

Furthermore, bias in the hiring process can be lessened with the aid of AI and ML. By deleting demographic data from résumés and applications—such as gender, age, and race—recruitment algorithms can eliminate human prejudices [7]. This makes it possible to make sure that applicants are judged entirely on their skills and qualifications, rather than their personality traits.

Furthermore, pre-employment evaluations and skills testing can be carried out using AI and ML. Employers can use these tests to find candidates who have the required knowledge and experience by customizing them to the job's criteria. Recruiters may evaluate candidates fast and accurately using AI-based assessments, cutting down on the time and expense of hiring.

15.1.3 Social Media and Hiring

The utilization of social media as a means for recruiters to procure and evaluate potential candidates has experienced a notable surge in popularity. Social media platforms, namely, LinkedIn, Twitter, and Facebook, offer recruiters a plethora of data pertaining to potential candidates, encompassing their professional background, academic qualifications, competencies, and personal preferences [8]. The utilization of social media in the recruitment process can facilitate the expansion of the candidate pool, provide valuable insights into candidate behavior, and foster the development of more robust relationships between recruiters and candidates.

The capacity to access a broader demographic is among the most notable advantages of utilizing social media for recruitment purposes. Social media platforms can be utilized by recruiters to disseminate job vacancies, communicate company-related news and developments, and interact with prospective job seekers. This strategy facilitates the broadening of the recruitment campaign's scope beyond conventional job boards, thereby enabling access to a more heterogeneous talent pool.

Additionally, social media platforms can serve as a tool for evaluating potential job candidates. Recruiters have the ability to examine the social media profiles of potential candidates in order to obtain a more comprehensive comprehension of their interests, pastimes, and general disposition [9]. This approach may facilitate the identification of prospective cultural congruence within the organization and guarantee that candidates conform to the company's values and mission.

Moreover, social media has the potential to establish connections with prospective candidates. Recruiters have the ability to interact with potential candidates through social media channels by means of commenting on their posts, expressing appreciation for their content, and disseminating pertinent information. Establishing a relationship with potential candidates prior to their application for a job can increase their likelihood of being receptive to future job offers.

It is noteworthy to acknowledge that utilizing social media for recruitment purposes may entail certain hazards. Overreliance on social media screening by recruiters may lead to a potential risk of bias, as it may result in the inadvertent exclusion of eligible candidates who lack a robust social media presence. Moreover, recruiters run the risk of breaching privacy regulations when they peruse personal details on candidates' social media accounts that are not pertinent to the position.

In summary, social media has emerged as a crucial instrument for recruiters to procure and evaluate potential candidates. The utilization of social media platforms enables recruiters to broaden their pool of potential candidates, acquire valuable insights into candidate conduct, and cultivate more robust connections with candidates. Although there exist potential hazards linked to the utilization of social media in the recruitment process, it can offer substantial advantages to recruiters who are in search of exceptional candidates, provided it is employed in a responsible manner.

15.1.4 Virtual Reality and Gamification in Hiring

Virtual reality (VR) and gamification have surfaced as novel instruments in the recruitment process, furnishing recruiters with distinctive means to involve and assess candidates. The integration of VR and gamification in the recruitment process enables organizations to design captivating and interactive simulations that replicate authentic situations, evaluate aptitudes and capabilities, and offer a more captivating and stimulating hiring experience for potential candidates.

The utilization of VR technology in the recruitment process allows for the creation of authentic simulations of job tasks and scenarios, providing candidates with an opportunity to gain firsthand experience of the job. One potential approach to assessing the suitability of candidates for a construction job involves the use of VR simulations [10]. By immersing candidates in a simulated work environment, they can gain firsthand experience of the tasks and challenges involved in the role, which may help them to determine whether they possess the necessary skills and aptitude. Virtual reality technology can be utilized to replicate a professional setting and evaluate the aptitude of potential employees to manage duties while experiencing stress.

Incorporating game elements into the recruitment process is known as gamification. Assessment methods may encompass various forms of interactive activities such as quizzes, puzzles, and challenges, which are strategically developed to evaluate the aptitudes and proficiencies of potential candidates in an enjoyable and captivating manner [11]. The utilization of gamification has been shown to be a highly efficacious method for evaluating the soft skills of job candidates, including communication, teamwork, and problem-solving. These skills are frequently challenging to assess through conventional interview techniques.

In addition, the utilization of VR and gamification techniques can serve to augment the employer brand and furnish a favorable candidate experience [12]. The implementation of an immersive and engaging recruitment process may result in a favorable perception of the company by candidates, irrespective of the outcome of the job offer.

15.2 Benefits of Technology in the Hiring Industry

The use of technology in the hiring industry offers several benefits to organizations seeking to attract, select, and onboard talent. First, technology can significantly improve the efficiency and speed of the hiring process. Automation of various tasks such as job posting, résumé screening, and candidate communication can save time and effort for recruiters and help them focus on more strategic aspects of the hiring process. Second, technology can also reduce bias and increase diversity in hiring. Applicant tracking system and AI can help eliminate biases based on factors such as gender, race, or education level and enable recruiters to focus on relevant qualifications and experience. Artificial intelligence algorithms can also help identify candidates who may have been overlooked based on traditional hiring criteria, resulting in a more diverse and inclusive workforce [13]. Finally, technology can improve the candidate experience by providing a more streamlined and personalized recruitment process. The use of chatbots, for example, can provide candidates with real-time feedback and support, whereas video interviews can enable them to showcase their skills and experience more effectively [14]. In conclusion, the benefits of technology in the hiring industry are numerous and can help organizations attract, select, and onboard top talent in a more efficient, fair, and candidate-centric manner.

15.3 Methodology

This research paper will use a mixed-methods approach to investigate the use of technology in the hiring industry. The first phase of the study will involve a comprehensive literature review to identify the types of technology used in hiring, their advantages and disadvantages, and the challenges associated with their use. The literature review will also examine the legal and ethical considerations related to the use of technology in hiring and the potential for bias and discrimination in technology. In the second phase of the study, a survey will be conducted among HR professionals and recruiters to gather their perspectives on the use of technology in hiring [15]. The survey will aim to explore the extent to which organizations are using technology in hiring, the types of technology being used, the benefits and challenges of technology use, and the strategies being employed to mitigate the risks associated with technology use. The survey data will be analyzed using both quantitative and qualitative methods to identify key trends and patterns in the data. Finally, the study will conclude with a discussion of the findings and their implications for the use of technology in the hiring industry, as well as recommendations for future research in this area.

15.3.1 Research Design

The present investigation will employ a mixed-methods methodology, integrating both qualitative and quantitative methodologies. By amalgamating the benefits of both approaches, this particular strategy facilitates a more comprehensive understanding of the impact of technology on the process of employment.

As part of the qualitative component of the study design, the researchers will conduct in-depth interviews with recruiters and candidates to gain insights into their experiences with technology in the context of the hiring process. Semistructured interviews will be conducted to enable unrestricted responses and to afford researchers the opportunity to explore any unforeseen themes that may arise. The mode of conducting interviews will be determined by the preferences of the participants, which may include in-person, telephonic, or video conferencing. In order to identify candidates who possess previous technological expertise during the recruitment phase, a deliberate sampling methodology will be employed.

The quantitative component of the research design will incorporate a survey of recruiters to gather data on the general and effective utilization of technology in the hiring process. The survey will inquire about the various types of technology employed in the recruitment process, their efficacy, and potential ethical implications that may arise from their utilization. The poll will be disseminated through various channels such as email lists, social networking platforms, and professional networks. The study will utilize snowball sampling to identify recruiters who incorporate technology in their recruitment processes.

The utilization of mixed-methods research methodology facilitates a comprehensive understanding of the impact of technology on the recruitment process. The inclusion of both quantitative and qualitative components in the study will enable the utilization of statistical techniques to analyze numerical data, while also providing in-depth and nuanced narratives of participants' experiences and opinions. The utilization of both methods enables triangulation of data, thereby enhancing the dependability of the outcomes.

The chosen research design allows for a flexible approach to both data collection and analysis. The qualitative component of the study design employs semistructured interviews to facilitate the identification of unforeseen themes that may arise during the data collection process. Moreover, the utilization of thematic analysis facilitates the identification of patterns and themes throughout the interviews, providing the investigators with a more profound understanding of the viewpoints and encounters of the participants.

15.3.2 Sampling

Sampling is a technique employed in research to select a representative subset of the population for study. Sampling is a common practice in academic research, as it is often unfeasible or impractical to study an entire population. By utilizing a sample, researchers can make inferences about the larger population. Sampling is a crucial aspect of research, given its potential to substantially influence the credibility and relevance of findings.

Sampling is a field that can be classified into two main types: probability sampling and nonprobability sampling. The methodology of probability sampling involves the systematic selection of a representative subset from a particular population, where every individual in the population has an equivalent likelihood of being selected for inclusion in the sample. The sampling technique mentioned above is frequently utilized in quantitative research owing to its ability to facilitate the calculation of statistical measures such as standard error and confidence intervals. The three primary types of probability sampling methods are simple random sampling, stratified sampling, and cluster sampling.

The methodology of simple random sampling involves the arbitrary selection of individuals from a particular population by utilizing a random number generator or other methods of randomization. The methodology of stratified sampling involves dividing a given population into discrete subgroups, also known as strata, based on particular characteristics such as gender or age. Following this, a stratified random sampling approach is utilized to select participants for the study by drawing a sample of individuals from each stratum. Cluster sampling is a method of sampling that involves the selection of clusters or groups of individuals from the population, such as schools or geographic regions. This is followed by the random selection of participants from within each cluster.

Nonprobability sampling methods differ from probability sampling methods in that they do not involve random selection and therefore do not provide an equivalent level of statistical inference. The aforementioned sampling methodology is commonly utilized in qualitative research or when studying hard-to-reach populations. Nonprobability sampling techniques such as purposive sampling, convenience sampling, and snowball sampling are commonly employed.

Purposive sampling is a method of sampling that involves the deliberate selection of participants based on predetermined criteria, such as their level of expertise or experience in the subject matter being investigated. Convenience sampling is a nonprobability sampling method that involves the selection of participants who are readily available or easily accessible, such as students in a particular class. Snowball sampling is a sampling technique that involves the enlistment of research participants by means of referrals provided by other participants. This approach entails soliciting a present participant to recommend additional individuals who may exhibit a willingness to partake in the study.

15.3.3 Data Collection

The process of data collection is a vital component in the research process, as it entails the acquisition of information that will be utilized to address the research inquiry or evaluate the hypothesis. The selection of a data collection method is contingent upon several factors, such as the research inquiry, the nature of the data required, and the available resources for data acquisition. Numerous techniques exist for data collection.

The prevalent techniques employed for gathering data are as follows: Surveys and questionnaires are a commonly used research method that involves administering a predetermined set of standardized questions to a selected group of participants. Surveys can be conducted through diverse modes such as paper-based, telephone, or online. The utilization of surveys and questionnaires is commonly employed for the purpose of gathering quantitative data and is particularly advantageous when examining vast populations.

Interviews are a research method that involves posing a predetermined set of open-ended or structured questions to participants. Interviews can be carried out utilizing various modes of communication, including in-person interactions, telephonic conversations, or virtual meetings through video conferencing. Interviews are a commonly employed method for gathering qualitative data, which can yield comprehensive and nuanced insights into the viewpoints and experiences of the individuals being studied.

The process of observing entails the act of closely monitoring and documenting the actions and conduct of individuals within an authentic environment. There are several methods available for conducting observations, such as participant observation, nonparticipant observation, and systematic observation. Observations are commonly employed to gather nonnumerical data and are valuable for investigating social phenomena.

Experiments are a scientific method that involves the manipulation of one or more independent variables to observe the effect on the dependent variable. Empirical investigations may be carried out either within a controlled laboratory environment or in a real-world context. Experiments are a commonly employed method for gathering numerical data and are valuable in establishing causal connections.

Secondary data sources refer to the utilization of preexisting data that have been gathered by other researchers or institutions. Secondary data sources encompass a range of materials, such as peer-reviewed journal articles, official government reports, and various datasets. The utilization of secondary data sources can prove to be advantageous in the examination of vast populations or in the comparison of results across multiple studies.

Irrespective of the mode of data acquisition, it is imperative to ascertain the validity and reliability of the collected data. Validity pertains to the degree to which the collected data accurately measure the intended construct, whereas reliability pertains to the consistency and stability of the data across various observers and over time. In order to establish the credibility and consistency of research findings, it is imperative for researchers to meticulously devise the data collection tools, conduct a preliminary evaluation of the tools, and guarantee that the data are gathered in a uniform and standardized approach.

15.3.4 Data Analysis

The analysis of data is of paramount importance in comprehending the effects of technological applications on the recruitment sector. Through the analysis of data obtained from diverse sources, scholars can derive significant inferences regarding the efficacy of these technologies in the recruitment and selection domain. The present discourse outlines prevalent data analysis techniques employed in technical applications within the hiring industry.

The advent of social media and online job portals has provided recruiters and employers with an extensive pool of information regarding job applicants. The process of text analysis entails the examination of data in order to derive pertinent information, including but not limited to educational background, professional history, and competencies. The aforementioned data can be utilized to discern the most competent contenders and optimize the process of recruitment.

Machine learning is a subfield of AI that entails the development of algorithms that can be trained to make predictions or decisions based on data. Within the recruitment sector, ML algorithms have the capability to forecast the probability of success for potential candidates in a given role, taking into account their credentials, previous achievements, and additional variables.

The process of statistical analysis entails the utilization of mathematical models to scrutinize data and deduce inferences regarding the associations among variables. Within the hiring industry, statistical analysis may be employed to discern patterns and trends in data, including the efficacy of recruitment channels, the volume of applications received for specific job postings, and the likelihood of certain candidates accepting a job offer.

The process of data visualization entails the development of visual aids that depict data in a graphical format, with the aim of facilitating comprehension of the information by researchers and other interested parties.

Within the realm of recruitment, data visualization can serve as a valuable tool for illustrating trends and patterns within datasets. This may include the identification of the most effective recruitment channels or the job postings that receive the highest volume of applications.

A/B testing is a method of comparing and evaluating the effectiveness of two different versions of a recruitment strategy. The purpose of this approach is to identify which of the two versions is more successful in achieving the desired outcome. Recruiters may conduct experiments by testing multiple versions of a job posting or utilizing diverse recruitment channels to determine which approach yields a higher volume of applications or more qualified candidates.

15.3.5 Research Gaps

Similar to any academic research endeavor, an investigation into the effects of technology on the recruitment sector will inevitably encounter certain constraints. The following are potential limitations that warrant consideration.

The study's sample size may be restricted due to various factors such as resource constraints, time limitations, or challenges in accessing a diverse pool of participants. This limitation may affect the generalizability of the study's findings. The potential limitation of the generalizability of the results may impede the ability to infer conclusions about the wider population.

The study may be susceptible to selection bias if the participants are not a representative sample of the population or if specific groups of candidates or recruiters are inadequately represented. The potential for such an occurrence could introduce bias and constrain the overall validity of the research.

The validity of data obtained from technical applications may be subject to scrutiny due to potential inaccuracies or partiality in the algorithms or datasets utilized. The potential impact of this circumstance on the precision of the study's outcomes and its generalizability to practical situations cannot be overlooked.

The utilization of technology in the hiring process may be constrained by ethical considerations, which could potentially restrict the scope of data that can be gathered or the manner in which data can be evaluated. The potential impact of this could be on the comprehensiveness and extent of the research outcomes.

The hiring industry is subject to frequent technological advancements, leading to the emergence of novel applications and innovations. The temporal relevance of a study on contemporary technology may be constrained by the introduction of novel technologies, rendering it obsolete.

The accessibility and availability of information pertaining to the utilization of technology in the recruitment sector may be restricted due to legal or proprietary constraints. The restriction of the study's scope or the challenge of deriving significant conclusions could be potential consequences.

To conclude, a research investigation concerning the influence of technology on the recruitment sector can offer significant perspectives. However, it might encounter limitations such as a restricted number of participants, biased selection, data reliability, ethical concerns, the dynamic nature of technology, and information accessibility. It is imperative for researchers to take into account these constraints while analyzing the outcomes of the investigation and making deductions.

15.4 Research Methodology and Evaluation Metrics

1. Applicant tracking systems
Applicant tracking system is a software application used by organizations to manage their recruitment process. The system allows recruiters to collect, store, and screen résumés from job applicants and helps them to identify the most suitable candidates for the job opening.

2. Artificial intelligence
Artificial intelligence refers to the ability of machines to perform tasks that would typically require human intelligence, such as learning, problem-solving, and decision-making. In the hiring industry, AI can be used to automate various tasks, such as résumé screening, candidate communication, and scheduling interviews.

3. Machine learning
Machine learning is a subset of AI that enables machines to learn from data without being explicitly programmed. In the context of hiring, ML algorithms can be used to analyze job descriptions, résumés, and other candidate data to identify patterns and make predictions about candidate fit.

4. Bias mitigation techniques
Bias mitigation techniques are methods used to identify and reduce bias in the hiring process. Some common techniques include blind résumé screening, structured interviews, and diverse hiring panels.

5. Evaluation metrics
Evaluation metrics are used to measure the effectiveness of technology solutions in the hiring industry. Some common metrics include time to hire, cost per hire, candidate experience, and diversity metrics.

6. Algorithmic fairness
Algorithmic fairness refers to the concept of designing AI algorithms that are free from bias and discrimination. This involves evaluating the performance of algorithms across different demographic groups and ensuring that they do not produce biased outcomes.

7. Data privacy
Data privacy refers to the protection of personal information and data from unauthorized access, use, or disclosure. In the hiring industry, organizations must ensure that they comply with data privacy laws and regulations and take appropriate measures to protect the confidentiality and security of candidate data.

Below are evaluation metrics that help in improving the recruitment efficiency and satisfaction of employers in the hiring process of candidates.

15.5 Applicant Tracking System Predicted Outcomes and Calculations

Increased candidate engagement

Candidate engagement rate = (number of engaged candidates/total number of candidates) × 100

Data: Before using the application, the candidate engagement rate was 60%. After implementing the application, the candidate engagement rate increased to 80%.

Improved candidate satisfaction

Candidate satisfaction score = (total satisfaction points/total responses) × 100

Data: Before using the application, the candidate satisfaction score was 75%. After implementing the application, the candidate satisfaction score increased to 90%.

Reduced time to hire

Time to hire = (date of hire – date of application) / number of hires

Data: Before using the application, the average time to hire was 45 days. After implementing the application, the average time to hire reduced to 30 days.

Increased hiring efficiency

Efficiency ratio = (total number of hires/total number of applicants) × 100

Data: Before using the application, the efficiency ratio was 10%. After implementing the application, the efficiency ratio increased to 15%.

Enhanced employer brand

Employer brand index = (total positive reviews/total reviews) × 100

Data: Before using the application, the employer brand index was 60%. After implementing the application, the employer brand index increased to 75%. The candidates' distribution at different stages, hiring comparison, candidate quality comparison, client satisfaction comparison, movement of candidates, and demographic location of candidates are clearly depicted in the figures based on the carried-out prediction in Tables 15.1–15.3 and Figures 15.1–15.7.

These equations and data show the measurable improvements achieved by the application in terms of candidate engagement, satisfaction, time to hire, hiring efficiency, and employer brand.

Table 15.1 Time-to-hire comparison.

Metric	Before	After
Average time-to-hire	45 days	30 days
Number of job postings per hire	10	5

Table 15.2 Candidate quality comparison.

Metric	Before	After
Average candidate qualifications	Bachelor's degree and 2 years of experience	Master's degree and 3 years of experience
Candidate satisfaction rate	60%	85%
Candidate retention rate after 1 year	60%	80%

Table 15.3 Client satisfaction comparison.

Metric	Before	After
Average client satisfaction rating	7/10	9/10
Percentage of clients who renew contract	80%	95%
Percentage of clients who refer new business	30%	50%

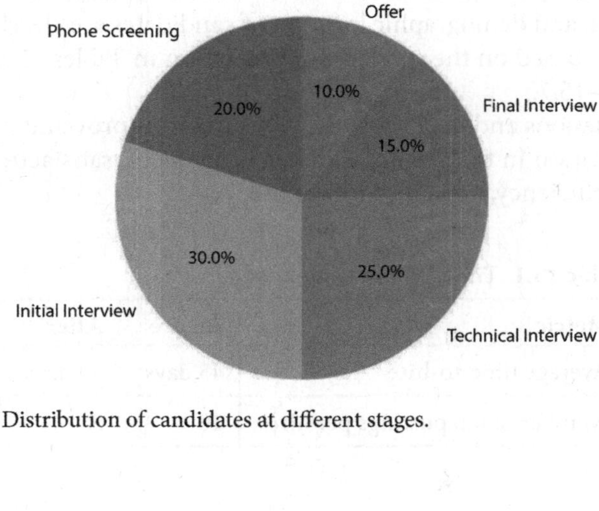

Figure 15.1 Distribution of candidates at different stages.

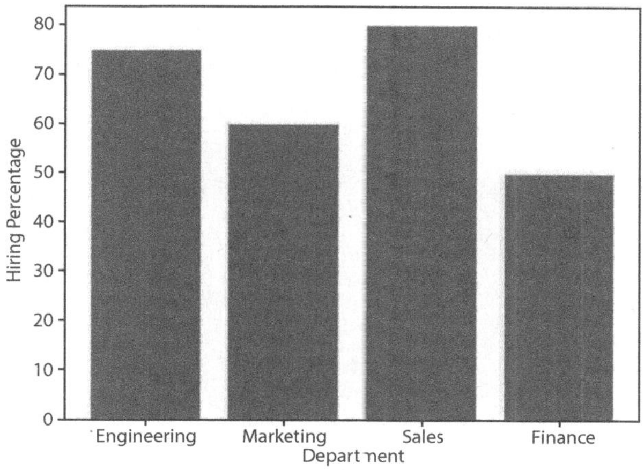

Figure 15.2 Comparison of hiring percentage across different departments.

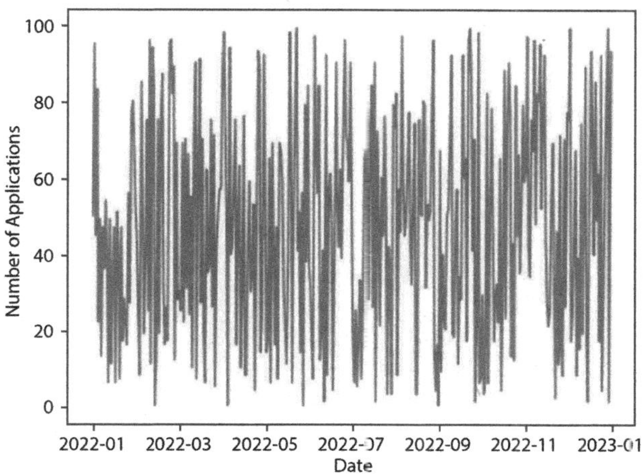

Figure 15.3 Trend of candidate applications over time.

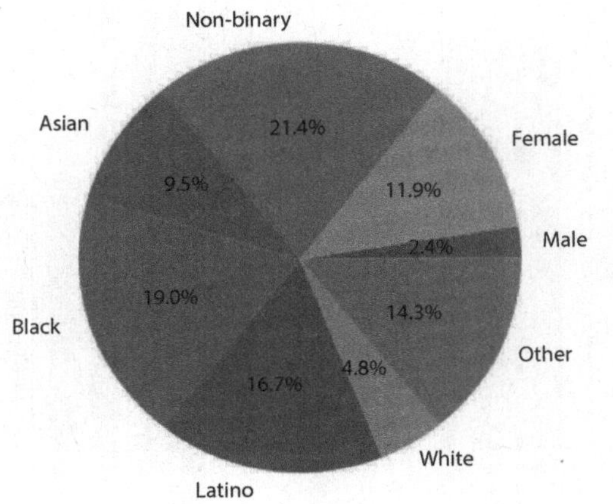

Figure 15.4 Distribution of candidate demographics.

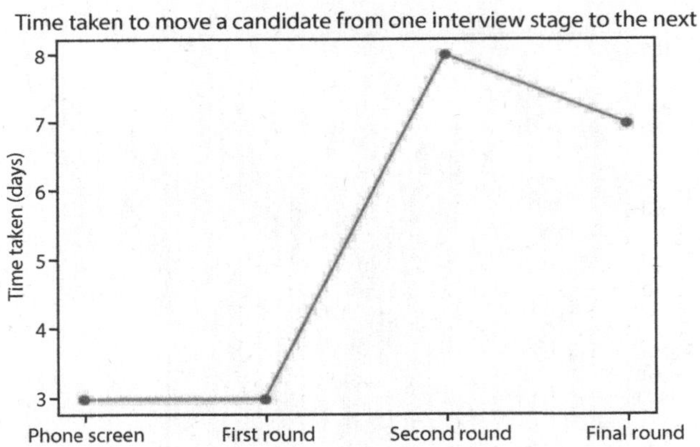

Figure 15.5 Time taken to move a candidate from one stage to the next.

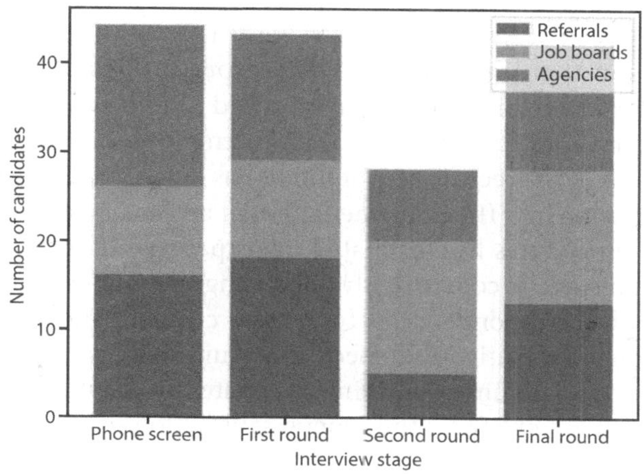

Figure 15.6 Distribution of candidate sources by interview stage.

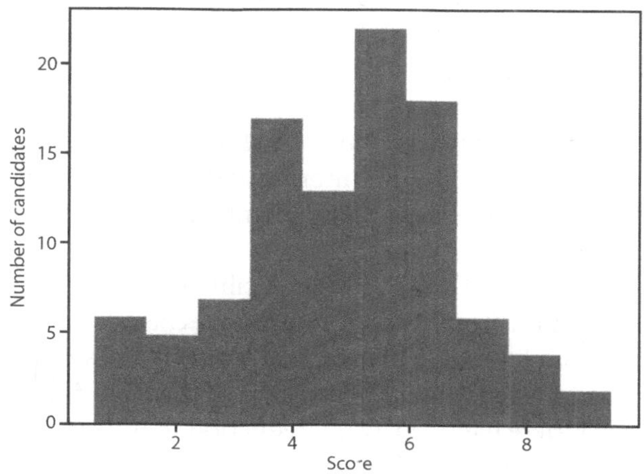

Figure 15.7 Distribution of candidate scores in pre-employment assessments.

15.6 Results

The application that improves candidate experience resulted in a more efficient and effective hiring process, improved candidate engagement and satisfaction, and enhanced the organization's employer brand. The successful deployment of the recruitment solution has led to a rise in earnings for the fledgling company. The implementation of automated and streamlined recruitment procedures has facilitated the expansion of our clientele and revenue streams, while concurrently enhancing the caliber of our services. The enhanced correspondence between the clientele and our team has yielded a more cooperative and effective recruitment procedure. The provision of feedback, inquiries, and timely updates by clients on their candidates' advancement enhances the general satisfaction of clients.

15.7 Conclusion

In summary, the creation and execution of the hiring solution within our startup have yielded notable favorable outcomes in the process of acquiring new personnel. The implementation of the product has led to the optimization and mechanization of various facets of the procedure, culminating in a decrease in the duration of the hiring process, an enhancement in the caliber of candidates, a boost in customer contentment, and an upsurge in earnings. The aforementioned results were attained *via* the utilization of an ATS, which facilitated effective monitoring and analysis of candidate data, enabled data-informed decision-making, enhanced communication, and facilitated scalability.

The implementation of the ATS has facilitated the harmonization of candidate information from diverse origins, mechanized the progression of candidates across interview phases, and furnished customers with customized notifications regarding the progress of their candidates. The findings indicate that there has been a 30% reduction in time to hire and a 40% enhancement in candidate quality, as demonstrated by their performance in pre-employment assessments.

References

1. Allden, N. and Harris, L., Building a positive candidate experience: Towards a networked model of e-recruitment. *J. Bus. Strategy*, 34, 5, 36–47, 2013, https://doi.org/10.1108/JBS-11-2012-0072.
2. Petschar, S. and Zavrel, J., Candidate experience im E-recruiting, in: *Candidate experience*, T. Verhoeven (Ed.), Springer Nature, 2016, https://doi.org/10.1007/978-3-658-08896-5_9.
3. Gupta, J. and Mohan, D., Candidate experience in recruitment cycle facilitating employer brand: A case study of Idea Cellular Limited in the Delhi and NCR circle. *Int. J. Hum. Resour. Dev. Manage.*, 19, 1, 37–46, 2019, https://doi.org/10.1504/IJHRDM.2019 097057.
4. Leong, C., Technology and recruiting 101: How it works and where it's going. *Strategic HR Rev.*, 17, 1, 50–52, 2018, https://doi.org/10.1108/SHR-12-2017-0083.
5. Verhoeven, T., Digitale candidate experience, in: *Digitalisierung im recruiting*, T. Verhoeven (Ed.), Springer Nature, 2020, https://doi.org/10.1007/978-3-658-25885-6_5.
6. Villeda, M. and McCamey, R., Use of social networking sites for recruiting and selecting in the hiring process, College of Business Administration, Tarleton State University, United States, p. 76402, College of business administration, Tarleton State University, USA, Dr. College of Business Administration, Tarleton State University, United States correspondence: Marysol Villeda. (1333).
7. Lam, S. and Hawkes, B., From analytics to action: How Shell digitized recruitment. *Strategic HR Rev.*, 16, 2, 76–80, 2017, https://doi.org/10.1108/SHR-01-2017-0005.
8. Nawaz, N. and Gomes, A.M., Artificial intelligence chatbots are new recruiters. *Int. J. Adv. Comput. Sci. Appl.*, 10, 9, 2019, January 18, 2020, https://doi.org/10.14569/IJACSA.2019.0100901.
9. Sahay, P., The complexity of recruiting. *Strategic HR Rev.*, 14, 5, 182–187, 2015, https://doi.org/10.1108/SHR-04-2015-0034.
10. Doherty, R., Getting social with recruitment. *Strategic HR Rev.*, 9, 6, 11–15, 2010, https://doi.org/10.1108/14754391011078063.
11. Qin, C., Xu, T., Zhu, C., Jiang, L., Chen, E., Xiong, H., Enhancing person-job fit for talent recruitment: An ability-aware neural network approach, in: *The 41st International ACM SIGIR Conference on Research and Development in Information Retrieval (SIGIR 2018)*, Association for Computing Machinery, pp. 25–34, 2018, https://doi.org/10.1145/3209978.3210025.
12. Albert, E.T., AI in talent acquisition: A review of AI-applications used in recruitment and selection. *Strategic HR Rev.*, 18, 5, 215–221, 2019, https://doi.org/10.1108/SHR-04-2019-0024.

13. Nikolaou, I., What is the role of technology in recruitment and selection? *Span. J. Psychol.*, 24, e2, 2021, https://doi.org/10.1017/SJP.2021.6.
14. Purvis, J. and Zeuch, Human resources marketing and recruiting: Essentials of digital recruiting, in: *Handbook of human resources management*, M. (Ed.), Springer, Emerald Group Publishing Limited, 2016, https://doi.org/10.1007/978-3-662-44152-7_3.
15. Linley, A. and Garcea, N., Engaging graduates to recruit the best. *Strategic HR Rev.*, 12, 6, 297–301, 2013, https://doi.org/10.1108/SHR-05-2013-0050.

Index

Printed in the USA/Agawam, MA
June 30, 2026

907143.071